THE ART OF
CHESS COMBINATION

A Guide for All Players of the Game

BY

EUGÈNE ZNOSKO-BOROVSKY

English Translation with an Introduction by
PHILIP W. SERGEANT

With New Introduction to the Dover Edition by
FRED REINFELD

With 200 Diagrams

DOVER PUBLICATIONS, INC.
NEW YORK

International Standard Book Number: 0-486-20583-5
Library of Congress Catalog Card Number: 60-1716

Manufactured in the United States of America

Dover Publications, Inc.
180 Varick Street
New York, N. Y. 10014

Contents

INTRODUCTION TO DOVER EDITION   vii

INTRODUCTION   xi

Part I
Combinations and their Study

CHAP. I. CAN THE ART OF COMBINATION BE LEARNT?   3

II. WHAT IS A COMBINATION ?   10

III. EXCEPTIONAL COMBINATIONS   20

IV. AN ATTEMPT AT CLASSIFICATION   30

Part II
Combinational Ideas

CHAP. I. COMBINATIONS, PROBLEMS, AND STUDIES   35

II. GEOMETRICAL IDEAS   38

III. THE KNIGHT IN COMBINATION   44

IV. THE OPENING OF LINES   51

V. THE INTERCEPTION OF LINES   58

VI. DISCOVERED CHECK   66

VII. STALEMATE INTO MATE   70

VIII. THE UNPROTECTED PIECE   80

IX. THE OVERWORKED PROTECTING PIECE   87

X. THE SUPPORTING PAWN   94

Part III
Combinations depending on Position

CHAP. I. COMBINATION IN RELATION TO POSITION   103

II. THE KING'S ROOK'S PAWN   105

Part III (continued)

PAGE

CHAP. III. THE SACRIFICE OF THE TWO BISHOPS   119

IV. THE PAWN AT KKт7 AND THE KKт FILE   125

V. KING'S BISHOP'S PAWN AND CASTLED
KING   136

VI. THE ATTACK ON KB7 AND K6, WITH THE
KNIGHT-COMBINATION   143

VII. COMBINATIONS IN THE CENTRE   150

VIII. THE ADVANCED KING'S BISHOP'S PAWN   163

Part IV

The Life and Death of a Combination

CHAP.   I. PREPARING THE COMBINATION   177

II. THE MECHANISM OF COMBINATIONS   184

III. REFUTING A COMBINATION   197

CONCLUSION   204

POSTSCRIPT: TWO EXAMPLES FROM THE
LATE CHAMPIONSHIP MATCH   206

INDEX OF ILLUSTRATIVE EXAMPLES   208

SOLUTIONS TO EXERCISES   210

INTRODUCTION TO DOVER EDITION

T HE reissue of Znosko-Borovsky's classic requires
no special pleading; it is a self-justifying event.
Yet the readers who are coming to this delightful book for the first time may want to share
with me some of the clashing ideas that were evoked
by its original publication.

Combination play, by common consent, is the most
enjoyable and thrilling aspect of chess. It is very
possibly also the most creative part of the game; to
conceive combinations and execute them properly
requires originality, imagination, insight. Above all
it requires that quality, common to great artists,
scientists, and statesmen, of seizing a number of
apparently disparate elements and combining them
into a harmonious unit. (The very word "combination" conveys this idea.)

But, we ask ourselves, can one *teach* the techniques
of conceiving and executing these glorious combinations, which we have been trained to see as the
attributes of genius? Dare we poach on the sacred
preserves of the great masters?

To express this problem in a slightly different
way: to make combinations is to synthesize—to put
together seemingly unrelated elements into a new
and effective relationship. To teach, to break down
the combination into its component parts—that is
analysis. So here we have two opposed processes—
analysis and synthesis. Can one shed light on the
other?

Before we answer this question, there is still
another division we must note. There are three
possible levels on which this book can be read. You

vii

can read it just for pleasure—very great pleasure, indeed, for the sacrificial combinations are enchanting. Or you can read the book with the specific purpose of improving your play; Znosko-Borovsky's explanations make an admirable guide. Or, and this is the best way, you can read it for both pleasure and profit.

And this brings us back to the original problem: can one teach a creative skill? As far as combination play is concerned, my answer has been "Yes!"

Consider the situations in Diagrams 96 and 97. In each case a crisp, astonishing sacrifice of the Queen leads to a quick win. If we play over these combinations for pleasure, we are handsomely rewarded. It was Richard Reti who pointed out that the enjoyment we get from these combinations "lies in the feeling that a human mind is behind the game dominating the inanimate pieces with which the game is carried on, and giving them the breath of life." Very well put, but the observation carries a moral:

Man is a thinking animal. No matter how discursively the reader glances at these combinations, he inevitably begins to perceive cause-and-effect relationships, he begins to see circumstances that are common to both examples, patterns that repeat themselves with certain variations.

In both cases we find a Rook "conveniently" (accidentally?—never!) and powerfully placed on a file where it can strike at the target King. We see two Bishops with long sweeping diagonals trained on the King. We note that an advanced Pawn becomes disproportionately powerful in the plot to lay low the enemy King. We see the unholy might of a discovered check, and even more brutal—a deadly double check. Here are all sorts of elements, like a child's building blocks, and perhaps even more instinctively than reflectively, we begin willy-nilly putting these elements together into a pattern. The point I am making is that analysis (taking apart) automatically links up at some point with synthesis (putting together). That is the way the human mind works, and not only in chess.

These were some of the ideas I had when I first read Znosko-Borovsky's book more than twenty years ago. In fact, I had used them earlier in a book of my own called *Elements of Combination Play*. My guiding thought was that it *is* possible to teach combinative play because its creative aspect is not so aristocratically remote as we think it is, and also because the learning process is by the same token not so humble and pedestrian as we think.

In the intervening years, we have learned from the electronic computers that the learning process, if broken down carefully and logically, can lead to stupendous successes even in fields that have been thought of as eminently creative. So, in the last analysis, such a book as *The Art of Chess Combination* stands or falls on the author's skill in manipulating the elements, in revealing the framework of a combination, in illuminating the details of the combination.

Judged by these standards, Znosko-Borovsky passes the test convincingly, for he is one of the great chess teachers. His book has withstood, and will continue to withstand, the passage of time. Its reappearance is good news for all chessplayers.

FRED REINFELD

EAST MEADOW, N. Y.,
September, 1959

INTRODUCTION

W HEN I was asked whether, in addition to preparing the English edition of my friend Eugène Znosko-Borovsky's new book, I would also write a brief introduction to it, I gladly accepted the task. I felt that in such an edition a few personal details about the author would be welcome to readers, which he himself would perhaps be reluctant to give over his own signature, whereas I might be able to elicit the facts from him, and from elsewhere, and to set them out with no undue reticence.

The following few pages are the result of my endeavour.

* * * * *

Eugène Alexandrovitch Znosko-Borovsky was born in St. Petersburg on August 16th, 1884, and was educated at the Lyceum of the Emperor Alexander I, which was considered the Russian equivalent of our Eton, but included also University courses. Here he was when the Russo-Japanese War broke out ; and, having passed his last examination on April 28th, 1904, on May 8th he took the train for the Manchurian front as a volunteer in the 1st East Siberian Regiment. He fought in the battles of Liaoyang (1904) and Mukden (1905), as well as in numerous smaller engagements. After Liaoyang he was decorated and received a commission. At Mukden he was severely wounded in the right hand.

To omit for the present the intervening years, in the Great War he again saw active military service, and was again wounded. After some work with the General Staff at St. Petersburg, he fell seriously ill, and in 1917 was sent to the Caucasus for a cure. The Revolution prevented his return to the capital, and he joined the " White" forces. Being still unfit for active service, however, he remained in employ at the base until early in 1920, when General Denikin's army was evacuated. With his family he was taken in a British ship to Constantinople, and thence proceeded to Paris, where, since June 1920, he has made his home.

We may now go back and look at the side of Znosko-Borovsky's life which is concerned with chess. He began his acquaintance with the game when a schoolboy, and went on to gain prizes in local and regional tournaments in Russia. It was not until the summer of 1906 that he made a reputation as a chess-player outside his own country. He was admitted to the great tournament of thirty-six players at Ostend in June ; but the system on which that was conducted involved the elimination of competitors by three stages before the final pool. He was knocked out in the third stage, though having the consolation of a brilliancy prize for his victory over the English master Amos Burn.

In August of the same year he met sixteen experts of the first rank in chess in the International Masters' Tournament promoted by the German Chess Association at Nuremberg. Here he had to be content with tieing for the last two prizes, the ninth and tenth ; but associated with him were no lesser masters than Dr. S. Tarrasch and Dr. M. Vidmar. Above them in the table were F. J. Marshall, O. Duras, L. Forgacs (Fleischmann), C. Schlechter, M. Tchigorin, G. Salwe, H. Wolf, and E. Cohn ; below, R. Spielmann, R. Swiderski, H. Fahrni, P. S. Leonhardt, D. Janowski, and D. Przepiórka. This was indeed high company for a young aspirant in chess. He defeated among others Spielmann and Janowsky, won another brilliancy prize, and altogether scored $7\frac{1}{2}$ points in 16 games.

He was again at Ostend in 1907, competing in the tournament of twenty-nine masters, all playing all on this occasion. With 15 points he tied with E. Cohn and Spielmann for twelfth to fourteenth prizes. Among his wins were those against A. Rubinstein (who tied with O. S. Bernstein for first place, with $19\frac{1}{2}$ points each), R. Teichmann, and O. Duras.

In his first and only International Masters' Tournament in Russia, that of St. Petersburg in 1909, Znosko-Borovsky showed lack of recent practice ; but the opposition was tremendously strong, including the world champion, Dr. Emanuel Lasker, and A. Rubinstein, who tied for first place.

Two years later he had the satisfaction of gaining the St. Petersburg city championship. In 1913 he further distinguished himself by winning an exhibition game against J. R. Capablanca, then on a visit to the Russian capital— the only game which the future world champion lost at that period against thirty masters in Europe.

At the beginning of 1914 he competed in the Russian national championship of eighteen players. In this A. Alekhine and A. Nimzovitch were equal first with 13 points, and Znosko-Borovsky tied for fifth place with $10\frac{1}{2}$.

Then came the Great War, and for seven years Znosko-Borovsky was out of touch with chess. When he settled in Paris in 1920 he took the game up again, and studied to recover his old strength at it. This was partly in order to enable him to make a living, supplementing what he could earn by writing upon literature and the drama in French and Russian papers. He still continues to write on these two subjects (being indeed an authority on the Russian theatre, and the author of plays acted there in the past), but has had more and more to devote himself to chess: practical play, tuition, and writing about the game.

His tournaments in the various European countries have been very numerous. In Britain, to which he paid his first visit at Broadstairs in 1922—a year in which he beat the late Belgian master, E. Colle, in a short match—he includes two equal firsts with the late J. A. J. Drewitt in the major open contests at Stratford-on-Avon, 1925, and Edinburgh, 1926, and first prize in the premier tournament at Folkestone, 1933. In Paris in 1929 he came out second to S. G. Tartakover, and equal with A. Baratz and E. Colle, in a tournament of twelve players, below him being J. Cukierman, Sir George Thomas, G. Koltanowski, etc.

In Paris again, in 1930, he came out first, without loss, in a tournament of eight players, below him being A. Gromer, Tartakover, A. Lilienthal, J. Mieses, etc. ; and at Nice in the same year, he was third, with 8 points, after Tartakover (9) and Sir George Thomas ($8\frac{1}{2}$), but above B. Kostich, Colle, G. Maróczy, and six others. In 1931 he won the Paris championship ; very appropriately, since that year in Paris there was a celebration of his jubilee as a chess-master, when he received congratulations and mementos from far and wide.   In 1935, on a visit to Bucarest, he played *hors concours* in the Rumanian national championship, and came out equal first.

As a simultaneous player he has an astonishingly good record, which will bear comparison with any master's, though he does not attempt the " Marathon " exhibitions, which perhaps are not so great a proof of skill as on the surface they appear.

As a lecturer, he has the gift of interesting and holding his audiences, and in consequence he has always been a success in this role.   In the teaching of chess he may claim to have no superior.

His contributions to chess literature, apart from articles in magazines all over the world, include *The Evolution of Chess* (1910), *Capablanca*, and *The Muzio Gambit* (1911), *Capablanca and Alekhine* (after the War), and the following works, which are known to English readers, having been published in our language among others : *The Middle Game in Chess*, *How not to play Chess*, and *How to play Chess Openings*.

In the present book the author's object, as stated in the Introduction to the French edition, has been pioneer work in a region hardly touched by explorers, with an attempt to make the results attractive and accessible to all.   He goes on to say:

" This is no matter of those general questions, for which a few examples are enough.   To reach conclusions, to furnish instruction capable of use in practical play, it has been necessary to accumulate examples until our little volume contains nearly two hundred diagrams—and as many brilliant combinations!

"As a minute examination of all these, however, demands much time and attention, the busy reader is advised at the start only to study the first examples in each group, reading the commentary at the same time, in order to arrive at the general idea; and then, to complete his instruction, let him proceed to the details of each combination by an examination of all the remaining examples."

With this piece of counsel from the author I leave my edition of his book to what I hope will be a very large number of students prepared to investigate what there is to be learnt from the printed page about the most fascinating side of a game for which I at least share Znosko-Borovsky's enthusiasm.

PHILIP W. SERGEANT

LONDON, *February* 1936

PART I

COMBINATIONS AND THEIR STUDY

CHAPTER 1

CAN THE ART OF COMBINATION BE LEARNT?

The Difficulties of the Problem

BEFORE I begin my fascinating journey into the mysterious realm of Combination, so little explored and therefore so much the more attractive, I hasten to state my full realisation of the difficulties that await me.

One might have supposed that the study of combinations in chess would be made pleasant and easy by the imaginative beauty therein displayed, that it was at all events much simpler than the study of other chess problems, which are governed by rigid laws and strict logic. But that would be an error; for it is precisely the apparent absence of logic which makes this particular study difficult. We can hardly deal in generalities. Can we even assert that there are here any general principles or governing ideas? Is not every combination a particular case, with its own special rules? At the risk of wearying the student, therefore, it is necessary to multiply examples, without even then feeling sure that convincing deductions can be made, to reward the labour involved in the attempt.

What has been Done

What we have said is the probable explanation why combinations have been so little studied by the technical writers. There is nothing ready to hand: no definitions, no terminology, not even a classification. All that we have in this domain is the collections of famous games and brilliant combinations. Some of these are deservedly favourites, but the combinations are hardly ever grouped under heads. It is as if mere chance had governed their selection and arrangement. When one spends much time over a mass of startling diagrams, must one not be driven to ask whether there is any instruction to be gained from the study, or whether these combinations are just exhibitions of luck, or at best of sheer inspiration?

Let us then look on these collections as the raw material from which new products are to be fashioned. Let us introduce order into this chaos, and throw the light of theoretical reason upon it. After we have examined the abundant material furnished by practical play, it will be our task to group it according to certain common features; and then perhaps we shall be able to disentangle some general conclusions.

Without depreciating what our predecessors have done, we are obliged to say that most of the writers dealing with this subject are too much under the sway of facts, and so appreciably lessen the value of their studies. We must, however, do homage, among these writers, to the late Dr. S. Tarrasch, to Dr. E. Vœllmy, and to P. Romanovsky.

Dr. Tarrasch had devoted to Combination several pages of his celebrated manual *Das Schachspiel*.[1] Those pages are unfortunately insufficient, for so complex a subject cannot be thoroughly dealt with in a manual. The study of combinations is also attempted in Dr. Vœllmy's masterly work *Schachtaktik*. Here we find a first essay in classification. But the author, having allowed but one chapter for the subject, has taken as his basis of classification rather the outward marks: mate-combinations, drawing combinations, Pawn-promotions, etc.—which cannot fully satisfy us.

Romanovsky's work on the Middle Game is divided into two parts: Plan and Combinations. The second part allows of a remarkable study of the mechanism of combination, as well as a praiseworthy attempt at terminology. But the absence of a reasoned classification is to be regretted. The different kinds of combinations are not completely set out. Let us hope that the author will pursue his researches in a region with which he is obviously familiar.[2]

<hr/>

[1] In the English edition, *The Game of Chess*, translated by G. E. Smith and T. G. Bone, published by Chatto and Windus.

[2] I must not omit to refer to R. Spielmann's marvellous little book, *Richting opfern!*, which will be the joy of its readers, as well as of the greatest service to them. But, as the author draws only upon his

All this seems to confirm the objection which many amateurs of the game raise against the study of combinations, saying that they cannot be, even ought not to be, studied.

Can we Study Combinations?

If it were a case of impossibility, it would be an extraordinary fact, of which we might indeed be proud. All things are studied, all the branches of human knowledge have their courses and their handbooks. Why alone should the combinations of the chessboard evade the enquiries of science? Certainly we cannot refuse to appreciate the part played by genius, the mystery of creation. Years of study cannot make up for the lack of imagination. And yet look at Légal's mate (see p. 22). The mediocre chessplayer will never invent anything like it; he will never ever think of such. But, when the mechanism of the stratagem has been explained to him, this same player will be able not only to reproduce it when occasion arises, but to apply it in other positions. It is probable, too, that he will not fall a victim to the snare when it is laid for him.

If the examination of combinations, in the whole mass of games, shows the ability of the great masters to create new types, the majority of players only reproduce old manœuvres, complicating them, adding variations to them, and sometimes also simplifying them and impoverishing them. This is because at the basis of every combination there shines an idea, and because, though combinations are without number, the number of ideas is limited.

The case is the same with problems; but it must be remarked that their "themes" are known and catalogued. Nothing like that has been done for combinations in the actual game, in spite of the advantage which a fine repertory of ideas displayed in them confers on the player. His task still remains very difficult, since the application of these ideas in quite dissimilar positions demands great experience. The game of the weak amateur, however, will be none the

own productions and gives only 37 examples, he cannot claim a great didactic value for his work, in spite of a remarkable attempt to classify sacrificial combinations.

less enriched, because it will be enough that he should know these creations of inventive genius to see his horizon enlarge and to produce himself games interesting in their variety. He will besides be forearmed against the trap-abounding manœuvres of an adversary bolder and more experienced than himself.

What can be Studied in Combinations

The study of combinations, then, should take first the ideas which inspire them.   As we advance, we shall arrive at other conclusions.

Let us establish first the relationship between certain kinds of combinations and certain kinds of positions, so that, when we see such and such a position, the corresponding combination will instinctively come to our mind.   Reciprocally, the combination of which we are thinking will suggest the type of position that we must bring about.   It goes without saying that it is not in the limited area of the first game which comes along that we can realise all our ideas.   We must be content with keeping a clear brain, to enable us occasionally, without striving after the impossible, to realise at least one idea, and not complain; for this partial success, in place of the shadowy "all that can be got", may be obtained, in infinitely varied ways, in the numberless games, with all their compromises and concessions, which still remain for us to play on earth.

It is well known how difficult it is to analyse all the variations of a simple ordinary combination.   The mediocre player cannot foresee them all.   What then, it may be asked, is the use of knowing the different types of combinations and positions, if we cannot prove the soundness of our conceptions when they are carried out?   This is precisely what should be studied.

The analysis of combinations of the same type gives us the necessary conditions for soundness.   This one cannot be sound, we know, unless the hostile King has no flight-square, unless we have a Bishop available for the attack, unless a certain square is unguarded.   Therefore we can not only see well in advance whether the combination is to be realised, but can manœuvre so as to bring about the position which makes it possible. Every move, it is true, brings features which may modify our views; but we shall examine them at the right time, with all the more ease when we know more clearly the general conditions necessary for success.

In this way then the problem of working up combinations confronts us.

Some players believe that a combination is a spontaneous creation, that the possibility of a sacrifice springs up in the mind like a flash of genius, as surprising to the player as to his opponent. The truth is that combinations due to pure chance are not merely fantastic. There are combinations based on the opponent's errors; and most "traps" may be classed among these. There is even a type of player, the coffee-house expert, who speculates on the ignorance and inexperience of his adversaries. But this is a detestable and inglorious style of play, based on others' weaknesses, not on one's own strength. True combination is quite another matter. The crown of a fine player's logical chess, it must be prepared, and not left to chance. The border-line amateur says, "It may be sound—in any case, I don't suppose my opponent can find the answer, so here goes!" But no; our play should be more intelligent, deeper, and more honest than that.

So study of the task of preparation is necessary. It will teach us how a champion is able to create the conditions favourable to his combinations and to mask his schemes to upset his opponent's calculations. We shall not, however, dwell on this, since it differs but little from all other preparatory work in chess. For the same reason we shall not discuss the exploitation of an advantage gained by a combination, nor other questions of the same kind. We shall even refrain from drawing distinctions between the combination and its execution. In our new elementary instruction we must banish all subtleties.

Ought we to Study Combinations?

If great masters opposed the study of combinations, we might say that it was not fashionable; but their attitude would be intelligible. As a matter of fact, surprising though it may be, the chief opposition comes from the moderate players. Listen to what they say. "What will become of our game if all its mystery and even its interest are to be destroyed by analysis under a microscope? We don't want the art to be contaminated by too much science, or creative genius to be spoilt by reasoning!"

May I be allowed to have a better opinion of chess? Its riches seem to me inexhaustible. It is indeed one of the strongest reasons for my increasing admiration for this intellectual distraction that, after centuries of analysis, it poses us with ever new and ever more profound questions. The further one advances in its study, the more one discovers fresh vistas and mysterious problems of which one did not even suspect the existence. If, too, we grant to the representatives of the art, to the players properly so called, the right to protest against excessive scientific research, the representatives of the science, that is to say the theorists, have also their interests, their ambitions, their ideal, which we must not despise.

To appreciate a combination at its true value it is not enough to admire the sacrifices which accompany it. Account must be taken of the difficulties which it presents, the risks and dangers which it involves, and the qualities which it demands of a player. It is science that reveals these to us. It is science, too, that gives us a just notion of its beauty, that teaches us to distinguish and appraise, without excessive admiration, the tinsel of certain combinations, hailed as brilliant, but often complicating the game without necessity and rendering victory doubtful, which are really useless, unsound, or the sequel of a gross blunder.

How far we are in them from the problem, properly so-called, with its strict conditions of purity and economy! And yet our satisfaction is great when we succeed in winning a fine game, forming a homogeneous whole, crowned with a final combination which attains its end by the surest, neatest, and quickest means. When, too, we finish with a "problem-mate", we feel that we have created, not indeed an immortal work, but a little art-treasure of our own. If, on the other hand, chance wills it that at a turn of the game we can profit by a hostile error to sacrifice our Queen and thereby snatch a doubtful victory, we have the winner's commonplace satisfaction, but none of the artist's inner joy.

There remains a last essential query: *Who* is able to profit by the study of combinations? Is it the grand masters? Certainly not, for they know by experience much more than is currently taught. The study of combinations is particularly for the moderate player, whom it will arm in his battles and will show that his admiration for some of his conquerors is often merely the result of ordinary ignorance; for his losses are frequently due not to his opponents' talents, but to their acquaintance with the works and ideas of others. We must distinguish between the genuine creators and the numerous imitators—who are really counterfeiters. If we thoroughly understand the structure of combinations and the mechanism which sets them going, when the part borne therein by genius flashes before our eyes, we shall appreciate it still better.

I shall therefore strive here, as in previous books of mine, to be as clear and simple as possible, to be accessible to all, to stifle nobody under the burden of a learning which aids in the preparation of the work, but should never make it crushing; to justify, in short, the sub-title which I have given to this book, "a guide for all players of the game".

CHAPTER II

WHAT IS A COMBINATION?

Definition

ALL chess players *know* what a combination is. Whether one makes it oneself, or is its victim, or reads of it, it stands out from the rest of the game and stirs one's admiration. Nevertheless, it is difficult to define the meaning of the word exactly. Definitions are either too wide or too narrow. The best of them convey very little to our mind, and do not correspond with the feeling which an actual combination inspires in us. Here, for example, is one of Dr. Vœllmy's most successful definitions: "A combination in chess is a transition (*Übergang*) in the game which, by its form, is distinguished from the general expected trend of the game".

We may substitute for the word "transition", which is not familiar to the majority of players, the phrase "series of moves between two positions" (between the middle and end games, for instance), and can then see that this definition includes the essence of a combination. Yet how inadequate it is! We cannot think of the decisive combination in the famous "Immortal Game" without feeling that such a definition does not cover it. If one were asked, in an inversion of the definition, "What is a series of moves which is distinguished from the general expected trend of the game?", would one answer offhand, "It is a combination"?

But is it necessary to find a definition? Why not simply give up the attempt? Before confessing our inability, however, let us see what are the indispensable conditions which make out of a series of moves a combination.

Are the Moves of a Combination forced?

Generally speaking, a combination, in the course of a game, has a quite distinct unity. Its beginning and its end can be determined. The moves which compose it are fairly closely linked with certain special characteristics, which we may sum up.

First let us ask whether the moves of a combination are forced. In comparison with the positional game of today, wherein a complete freedom of movement prevails, where often the next move cannot be foreseen, the combinational game seems to be governed by some inevitable necessity. Yet, really, it is not only in combinations that the moves are forced. Remember those end-games in which every move is compulsory, those blocked positions where there is no choice, those immediate direct threats which allow but one reply. There is no question of combination in these cases. And, besides, forced continuations are only found in simple short combinations. The longer and more complicated they are, the more freedom the defence has, even to the point of having almost as much as in the normal course of the game.

Our first example shows one of the most complicated combinations ever seen. Black sacrifices a Rook, although he had not completed his development. The consequent difficulties can be imagined. Pieces are lacking for the attack, and the decision can only be reached by an increase of development. Quiet moves, without a direct threat, leave White freedom to do much as he wishes,

No. 1

Teplitz-Schönau Tournament, 1922

S. G. Tartakover

G. Maróczy

1.. R×P; 2 K×R, Q×P ch; 3 K—R1 (3 B—Kt2 is the alternative), Kt—B3; 4 R—K2, Q×KtP; 5 Kt—Kt1 (or R—Kt2), Kt—R4; 6 Q—Q2 (or again R—Kt2), B—Q2; 7 R—B2 (or Q—K1), Q—R5 ch; 8 K—Kt1, B—Kt6; 9 B—B3 (or R—Kt2 or R2), B×R ch; 10Q×B, P—Kt6; 11 Q—KKt2, R—KB1, and Black won on the 18th move.

and to make his choice, on almost every move, between several replies.

We give 11 of the 18 moves required to secure the win. It is clearly impossible to foresee all the moves precisely. The combination is therefore based on a fine understanding of the opportunities of the position, without our being able to say that we have before us a magnificent positional combination.

Absolute freedom, alas! never exists on the chess-board; no more there than elsewhere in this life of ours. It is just a question of degrees of constraint. In the deepest and most positional combinations constraint is the more accentuated, because the threats, though not necessarily direct, are localised. In the example before us, where there is hardly any immediate threat, the attack is aimed at certain King-side squares, and the question to be solved is what course will first bring up the reserves to decide the fate of the struggle.

One may say, therefore, that in combinations the element of constraint is more marked than in the ordinary course of the game, without claiming that the moves are absolutely forced, or that forced moves inevitably make a combination. This conclusion is of little weight, it may be said; but nevertheless it is something gained.

Must a Combination lead to an Advantage?

What is the worth of a combination of exceptional brilliance, if it is refuted? Of what use is the brilliant flash, if it is to end in extinction? It sometimes happens that we have foreseen everything, have minutely analysed all the variations, and have attained our objects, when a counter-combination by our opponent suddenly puts us at his mercy. Our daring and ingenuity have been entirely wasted. Although unsound combinations are still combinations, they are stamped with the original sin of chess, for they do not attain the essential object, which is victory. But, while without interest from the theoretical point of view, they can still sometimes serve as examples. We should always give the preference to a daring combination over a tame continuation, but the least that we can ask of the combination is that it shall not lead us away from victory. ⋅This is the theoretical view-point; for in practice the daring player is to be encouraged, whatever may be the results of his boldness.

In our second example Black could have chosen a pretty combination, with several very uncertain variations, one of which is extremely brilliant, viz. 2..P – K5 (instead of R × P); 3 P × P, Kt – K4; 4 Q – B3, B × P; 5 Q × B, Q × B; 6 Q × Q, Kt – B6 ch; 7 K – Kt2, Kt × Q; 8 KR – K1, Kt × P.

All the sacrificed material has been regained—but that is all, for after 9 Kt – B4 the advantage is distinctly White's.

So this firework display would have ended in disaster. One must resist the temptation to be brilliant beyond reason. In a game of chess one is obliged to be a materialist. Everything must be subordinated to the idea of victory, and useless or dangerous beauty, which compromises the result, must be considered a fault.

Nevertheless, the moves

No. 2

Paris Inter-club Match, 1934

E. Znosko-Borovsky

J. Cukierman

Black played 1..P – KB4; 2 P × P, R × P.

of this combination may serve as an example. We have (1) the sacrifice of the KBP, to open a file for the QR; (2) the sacrifice of the KP, to open a diagonal for the B and to allow Kt – K4; (3) the sacrifice of the B, to open the file for the Q; (4) the sacrifice of the Q, to allow the Kt's check, with the win of White's Q. But this is all vanity, only worthy of a place in the annotations! What we have to occupy ourselves with here is the sound combination, which is much less frequent than enterprises of this kind.

The advantages which may be gained by a combination are very various, from a forced mate to an infinitesimal superiority in position. The consequences depend on the

opponent's play, and on the initial position.   If the latter
gives scope for a real advantage, the combination ought to
be decisive.   When there is initial equality we must be less
exacting; and when we stand in inferiority we should thank
Heaven for being able to secure a draw!

Can we blame the player who, by an elegant combination
in a level position, forces a draw against a tenacious op-

No. 3
New York Tournament, 1927
M. Vidmar

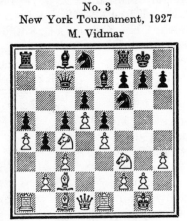

J. R. Capablanca

1 KKt×P, B−R3; 2 B−Kt3, P×Kt; 3 P−Q6, B×P; 4 Q×B, Q×Q;
5 Kt×Q, Kt−Kt2; 6 Kt×Kt, B×Kt; 7 P×P, BP×P; 8 P−B3, etc.

ponent?   We should praise him who has the courage to
venture on a complicated combination, of which the consequences are hard to foresee, even if he fails to arrive at a
definite result.   Is the calm positional game all peace?
Certainly not.   So why should we be more exacting where
a combination is concerned?

In Example No. 3 the game is still in its beginnings.
There is no superiority to be noted on either side.   Yet
White ventures on a Knight-sacrifice.   Several exchanges
follow, and finally, without any gain in material, White
obtains almost a winning position.   This combination, so
different from those which result in mate after a few moves
or in some big gain, is therefore justified.

Good judgement of position decides.   To bring off a
brilliant combination one must be a subtle positional player.

We see that, from the standpoint of advantage gained, combinations resemble other manœuvres. But the latter transform a position imperceptibly, while the former, being limited in their object, transform it swiftly. That is why Dr. Vœllmy calls a combination a "transition". It is, in fact, like a bridge thrown over between two positions. The bridge once crossed, the landscape changes. And, since we are indulging in metaphor, let us think of the uplift of some immortal poem, of the phrase which illuminates some spell-binding speech, or, better still, of the thunder-clap that brings about a gigantic collapse.

Does a Combination necessarily involve Sacrifices?

It is unjust, and sometimes very untrue, though it is a common theory, to hold that it is sacrifices which make the beauty of a combination, and that the combination is prettier by the magnitude of the sacrifices. In reality, when one sacrifices a major piece, the risk is but apparent, for it is seldom that there is delay in the result. One compels resignation, surely and precisely, with few variations possible. Pawn-sacrifices, on the contrary, are often of remarkable subtlety and, since the advantage is not assured, one runs a great risk.

In judging a combination from the artistic point of view, we must consider, besides, the variety of defences, the number of variations, the originality of the positions, the disparity between the attacking and defending forces, the purity of the mates, etc. It is possible to imagine a very beautiful combination which involves no sacrifice. But all must be subordinated to the essential principle of victory. To insure that, the path chosen must be the shortest and the most decisive. A player who does not despise the flash of doubtful combinations exhibits bad taste. We must resist the temptation to sacrifice and give the preference at need to a simple continuation, with no ostentation, which leads inevitably to a win. Chess must not shun that bareness of style which is so sought after today in the realm of the arts. Compared with classic beauty, the prettiness of certain combinations may be likened to that eloquence, mere

words, of which Paul Verlaine in his *Art poétique* expressed
his desire to "wring the neck".

All conditions being equal, however, let us prefer to the
tame and ordinary game those beautiful combinations,
demanding imagination, risk, fighting spirit, bravery, which
venture beyond the rut of patience and of memory.   Nowadays it would be a good thing for many players, even the

No. 4
St. Petersburg Tournament, 1914
J. R. Capablanca

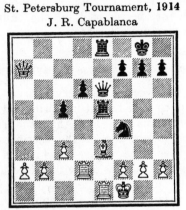

A. Alekhine

1..Kt × P; 2 K × Kt, Q − Kt5 ch; 3 K − B1, Q − R6 ch; 4 K − K2, R × B ch;
5 P × R, Q × P ch; 6 K − Q1, Q × R ch, etc.

finest of them, to take a "cure" of combinations, to liven
them up, to induce them to leave a little the sure and beaten
tracks wherein they step slowly, with relentless logic,
towards the nullity of the draw.

In No. 4 Black has sacrificed a Pawn.   He has two continuations that clearly lead to gain, one slow but sure, the
other in the grand style:

(1) The variation without a surprise, 1..Q – Kt5;
2 Q – Kt7, P – Q4; 3 P – B3, Q – K3; 4 B × Kt, R × R ch,
winning the Exchange at the price of the menace to his QP.

(2) The variation chosen, beginning with a Knight-
sacrifice and leading to the win of two Pawns.

In such a case the Knight-sacrifice is justified, and the
continuation is the better one.   Only the uninspired player
would prefer the first variation.

If, on the other hand, analysis had demonstrated that the possession of a Pawn to the good did not lead to a win, whereas the gain of the Exchange made sure of it, it would have been necessary, with a heavy heart, to reject the alluring sacrifice, and to choose the tame continuation.

We see here what distinguishes a combination from an ordinary manœuvre; not so much the sacrifice as the surprise. Is it not this which best characterises the combination?

Surprise

Let us be precise.   It is not a question merely of the kind of surprise excited by a battering blow at an opponent who never dreamt of his game suddenly falling in ruins.   The student is affected by the same surprise, which springs from an upset of the natural and logical course of events.   What a sweet satisfaction it is to our adversary when an unexpected sacrifice makes us jump!   For instance, we may have a Pawn protected by another Pawn, seemingly invulnerable and safe from attack by pieces.   If a piece captures it, we are disconcerted; which is logical, since the superiority of pieces to Pawns is one of the fundamental rules of chess. But there are special cases, and exceptions which prove the rule.   Our judgement, in short, was superficial, for strict analysis would show the sacrifice to be justified.   Under the surprise-blow the game may take a different turn, to the shortening of its duration.

Let us go back to Example No. 1.   White's King-side Pawns there seemed sufficiently defended before the surprise sacrifice of Black's Rook, which led to the fall of all those Pawns.   Although the attack had still to go on against the King's position, the upset was caused by the breaking of the Pawn-barrier.   A new defence was called for, by pieces, to stop a mate on one of the unsheltered squares.

Distinguished as it is from a mere manœuvre by this element of surprise, a "combination" may be very beautiful and absolutely forced, may give a decisive superiority and may consist of a limited number of moves, yet if there is no surprise there is no reason for considering it a combination.

So with the position in our fifth example, Black has an isolated Pawn at R4, attacked by a Knight, defended by a Rook. White attacks the Rook four times and at last wins the Pawn. The manœuvre is fine, ingenious, and decisive, and every move is almost forced. But the element of surprise is lacking, and it is better not to classify this manœuvre among combinations, for otherwise we could not draw the

No. 5
New York Tournament, 1924
F. D. Yates

J. R. Capablanca

1 Kt—B3, R—B4; 2 Kt—K4, R—Kt4; 3 Kt(K4)—Q6, R—B4;
4 Kt—Kt7, R—B2; 5 Kt(Kt7)×P, etc.

line of demarcation between manœuvres and combinations. The latter coming within the general category of the former, it is necessary to make a sharp distinction.

We may go further, and say that combinations based on surprises which are too well known, indeed hackneyed, are not real combinations, since the idea of the unforeseen is excluded. A well-known air when made popular on the street-organs loses thereby much of its charm.

The manœuvre called commonly in England "Philidor's Legacy" (though it really dated from Lucena in 1497, at the latest) is just a well-known case of smothered mate. When this manœuvre was brought off for the first time, the sacrifice of the Queen, to allow the Knight to administer smothered mate, must certainly have caused immense surprise. Though today many amateurs may, through ignorance, content themselves in the position with a perpetual check, we must allow that " Philidor's Legacy" is universally known and can excite no surprise.   Consequently we need pay no more attention to it.

Let us sum up our observations on the essence of combinations.

A combination is distinguished from other manœuvres by a surprise, springing as a rule from a sacrifice.   It brings about a sudden change in the position, and should gain some advantage for the player.   It is composed of a series of more or less forced moves, and satisfies an aesthetic demand.

We must be content with this definition; which does not, however, prevent us from feeling that in a combination there is all this—and something more!

No. 6

Lucena's Mate (or "Philidor's Legacy")

1 Q — K6 ch, K — R1; 2 Kt — B7 ch, K — Kt1; 3 Kt — R6 dbl. ch K — R1; 4 Q — Kt8 ch, R × Q; 5 Kt — B7 mate.

CHAPTER III

EXCEPTIONAL COMBINATIONS

THERE is no limit to the number of combinations. To see clearly into their diversity and to perform work that will be of service, a judicious classification is necessary. As the French proverb says, *Qui trop embrasse, mal étreint*; or, in English, one should not bite off more than one can chew. We must therefore exclude from examination, for various reasons, combinations which fall under the following three categories, though not forbidding ourselves to choose examples from among them:

(1) Combinations due to chance, as based chiefly on opponents' errors;

(2) Traps in the openings, since they cannot succeed except through the like errors, and are, moreover, too simple and well known to deserve the name of combinations;

(3) Positional sacrifices, because they only differ from ordinary combinations in the end sought, and that end is often difficult to set out precisely.

Combinations due to Chance

If it is pleasant to receive a godsend and to feel that the powers above are working in our favour, we must recognise that our personal merit in the matter is none. A combination in like circumstances, however charming, is hardly ever instructive. To be preferred is one that rewards our industry like a fruit which we have tended, to gather when it is ripe.

In No. 7, White's inferiority is manifest. Three Black pieces are developed, whilst White has developed only a Bishop and the Queen, which has come from K3 to escape the Bishop (if Q × B, of course Kt – Q6 ch) and is exposed to all sorts of surprises. If she had gone to K2, the pretty combination—a good example of the Knight's manœuvre, which we shall deal with—would not have been possible.

In No. 8 we see the rather exceptional case where two combinations unexpectedly present themselves in consequence of the opponent's errors. It must be admitted that White has some attack against the hostile King, but a sound defence is possible. Moreover, having provoked the sacrifice of the Exchange by his first imprudent move, Black might

No. 7
Leipzig, 1903
R. Swiderski

No. 8
Ostend Tournament, 1906
J. Taubenhaus

X.

J. Mieses

1..B × P ch; 2 Q × B, Kt − Q6 ch. Or 2 K × B, Kt × P ch. In any case the Queen is lost.

1 Kt − QKt5, Kt − K5?; 2 R × Kt!, P × R; 3 Kt × P ch, K − Q2?; 4 Kt − K5 ch, and wins.

still have escaped ruin by playing 3..K – Kt2. 3..K – Q2 provoked a second, very pretty sacrifice. The manœuvre might have been given to illustrate a certain type of combination. But combinations which are at once pretty and unaided by the opponent's errors are numerous enough to make it unnecessary to choose examples marred by faults. I have little taste for combinations of this kind. We should improve and refine our taste, and not just placidly admire sacrifices based on bad blunders by the opponent.

Traps

Traps in the opening are so many that we have a positively embarrassing choice. We must limit ourselves to a few examples wherein, despite errors, true combinations manifest themselves.

First we may take "Légal's Mate", of which Example No. 9 is an illustration. The position was brought about as follows: 1 P – K4, P – K4; 2 B – B4, P – Q3; 3 Kt – KB3, B – Kt5; 4 Kt – B3, Kt – QB3; 5 P – Q4, P – KR3. White's combination has been made possible by an accumu-

No. 9
Philadelphia, 1882

X.

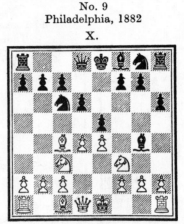

W. Steinitz

It was White's 6th move. Then, 6 P × P, Kt × P; 7 Kt × Kt, B × Q; 8 B × P ch, K – K2; 9 Kt – Q5 mate.

lation of faults on Black's part. Why, for instance, P – KR3? Why, next, Kt × P? Black could have played 6 . . P × P or, better still, B × Kt, and if 7 Q × B, then Kt × P, defending the KBP and forking Queen and Bishop. The number of errors which enable White's combination might have made us suppose that it could only occur once. But no; since its baptismal in the Eighteenth Century the combination has been often reproduced in serious games, and it reappears frequently in club-circles over the world, especially as the trap can occur in various openings—a fact which leads the novice astray. Here are a few examples:

Game won in 1847 by the celebrated Ernest Falkbeer (*Danish Gambit*): 1 P – K4, P – K4; 2 P – Q4, P × P; 3 P – QB3, P × P; 4 Kt × P, P – Q3; 5 B – QB4, Kt – QB3; 6 Kt – B3, B – Kt5; 7 Castles, Kt – K4?; 8 Kt × Kt, B × Q;

9 B × P ch, K – K2; 10 Kt – Q5 mate.

Game played in 1896 (*Vienna Game*): 1 P – K4, P – K4;
2 Kt – QB3, Kt – QB3; 3 P – B4, P – Q3; 4 Kt – B3,
P – QR3; 5 B – B4, B – Kt5; 6 Castles, Kt – Q5; 7 Kt × P,
B × Q; 8 B × P ch, K – K2; 9 Kt – Q5 mate.

Game played by H. N. Pillsbury in 1900, with the same
first 5 moves as in the preceding example: 6 P × P, Kt × P;
7 Kt × Kt, B × Q; 8 B × P ch, K – K2; 9 Kt – Q5 mate.

Game played in 1915 (*King's Gambit Declined*): 1 P – K4,
P – K4; 2 P – KB4, P – Q3; 3 Kt – KB3, Kt – QB3; 4 B – B4,
B – Kt5; 5 Kt – B3, Kt – Q5; 6 Kt × P, B × Q; 7 B × P ch,
K – K2; 8 Kt – Q5 mate.

So this flagrant, almost "twopenny" trap continues its successes through time and space!   In simultaneous exhibitions
the masters have frequent chances to set it for the unwary.

Finally, here is Légal's own mate, the *editio princeps*, so
to speak, of the trap.   Philidor's celebrated teacher once
played a *Bishop's Opening* thus: 1 P – K4, P – K4; 2 B – B4,
P – Q3; 3 Kt – KB3, B – Kt5; 4 Kt – B3, P – KKt3?;
5 Kt × P, B × Q; 6 B × P ch, K – K2; 7 Kt – Q5 mate.   On
another occasion, giving the odds of QR, he brought it off
still more flagrantly: 1 P – K4, P – K4; 2 B – B4, P – Q3;
3 Kt – KB3, Kt – QB3; 4 Kt – B3, B – Kt5; 5 Kt × P,
B × Q; 6 B × P ch, K – K2; 7 Kt – Q5 mate.   It is obvious
that if Black had played 5 . . Kt × Kt he could hardly have
lost, with B and Kt to the good.   White reckoned on a
blunder, and that is precisely why we cannot commend
play based on such petty traps, which take almost for
granted the stupidity of the other player.

A somewhat similar trap occurs in the *Queen's Gambit
Declined*.   After 1 P – Q4, P – Q4; 2 P – QB4, P – K3;
3 Kt – QB3, Kt – KB3; 4 B – Kt5, Black can unpin by
B – K2 or defend by QKt – Q2.   The latter move cuts off
the defence of the QP by his Queen, so that White can win
a Pawn—and fall into the trap: 5 P × P, P × P; 6 Kt × P?,
Kt × Kt; 7 B × Q, B – Kt5 ch; 8 Q – Q2, B × Q ch; 9 K × B,
K × B, Black being a piece ahead.

This combination may occur in various openings, in
more subtle form, and sometimes with colours inverted.

For instance, in the *Queen's Gambit Declined*: 1 P – Q4,
P – Q4; 2 P – QB4, P – K3; 3 Kt – KB3, Kt – KB3;
4 Kt – B3, P – B4; 5 B – Kt5, BP × P; 6 KKt × P, P – K4;
7 KKt – Kt5, P – Q5; 8 Kt – Q5?, Kt × Kt; 9 B × Q,
B – Kt5 ch; 10 Kt – B3, P × Kt, and Black wins.

The same combination, but more complicated and finer,
is demonstrated in Example No. 10. If on his 4th move

No. 10
Vienna Tournament, 1908
O. Duras

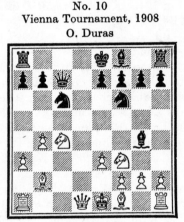

A. Rubinstein

1 . . P × QKt4; 2 QKt – K5, Kt × Kt; 3 Kt × Kt, B × Q; 4 B × P ch, Kt – Q2;
    5 B × Kt ch, Q × B; 6 Kt × Q, B – R4; 7 Kt – K5, and wins.

Black had played K – Q1, then would have followed the
magnificent variation 5 R × B ch, K – B1; 6 B – R6 ch,
K – Kt1; 7 Kt – B6 ch, Q × Kt; 8 B – K5 ch, Q – Q3;
9 R – QB1, and mate next move. And if on his 5th move
K – Q1, then 6 R × B, etc.

Laborious analysis was here necessary to establish the
certainty of a mate or a win of Black's Queen. The
essential point always is to hit upon the idea of the combination, for then one knows where one is going, and the
variations are capable of proof. There is nothing to be
said against a "trap" of such subtlety, which calls for ingenuity and no small measure of courage; and praise is due
to the player who can conceive the trap, set it, and secure
the prize in elegant style.

Inspired by the idea which we have just been examining, the author once attempted to elaborate a combination of the same kind, and succeeded in arriving at a final mating position which is really charming; an economic mate, wherein every piece engaged is necessary. Some duals are inevitable. The many opening errors, however, that are required to bring off the combination militate against its

No. 11
Study by E. Znosko-Borovsky

No. 12
Cologne, 1912
B. Kostich

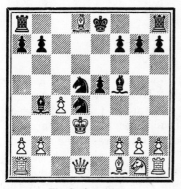

The final position.

Mühlock
The final position.

classification among artistic studies. The reader may judge. It is a *Caro-Kann Defence*: 1 P – K4, P – QB3; 2 P – Q4, P – Q4; 3 P × P, P × P; 4 P – QB4, Kt – QB3; 5 Kt – QB3, Kt – B3; 6 B – Kt5, P – K4; 7 Kt × P, Kt × Kt; 8 B × Q, B – Kt5 ch; 9 K – K2, Kt × P ch; 10 K – Q3, B – B4 mate. (See diagram No. 11.)

Another game of the same kind follows, played by Dr. B. Lasker, as Black, in Berlin in 1896, against a weak opponent: 1 P – K4, P – K4; 2 Kt – QB3, Kt – QB3; 3 P – Q3, Kt – B3; 4 P – QKt3, P – Q4; 5 B – Kt5, P × P; 6 Kt × P, Kt × Kt; 7 B × Q, B – Kt5 ch; 8 K – K2, Kt – B6 ch; 9 K – K1, Kt – Q5; 10 Q – Q2, B – Kt5; 11 B – Kt5, Kt – K5; 12 P × Kt, Kt × P mate.

Let us see another well-known opening trap. A win by Kostich will serve as an example (No. 12). He was

Black in a *King's Knight's Opening*: 1 P – K4, P – K4; 2 Kt – KB3, Kt – QB3; 3 B – B4, Kt – Q5; 4 Kt × P, Q – Kt4; 5 Kt × BP, Q × KtP; 6 R – B1, Q × KP ch; 7 B – K2, Kt – B6 mate.

Two other games of the same kind show that a similar trap can be met in different openings. (1) McGrouther–McCann (*Sicilian Defence*): 1 P – K4, P – QB4; 2 Kt – KB3, Kt – QB3; 3 P – Q4, P × P; 4 Kt × P, P – K4?; 5 Kt – B5, KKt – K2??; 6 Kt – Q6 mate. (2) X.–Jankovitch (*Irregular*): 1 P – K4, P – K4; 2 Kt – K2, B – B4; 3 P – KB4, Q – B3; 4 P – B3, Kt – B3; 5 P – KKt3, Kt – R3; 6 B – Kt2, Kt – KKt5; 7 R – B1, Kt × P; 8 P × P, Q × R ch; 9 B × Q, Kt – B6 mate.

Positional Sacrifices

A sacrifice is called positional, when it does not lead to a rapid gain by violent attack. It aims at advantage in position. Therefore the various gambits might be classed under the heading of positional sacrifices, for at the moment when they are offered it is impossible to foresee the outcome of the attack that is initiated. The sole object in view is to speed up development and get ahead of one's opponent. But we must draw a distinction. In the majority of the old gambits it was the hostile King that was aimed at, and there was nothing of positional sacrifice in the attack delivered. There is a vast difference in the modern openings, where the only object of the gambit is advantage in position.

Take, for instance, the *Blumenfeld Counter-Gambit*: 1 P – Q4, Kt – KB3; 2 Kt – KB3 (or P – QB4 first), P – K3; 3 P – B4, P – B4; 4 P – Q5, *P – QKt4*; 5 QP × P, BP × P; 6 P × P, P – Q4! (continued below diagram No. 13).

Black has sacrificed a Pawn to obtain a strong centre, but there is no indication how the game will go. In fact, it will take not less than 15 moves for the form of the attack to be seen, and this attack has no relation to the initial sacrifice. But it is precisely that which distinguishes such a sacrifice. The Pawn on White's QKt5 does not count, while his strength in the centre gives an immediate advantage to Black, and allows him to combine central pressure with an attack on the hostile King.

In this sacrifice, which recalls the *Wing Gambit* in the *Sicilian Defence*, there is not yet a question of a positional sacrifice, in the strict sense of the term. A strong centre and a better development are appreciable advantages; but the positional game, which is concerned rather with *squares*, and does not contemplate the attack on the hostile King, is a more subtle affair.

<table>
<tr><td>No. 13</td><td>No. 14</td></tr>
<tr><td>Pistyan Tournament, 1922</td><td>Copenhagen Tournament, 1923</td></tr>
<tr><td>A. Alekhine</td><td>A. Nimzovitch</td></tr>
</table>

S. Tarrasch   F. Sämisch

7 P – K3, B – Q3;   8 Kt – B3, Castles;
9 B – K2,   B – Kt2;   10 P – QKt3,
QKt – Q2; 11 B – Kt2, Q – K2, etc.

1 P – K4, BP × P;   2 Q × Kt, R × P;
3 Q – Kt5,   QR – KB1;   4 K – R1,
QR – B4; 5 Q – K3, B – Q6; 6 QR – K1,
P – R3.

The next example, No. 14, is still more striking. White has a cramped position, and to free himself plays P – K4. But Black, by sacrificing the Knight, closes up his opponent's game still further, to such an extent indeed that he has no move to make, and is obliged to give up. Here we have sacrifice and combination with a purely positional object. Nevertheless this example, though coming under the game of position, is akin to the old-style combinative game.

In Example No. 15 the positional game has a sensational triumph. Why does White sacrifice a Pawn? No attack results from it; indeed, one might suppose, no advantage, since Black keeps his two Bishops. But White's Knight on Kt6 forces the hostile QR to occupy the unfavourable square, R2, to protect his threatened Pawn. Moreover, White holds the open QB file and can, if he wishes, get both Rooks on it. These are pure positional advantages.

No. 16 is a comparatively recent English example, from the B.C.F. championship contest two years ago. White has already a decided advantage in position, with his strong Pawn-centre, and with two of Black's pieces badly placed

No. 15
World Championship Match, 1934

E. D. Bogoljuboff

A. Alekhine

1 P—K4, P×P; 2 P—R3, KKt—K4; 3 KKt×Kt, Kt×Kt; 4 B—KB4, B—Q3; 5 B×Kt, B×B; 6 Kt—Kt6, R—R2; 7 QR—B1, Q—Q3; 8 R—B4, etc.

No. 16
Hastings Tournament, 1933

Sultan Khan

W. Winter

1 KR—Kt1, P×P; 2 B×P ch, K—Q2; 3 P×P, R×P ch; 4 K—Q3, R×P ch; 5 K—B4, R—B4; 6 R—Q1 ch, K—B2; 7 KR—K1, R—B2; 8 B×P, R—R1 (he could not catch the Bishop by P—Kt3); 9 R—K5, K—B1; 10 P—Kt6, R—B3; 11 R—B5 ch, R—B3; 12 R×R ch, P×R; 13 P—R5, and the Q-side Pawns win.

on the King's side. He lets all of his Pawn-centre be swept away, in order to decide the game on the Queen's side. His initial move of KR – Kt1 was so far part of his combination that by the threat of R × P he forced Black to counter-attack in the centre.

In the chess of to-day sacrifices of this kind, differing so much from those that were the glory of the old-school combinationists, are plentiful. But it is useless to accumu-late examples. We shall not study in our book this type of combination, for the simple reason that such sacrifices are completely subordinate to the positional game, and it is the combinational game with which we are concerned.

We submit, however, one final example of a sacrifice which has in view a superiority in the end-game sufficient to secure a win.

As the sacrifice is of the Queen for two Rooks, it might be regarded in the light rather of an exchange—and in this

No. 17
Folkestone Team Tournament,
1933
Sir George Thomas

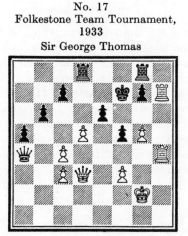

J. Enevoldsen

1 . . Q − Q2; 2 R(R4) − R6, K − B1; 3 Q − Q4, Q − K2; 4 R − B6 ch (4 P − B4, P − K4),
   P × R; 5 R × Q, R × P ch; 6 K − B2, K × R, with a winning end-game.

case, owing to the mobility of the Rooks, a decidedly advantageous exchange.   Black declares his intention by his first move, which, but for the fact that he was already a Pawn down, might have deterred White from continuing with his operations against the hostile King's position.

CHAPTER IV

AN ATTEMPT AT CLASSIFICATION

Order in Chaos

To give our work an interest which is not only theoretical and scientific but also practical, it is necessary to group the innumerable combinations in such a way that the student can see clearly into the welter and derive instruction from his contemplation. It would be impossible to take into consideration the whole mass of combinations, or even those which have been recorded. But the result will be sufficiently remarkable if we can arrive at a methodical classification of the most important and most frequently occurring. We must be content with marking our first steps into a virgin forest and blazing a trail for future explorers.

What principle, then, will allow us to establish this classification?

The study of combinations teaches us that some of them do not seem to depend upon the position, that they apply to all parts of the chess-board. Others, on the contrary, can only be carried out in certain parts, as for example the combination against the castled King.

We have, therefore, two main groups, each of them demanding a special study.

In the first group we have pure ideas, which recall the themes of problems. It will be sufficient to examine briefly a series of combinations, in order to extract from them their principal basic ideas.

In the second group these ideas are always subordinate to the peculiarities of the position, which also give rise to other special ideas, so that we have to analyse the various positions which we meet.

Although one may say that every combination depends upon the position, and is governed by it, the difference between the two groups is not to be denied. Thus an idea of combination depending on an unprotected piece, or on a piece which protects two or three important squares, may be developed at any point on the board and in very different positions, whereas a certain definite structural position is necessary for the development of a combination of the second group.

Terminology

To avoid confusion we shall employ as few technical terms as possible; in fact, only one, the idea of combination, of which we have just been speaking. We must, however, make a distinction between the principal and the secondary idea, between the idea of combination and the idea which justifies it, the combination itself and the accessory incident, etc. Appropriate terms must be found for all these special features. But the reader assuredly is looking for a study in chess, not in linguistics; and the time which might have been devoted to the search for terms would have been detrimental to the prosecution of chess analysis. We should deserve no thanks for distracting attention to terminological matters instead of a full discussion of what is the subject of this book—Combinations.

It is to be hoped that the almost complete avoidance of technical terms will not in any way detract from the clearness and precision of our exposition.

PART II

COMBINATIONAL IDEAS

CHAPTER 1

COMBINATIONS, PROBLEMS, AND STUDIES

The Basic Idea

EVERY combination has as its basis an idea to be developed. This idea is usually simple, even when the combination is complicated; such as an undefended piece, the bad position of the hostile King, the promotion of a Pawn, a discovered check, and so on. Not depending on position, this simple idea may apply to all parts of the board, though a certain positional arrangement is necessary for its success.

Combinational Ideas and Problem Themes

Combinational ideas, we have said, recall the themes of artistic compositions, problems, and studies. There are, however, certain essential differences to be noted.

When we play we do not choose the position, we can only make those combinations which present themselves to us after a preparation that is full of chance. We hardly ever, like the composer, have the complete material at our disposal. The composer always starts with an idea, which he strives to realise in its best shape, whereas the player strives to find the idea contained in a position that occurs in the actual game he is playing. The player brings out the idea as the sculptor reveals the statue which sleeps in the block of marble.

Certain themes, therefore, which are currently used in problems, are hardly ever met in games, while an idea fertile in combinations may be devoid of interest for the problem-composer. But a problem can suggest to a player a combinational idea, just as a remarkable turn in a game may inspire a composer. Thus Dr. Tarrasch evolved a combination which is nothing but an application of the celebrated Indian theme. See No. 55.

Let us take from the Russian problemist A. Herbstman, in his work on the subject, a few examples of the mutual influence on one another of players and composers.

The position in No. 18 occurred in a simultaneous display (which excuses his error) by the then champion of the world. Black's idea is simple: to drive the White King to a square on which his KtP can administer a check, so as to allow his own King to move to KKt2 and catch White's advanced Pawn.

No. 18
London, 1914
R. J. Loman

Dr. Emanuel Lasker

1 . . R − B6 ch;   2 K − Kt4?, R − B5 ch;
3 K − Kt5,   R − KR5!;   4 K × R,
P − Kt4 ch;   5 K × P,   K − Kt2, and
wins.

No. 19
Study by F. Sehwers
(Collection of Studies, 1921)

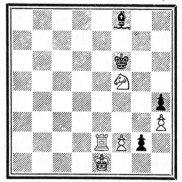

White to play and draw

1 R − K6 ch,   K × Kt   (if   K × R,
2 Kt − Q4 ch   and   3 Kt − B3);
2 R − K5 ch,   K − B3   (if   K × R,
3 P − B4 ch and 4 K − B2); 3 R − KKt5,
K × R; 4 P − B4 ch, K moves; 5 K − B2.
Drawn game.

The combination depended on an error, but was so pleasing that the great composer F. Sehwers set himself to exhibit it in conjunction with the best defence (No. 19). It can be seen from the result he obtained that the idea is still the same: to bring the hostile King to a square on which he can be checked by the KBP, allowing White to catch the KtP. The superiority of the study over the actual ending is notable. The idea is less simple, because a third sacrifice, the Knight's, is added, and it is only the Knight, in one variation, which can stop the Pawn. A clear example of that idea of combination of which we have so far only spoken theoretically.

Here now, in No. 20, is an example of a study inspiring a player and enabling him to win a game.

White wins by promoting a Pawn to a Knight instead of a Queen, such promotion leading to immediate mate.

The Knight in certain positions is more powerful than any other piece.

This choice of the Knight-promotion is illustrated again in game played nineteen years after the study was published

No. 20
Study by H. Rinck
(*Deutsche Schachzeitung*, 1905)

No. 21
Frankfurt, 1924
F. Präger

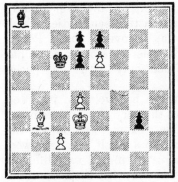

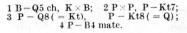

White to play and win

1 B – Q5 ch, K × B;   2 P × P, P – Kt7;
3 P – Q8 (= Kt),   P – Kt8 (= Q);
              4 P – B4 mate.

X.

1 . . Q – R1 ch; 2 P – K8(= Q?), Q – B3 ch;
and, whichever way White covers,
3 Q × P ch or Q – R1 ch leads to a perpetual.

(No. 21).   Black had here perpetual check after the promotion to Queen, whereas after 2P – K8(= Kt) he was lost, having no check, and no guard against White's Q × P ch.

Dr. Lasker conceived a similar idea of under-promotion to advantage, in an early stage of the game: 1 P – Q4, P – Q4; 2 P – QB4, P – K4; 3 QP × P, P – Q5; 4 P – K3?, B – Kt5 ch; 5 B – Q2, P × P!; 6 B × B, P × P ch; 7 K – K2, P × Kt(= Kt) ch. The Knight cannot be taken, for then B – Kt5 ch wins the Queen. But 7 . . P × Kt(= Q) would allow 8 Q × Q ch, K × Q; 9 R × Q.

CHAPTER II

GEOMETRICAL IDEAS

The Geometrical Basis

ALL conceptions in the game of chess have a geometrical basis. It is impossible to make an abstraction of the linear relations on the board, for into very many combinations there enter characteristic peculiarities which belong purely to the game, such as discovered check, Pawn-promotions, stalemate, etc. But there are other combinations in which we are concerned only with the special geometry of the chess-board.

It was Dr. Emanuel Lasker, we believe, who invented for the last class of combinations the very appropriate name of geometrical ideas. The simplest example perhaps is the "fork", a manœuvre which reduces itself, in its lowest terms, to the Pawn's power of capturing in two different directions, and which can be executed with all pieces in all positions. These combinations are frequently feasible in the end-game, when the Pawns are going on to queen. Every player knows the importance of arriving first to prevent the promotion of a hostile Pawn or to give check, if not at once at least on the next move, with a capture of the new Queen after the opponent's King has moved. In all such cases the idea is just "linear", though very simple positions are sometimes complicated as much as one could wish, so as to yield hidden combinations that delight us, especially when our opponent is gradually forced into the position we have planned for him.

No. 22 shows us an instance of a geometrical idea. Black's KRP queens on the same diagonal on which his King now stands. It suffices therefore for White to queen first and win Black's Queen by a check on QR8. But this diagonal is at present obstructed by a White Pawn and the Black Rook. The combination is only made possible by clearing the diagonal completely, which explains White's first two moves.

As soon as we have grasped a geometrical idea of this kind, the game becomes easy, logical, and concentrated on a precise object. In the last example, Dr. Alekhine could not have conceived the combination until after Black's P – QKt4, opening a long diagonal. Without that move it

No. 22
World Championship Match,
1927
J. R. Capablanca

No. 23
Study by K. A. L. Kubbel
28 *Rijen*, 1924

A. Alekhine

White to play and win

1 R – B5, R × R; 2 P × R, P – R7;
3 P – B8(= Q), P – R8(= Q); Q – R8 ch,
and wins.

1 Kt – K2 (threatening Kt – Kt3 ch),
K × Kt; 2 B – Q1 ch (threatening
B – B3), K × B; 3 P – Kt8(= Q),
P – R8(= Q); 4 Q – Kt1 ch, etc. If
here 1 . . K – B2; 2 P – Kt8(= Q),
P – R8(= Q); 3 Q – Kt6 ch, K – Kt2
(K × Kt; 4 B – Kt5 ch, with mate to
follow); 4 B – B6 ch, P × B; 5 Q × P ch,
and mate in 9 moves on KKt2! On
move 2, if K anywhere else, then 3 B – B3,
K × B; 4 P – Kt8(= Q), etc.

would have been necessary to look for another method of winning; and it is the characteristic of genius to seize immediately upon the opportunity of a win in the most decisive and elegant manner.

No. 23.—In this end-game study Kubbel exploits the same theme with much more variety, as befits an artistic composition.

It is not only on the diagonal that the coming Black Queen will be threatened, but also on the rank. Besides, the threats against her are by Knight or Bishop; and the manœuvres which force Black's King to occupy dangerous squares, so as to exploit the geometrical idea, exhaust almost all the linear possibilities of the chess-board.

In No. 24 is a combination of another kind, but still based on the same idea. Black's first move threatens immediate mate. White seems lost, for his Rook is immobilised by

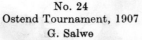

No. 24
Ostend Tournament, 1907
G. Salwe

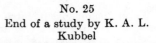

No. 25
End of a study by K. A. L.
Kubbel

E. Znosko-Borovsky

1..K—B6; 2 R—R8!, R×R; 3 P—R8   1 Q—R3 ch, K×Q; 2 Kt—B2 mate..
  (=Q)!, R×Q.   Stalemate.

his passed Pawn, his only hope. The geometrical idea comes into play. As his Pawn on promotion to Queen would command his QR1, the combination is clear; to sacrifice the Rook, which on QR8 commands QR1 vertically, and then the Queen, which commands it diagonally, and then—stalemate, the tragi-comedy of chess, as Dr. Tartakover styles it. It may be noted that if Black's Rook were at QKt2 instead of QR2 there would be no stalemate, for White's Queen would not command the mating-square. It was a mistake for Black to place his Rook on his R7.

Linear Relations

We must keep the geometrical idea, therefore, always at the back of our minds. Thanks to it, we shall be able not only to save a lost game, but also to gain at any moment an appreciable advantage.

It looks in No. 25 as if there were no connection between the pieces, and that therefore the geometrical idea is not applicable. But, if we note that the Black King and Queen are on the same diagonal, we can make use of this fact. It is the Queen's position which makes the combination possible. White's sacrifice must be accepted, on penalty of losing the Queen and the game; and the result is mate.

In actual practice it is almost impossible to think every moment of the reciprocal position of the various pieces. It is best, therefore, to develop a general feeling of these relations, especially when confronted by certain hostile pieces which are dangerous in some positions. We do not, for instance, put our King and Queen on the same diagonal when the adversary has a Bishop of the colour of that diagonal.

Let us look again at the study of which No. 25 showed only the final manœuvre. Everything already depends on the position of the Black Queen. The Black King is in trouble, under the threat of mate by an eventual Q – Kt4 or Kt2. He cannot go to other squares than those shown, or he would lose his Queen. The capture of the Knight is impossible for the same reason (King and Queen on the same file). Lastly, if he went to Q5, Kt – B5 would win the Queen; the geometrical threat of the Knight, always full of surprises, to which we shall give special attention.

In this fine study the hunted King is exposed to the risk of putting himself in geo-metrical relation with his Queen vertically and diagonally, as well as by the Knight's fork.

Note also that the Black Queen is undefended, which

No. 26
Study by K. A. L. Kubbel
150 *Endspielstudien*, 1925

White to play and win

1 Kt – K3 dis. ch, K – Kt6; 2 Q – Kt4 ch,
K – B7;   3 Q – B4 ch,   K – K7;
4 Q – B1 ch,   K – Q7;   5 Q – Q1 ch,
K – B6;   6 Q – B2 ch,   K – Kt5;
7 Q – Kt2 ch, Kt – Kt6.

makes her a glorious prey. What the geometrical idea does
here is to make use of another idea for its ends. We shall
often have occasion to observe that, whatever the idea of
the combination, the geometrical motive is never excluded
from it. It is therefore indispensable for us to be familiar
with the geometrical idea before we can undertake combinations. In complicated positions, in combinations full
of "chess", the geometrical idea is always present, though
it may be disguised, as in the following example, No. 27.

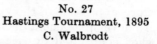

No. 27
Hastings Tournament, 1895
C. Walbrodt

S. Tarrasch

1 R × P!, Kt × P; 2 Kt × Kt, R × Kt ch; 3 P × R, R × P ch; 4 K − B1,
R × Q; 5 R − Kt4!, and wins.

In this complex combination the geometrical idea is hard
to disentangle. It is there, however, in the fact that Black's
King and Queen are on the same diagonal. The whole
combination aims at opening this diagonal for the White
Bishop. Hence the sacrifice first offered of a Rook. As
White has a Bishop of the colour of the crucial diagonal, we
have the two essential conditions of such a combination; a
line completely free of pieces, and a piece commanding this
line.

Thus, in playing, we must always keep geometrical ideas
in mind. But we know also in what circumstances we must
be careful, and of what we can take advantage. A pretty
combination will therefore be the reward for one player's

sound judgement of the position, and the just punishment for the other's positional carelessness.

Exercise

To enable the reader to learn the art of combination and to improve his gifts of imagination and analysis, we propose at the end of each chapter from now onward to submit an exercise or two, of which the solutions will be found at the end of the book.   Here is the first, the work of a composer from Aleppo, whom the British Government of his day employed in London as a translator.

No. 28

Study by P. Stamma (1737)

White to play and win.

CHAPTER III

THE KNIGHT IN COMBINATION

The "Mysterious" Knight

THE combinational value of the Knight is only one particular instance of the geometrical idea; but it is so important that we must devote a special chapter to it.

Inexperienced players have a fear of this piece, which seems to them enigmatic, mysterious, and astonishing in its power. We must admit that it has remarkable characteristics which compel respect and occasionally surprise the most wary players.

The Knight's move has the appearance of a leap or a crook, but in reality it is subject, like the other pieces' moves, to the geometry of the chess-board. Mathematicians have devoted some attention to it.

Weaker than the Rook, and even than the Bishop, both of which command whole lines, the Knight has nevertheless a special power, that of acting, like the Queen, in eight directions, while the Rook and Bishop never have more than four in which to act. It has further, over the Bishop, the advantage of being able to visit all the squares of the board, regardless of colour. These two peculiarities make its attacks much more difficult to foresee and parry. It is impossible to block its way and cut its line. As its movements are not marked on the board (*i.e.*, by intervening squares traversed), they more easily take by surprise. The Knight, as it were, mocks the rest of the men by passing over or under them!

From all this there results a certain magic power which gives Knight-combinations a special beauty. The simultaneous threat to King and Queen by Bishop seems very ordinary beside that by Knight. In Example No. 23 we saw the Knight on Kt1 threaten by a subtle manœuvre R1

—which would be impossible for a Bishop, though child's play for a Rook. The Knight goes to K2, threatening to give from Kt3 a "double check" to King on B1(8) and Queen on R1(8)—if we may be allowed such licence in chess language.[1]

All Knight-combinations are really movements which recall the "fork", the most simple of geometrical ideas. But

No. 29
Match-game in Holland, 1925
J. Davidson

M. Euwe

1 Q – Q8 ch, K – Kt2; 2 Q × Kt ch, K × Q; 3 Kt × P ch, K – K4;
4 Kt × Q, and wins.

whereas the Pawn's fork has no element of beauty in it, the fork by the Knight is always attractive, and lends itself to startling combinations, through this piece's wide power of acting in eight directions.

A simple introduction to this particular combination, in which the Knight plays a very secondary part, reaping the benefit of another piece's work, is No. 29. It is the Queen that sacrifices herself to create the position wherein the Knight displays his value. Compare "Philidor's Legacy", so-called.

This example shows how unexpected the Knight-combination can be. If the respective situation of the Black Queen and Knight leads one to suppose that it is favourable

[1] Bogoljuboff wrote of a "family check" administered by Knight to King, Queen, and two Rooks!

to an application of "double check", the attraction of the Black King to his B3 calls for that positional sense, that instinct of the linear relations between the pieces, upon which we cannot too much insist. Possessed of it, one can avoid terrible situations; without it one will not dream of them and will fall into all the traps laid, the inter-relation of the pieces in the various phases of the game being completely ignored.

It is in this that the comparative strength of players can be seen. One grasps immediately these relations and often engages in laborious manœuvres to score at the decisive moment. Another does not suspect the defective position of his pieces and will only realise the sad truth after a surprise move. It is not enough to know that there is a connection, for instance, between the squares QB5, K4, KB6, one must feel it and, in the common vulgarism, "have it in one's bones".

No. 30 exhibits a more hidden combination. By the move which compels resignation White threatens either Kt × KBP, and R – R8 mate. If 1..P – B3, to avoid this, 2 Kt × KtP, threatening both Kt × Q and R – R8 mate; or 2 R – R8 ch and 3 Kt × P ch. If 1.. R – KB1, then 2 Kt (Kt5) × BP, R × Kt; 3 Kt × KtP, threatening again both Queen and mate. Finally, if 1..Q × Kt, then 2 R – R8 ch, K × R; 3 Kt × BP ch. The Rook-sacrifice at R8, it is to be noted, brings Black's King into relationship with his Queen at K2 or KKt4 by the move of a Knight (to KKt6 or KB7).

How many inexperienced players, faced with this position, would fail to see the possibility of the mate by R – R8, supported by a Knight? The mutual aid of the two Knights here is a decisive factor, and there is no parallel action with two Bishops.

Being already familiar with the geometrical idea, we grasp at once in No. 31 the threats R × B and R × P ch, with the link by Knight's move between K6, Kt5, and R7. The sacrifice of one Rook at K6 and the other at R7, taking Black's Queen to K3 and King to R2, allows the double check by Kt – Kt5, winning the Queen. But there is the grave objection that it is at the price of two Rooks. There is a better prospect, the stalemate position of the Black

King enhancing the combination. Instead of sacrificing the second Rook at R7 White attacks first the Queen and menaces mate. The Queen is therefore obliged to defend the RP, enabling White now to sacrifice the second Rook and give a smothered mate.

Here we see the two lines referred to above, with White's Kt5 as the point of junction. The stalemate position of

No. 30
New York Tournament, 1924
R. Réti

F. D. Yates
1 Kt — Kt5!, Black resigns.

No. 31
Manchester, 1929 (?)
X.

G. T. Atkinson
1 R × B!, Q × R;   2 Kt — Kt5, Q — Kt3;
3 R × P ch, Q × R;   4 Kt — B7 mate.

Black's King is a necessary ingredient in the combination, forcing as it does 3 . . Q × R. Further, the mate on B7 could not be given if that square were protected, in which case White would probably have to be content with winning Queen and Pawn for two Rooks. This complication of the initial theme, without changing anything in the idea of the combination, increases its beauty. Note that White's Knight at Kt5 exploits half of its "star" (K6, B7, R7), and already the combination is wonderful. What shall we say of a combination with the full display of the eight-pointed star?

The Knight's Star

To the advice already given, to study the relations of the Knight's move among the hostile pieces, may be added now the advice to attract the pieces to squares where those relations exist. This is the double aspect of the same problem, the passive and the active, and it is the whole secret of this type of combination.

In Example No. 32 Black's Queen is attracted to a dangerous square long before the decisive move of the combination.

No. 32

Theoretical Study in the *French Defence*

No. 33

Ramsgate Tournament, 1929

H. E. Price

E. Znosko-Borovsky

1 B—Kt5!, Q×B; 2 Kt—K5!, Kt—K2; 3 Kt—B7, R—KKt1; 4 Q×R ch!, Kt×Q; 5 Kt—Q6 ch, winning the Q.

1 Q—R3, Q×B; 2 Q—R7 ch, K—B1; 3 R—K1, Kt—K4 (Kt—K2; 4 Q—R8 ch, Kt—Kt1; 5 Kt—R7 mate) 4 R×Kt!, Q×R; 5 Q—R8 ch, K—K2; 6 Q×R ch!, K×Q; 7 Kt—B7 ch, and wins.

The Bishop is sacrificed in order to draw the Queen into relation to the King by a Knight's move, the line K8 – Q6 – Kt5. Then comes the threat to win the Exchange by 3 Kt×Kt or Kt–B7. This makes Black's moves forced, and so is carried out the principal threat, very abstruse, of winning the Queen. It is hard to see such a threat when the time is limited. It was only, as a matter of fact, after the finish of an actual game that the winning combination was here discovered. It is the first two innocent - looking moves and the Knight's progress, B3 – K5 – B7 – Q6 – Kt5, that make it so charming.

Now let us take a still more complex example, No. 33, where almost the whole of the Knight's star is used for the purpose of the win.

White has won the Exchange; but his Bishop is *en prise*, and if B – Kt3, Kt – K6 wins back the Exchange.   By playing Q – R3 White protects his KKt2, and makes possible the retreat B – Kt3, unless Black captures at once.   Having captured, Black falls victim to the Knight-combination.

The difficulty of the position is that on his KKt1 the Black King is at a distance from the critical square.   He must be driven to his Q1, where he will be in the relation of a Knight's check with his Queen at Q3.   But, if White were content with the continuation 3 Q – R8 ch, K – K2; 4 Q × R ch, K × Q; 5 Kt × P ch, K – B2; 6 Kt × Q, K × Kt, he would have lost Bishop and Knight for Rook and Pawn. It is necessary, therefore, to draw the Black Queen to another square in the same relationship with her Q1.   This is K4, linked with it by the line K4 – B2 – Q1 (K5 – B7 – Q8).

Let us not forget, too, that the same Knight supported the Queen on R7 and gave mate on B8.   Thus we have the lines, Kt5 – R7 – B8, Kt5 – B7 – Q8, Kt5 – B7 – Q6, and Kt5 – B7 – K5.   Could one adduce a finer example of the Knight's play?

No. 34

Study (original source uncertain)

The Knight's manifold resources make these combinations very attractive.   Consider the cases that frequently occur in end-game studies and problems, where a Pawn is promoted to Knight, of which we have already given an instance.

No. 34. — This study, of which several versions exist,[1] shows a position that might well occur in actual play.   A

1 R – B8 ch,   R × R;   2 Q – R7 ch!
K × Q; 3 P × R (= Kt) ch, and 4 Kt × Q, winning.

draw seems problematical for White, under the threat of mate.   And yet he wins by preparing the line R7 – B8 – K7

[1] See, *e.g.*, Lasker's *Common Sense in Chess*, p. 113; Tattersall's *Thousand End-Games*, II. p. 122; and O. Labone's *A B C of Chess*, p. 94.

for a Knight's move. There are two sacrifices, of Queen and Rook; and a Knight springs up instead of a Queen, to accomplish a miracle. One is tempted to call this a marvellous Knight-combination without a Knight!

Exercises

Of the two exercises that follow, the first is a superb specimen, which recalls to some extent our No. 32. The

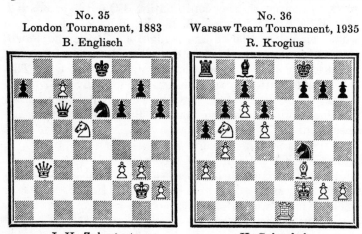

No. 35
London Tournament, 1883
B. Englisch

No. 36
Warsaw Team Tournament, 1935
R. Krogius

J. H. Zukertort
White to play and win.

H. Golombek
White to play and win.

second is given as an illustration of how the Knight's power is sometimes nullified, the "star" becoming here in fact an extinct one. Both players go out for the win of the Exchange, and secure it. But White rightly calculated that his opponent would regret his bargain; which justifies us to some extent in talking of a combination.

CHAPTER IV

THE OPENING OF LINES

Lines

W E have already called attention to the fact that combinations call for the opening of lines. It is particularly with a view to realising the geometrical idea that one must free the line through which one aims at advantage. The opening of a line, therefore, is sufficient to create a combinational idea, whether it be to give full play to some piece commanding this line or to allow the pieces to obtain the desired object. The more important this object is, the more heavy may be the sacrifices in order to open the line. We shall not expatiate on the importance of the various lines, which is a secondary matter in our study; but it is useful to remember the importance of the ranks for the Rooks, which are generally concerned with the files. Every player knows that the most efficacious rank for attack is the seventh. To get control of this line we may have recourse to most extravagant manœuvres.

Being a special sort of combination, the opening of one line is usually only a preparatory manœuvre for the decisive attack on another coveted line. For instance, a file is opened to obtain command of a rank.

In the following example White wished to seize the seventh rank, which at present is impossible. Since on the only open file the square B7 is guarded by Rook and Knight, either other files must be opened or at least Black's Knight must be removed. The two White Bishops, which in the diagrammed position are paralysed by many Pawns, have an important part to play, one on KR4, the other on KKt6, when the diagonals are opened. All this cannot be done without a sacrifice, which the almost unprotected state of Black's QB, moreover, justifies. Finally a White Rook establishes itself on the seventh rank, and, aided by a passed

Pawn which exchanges yield to White, decides the fate of the game.

Sacrifice therefore has had but one object, the attainment of the seventh rank. The opening of lines is only a means. It would be useless to get control of a line on which there is no weak square or piece. In No. 37 the vulnerable point is the Black QB, passive and insufficiently guarded. The

No. 37
World's Championship Match, 1934
E. D. Bogoljuboff

A. Alekhine

1 P—Kt4, Kt × P; 2 Kt × Kt, P × Kt; 3 P × P, P—K4? (not realising his opponent's intention; but it is hard to find a good move); 4 R—K1, P × P; 5 R × B ch, R × R; 6 B—R4, K—B2; 7 B × R, K × B; 8 R—B7 ch, R—Q2; 9 P—B6 ch, K—K1; 10 B—Kt6 ch, K—Q1; 11 P—B7, and wins.

geometrical motive is not absent, in Black's K on KKt2, B on QKt2. Though the Bishop has some protection, a grand master knows how to create weaknesses which a moderate player cannot foresee. We may marvel at the means employed to bring about the desired weakness and profit by it.

The student can see how numerous are the different elements that make up a combination. Analysis permits their separation; but what vigilance and attention are required to pick out the weaknesses in the enemy's position, and not to dismiss as insignificant the least signs of a weakness!

A shorter and much less complex example is No. 38. White has already obtained great positional superiority, but requires to open lines for his two Bishops to clinch matters.

The QB's range is easily extended; for the KB, at present quiescent, a sacrifice of the Exchange is necessary, for which Black incautiously offers the chance. This effected, White follows up with the vertical movement of the KKtP. As we see in so many of our examples, action in one direction facilitates action in another.

In No. 39 we see the opening up of several lines on which

W. Winter

1 P—B4, Kt—Kt5? (better was Kt—Kt3); 2 KR—Kt1, R(K1)—B1; 3 R×Kt, P×R; 4 P—Kt6, R—Kt2; 5 B×R, K×B; 6 Q×P ch, etc.

P. Biscay

1 .. P—QR4; 2 R—Kt1, P×P; 3 P×P, R—R7; 4 P—Kt4, R—K1; 5 K—R1?, R—K5!; 6 Kt—K2, P—Q5; 7 K—Kt1, R—K1; 8 R—R3, Q—Q4; 9 K—B1, Q—R8 ch; 10 Kt—Kt1, R—K6!; 11 R×R, P×R; 12 Q×P, Q—Kt7 ch; 13 K—K1, R×BP and wins, for if 14 B×R, Q×B; 15 R—B1, B—R5 ch, etc.

pieces are reposing peacefully at present, only to become suddenly most aggressive.

A whole network of lines here open for Black's Rooks and Bishops. The action unfolds on the seventh rank, with combinations all based on the idea of the opening of lines. The essential feature is certainly the advance of the QP, which obstructs the long diagonal of the QB. At Q5 this Pawn obstructs the other Bishop's long diagonal, so that it must still advance, even at the price of a sacrifice. But the whole manœuvre is hindered by the position of White's Knight. This gives the key to the play. The Knight must be dislodged by a sapping of White's position, through the opening of the QR file, when Black's Rook at R7 fastens on White's QBP.

This example shows that the opening of lines is a piece of strategy in the game of combination, but also in that of position; which is a fresh proof that combinations have their logic, and that they should be studied like other branches of chess.

We cannot claim that all the variations of this example could be foreseen; but the necessary move can always be found when one is inspired by a correct idea, the combination in the emergency allowing the opening up of lines for the decisive attack.

The Complexity of Combinations

A combination may be a complex of several ideas.   The mark of genius is to extract from them their full value by developing them successively, measuring them out, passing at the right moment from one to another.   The first condition for handling them is obviously to know them well. We must, therefore, in this chapter devoted to pure ideas, fix the student's attention upon them; for it seems to us that very many players, faced with a combination, are ignorant of the ideas which enable it to be realised.   Has no one ever talked to them of these ideas?   In my forty years' chess career, I must confess, for my part, that the subject was very rarely brought to my notice.

Example No 40 might be called "the combination of combinations".   First there is an opening of a line for a Knight-combination such as we already know.   The Knight threatens, at K6, White's Queen and King, whom it is easy to attract to his KB1.   But the square K6(3) is guarded by Rook and Knight.   It is necessary, therefore, to drive them off or to suppress them by a timely sacrifice.

This is a new idea, how to drive off a piece guarding an important square, and we will study it later.   What concerns us at the moment is to observe the various ideas that mingle in one and the same combination, and especially to note in what order the sacrifices are effected.   For instance, if the Queen is sacrificed before the Rook, inverting moves 4 and 5, the result is different, for White's King can escape to K2, and the Rook-sacrifice will not be accepted.

The amateur may say that he can never arrive at the point of making such complicated combinations.   It is true that we can give him no guarantee on this subject.   Never-

No. 40
St. Petersburg Tournament, 1909
J. Mieses

C. Schlechter

1..B×KP; 2 P×B, Q−R5; 3 R−KKt3 (if 3 P−R3, Q−K8 ch; 4 R−B1, Q×R ch; 5 K×Q, R×Kt ch; 6 R×R, Kt−K6 ch, etc.), Q×P ch; 4 K−B1, R×Kt ch; 5 R×R, Q×R!; 6 Kt×Q, Kt−K6 ch, and Black wins.

theless, if he will study carefully each of the elements of which the combination is composed, from the simple to the complex, he will acquire the practice of various combinations and will be able thereafter to handle them simultaneously.   Especially, let him not be disheartened.   Our example, which he finds so complicated, is relatively simplified by the fact that all happens in the same section of the board.

A combination is far prettier when it develops in several quarters.   In close analysis all is simple, but during the game conception becomes sometimes superhumanly difficult. It is by keeping always in mind the essential ideas which constitute combinations that we reach the imagination of those splendid manœuvres wherein gain of time and space is the result of sacrifice.

After all, if things do not go as we wish, we can console ourselves by saying that we must leave some superiority

to the great champions, in order that they may preserve
their prestige!

Example 41 is very instructive. How is White to profit
by his open KKt file? And how, having his Queen on the left
wing, is he to bring her over to the other to participate in
the attack? His Bishop is of the opposite colour to Black's
KKtP, is useless against it, and is rather in the way. A

No. 41
Baden-Baden Tournament,
1926
J. Mieses

No. 42
London, 1858

P. Morphy

E. D. Bogoljuboff

1 B × P!, P × B;   2 R × P ch!, K × R;
3 Q − B6 ch, K − Kt1;   4 R − Kt1 ch,
Q − Kt5; 5 R × Q ch, P × R; 6 P − B5,
and wins through the strength of the
united passed Pawns.

H. E. Bird

1 . . KR × P!; 2 B × R, Q − R6!; 3 P − B3
(analysis has proved that 2 Q − Kt5 does
not save White), Q × RP;   4 P − Kt4,
Q − R8 ch; 5 K − B2, Q − R5 ch, and Black
won, though the analysts are of opinion
that the legitimate result was a draw.

sacrifice resolves the problem. B × P opens the rank for the
Queen when Black retakes; but if 2 Q − KB6, Q − B6 ch
would win for Black. Therefore another tempo must be
gained, by a fresh sacrifice, R × P ch, much easier to see
than the last, which was based on a line-opening.

The same reasoning applies to Morphy's famous sacrifice
against Bird (No. 42), the precursor of Bogoljuboff's combination. The Rook-sacrifice is surprising, and the move Q − R6
is difficult to find; but the idea is the same as in the preceding
example, to transfer the Queen from a wing where she has
nothing to do to the other, where the train of an attack is
ready laid. In both cases the Kt file is open, but it is the

opening of a rank which allows the realisation of the combination, by the transfer of the Queen from one wing to the other. Note that if Morphy had not sacrificed his Rook it was Bird who would have had the attack on the KKt file, with Queen, two Rooks, and two Bishops in action. The sacrifice is not only one of beautiful ingenuity, it is also very positional. It shows that the distinction between the positional and combinational games is very arbitrary, and that in reality the good player knows how to handle both of them. The game of chess constitutes a whole, of which it is unreasonable to break the unity by opposing the game of position to the game of combination.

Exercises

Diagram No. 43 presents a charming instance of the opening of a column. It is very instructive to discover how Black obtains command of the seventh rank. In No. 44

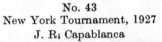

No. 43	No. 44
New York Tournament, 1927	Warsaw Team Tournament, 1935
J. R₁ Capablanca	G. Stoltz

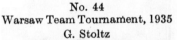

A. Nimzovitch	F. J. Marshall
Black to play and win.	Black to play and win.

Black makes a fine initial move, opening up a diagonal for his Queen and a rank for his QR. If White accepts (as he did) what is offered him he has to lose his Queen to save a mate. But even if he declines his positional inferiority is manifest.

CHAPTER V

THE INTERCEPTION OF LINES

A Notion dear to the Problemist

THE simple operation consisting of the cutting a line of defence or attack may give birth to a real masterpiece. It is especially in artistic compositions illustrating the crossing of two lines that this idea is realised. Under

No. 45
Study by H. Rinck
Deutsche Schachzeitung, 1906

White to play and win.

1 P − R7, B − Kt7; 2 P − Q7, R − Q7;
3 B − Q5, R × B (B × B, 4 P − Q8(= Q),
etc.); 4 P − R8 (= Q), R × P; 5 Q − B8 ch,
K − Kt3;   6 Q − Kt8 ch,   K − R3;
     7 Q − K6 ch, and wins.

No. 46
Match-game, Moscow, 1923
V. Grigorieff

V. J. Nenarokoff

1 . . B − Q3; 2 R × B(2 B × B, P − Q8 = Q,
     etc.), P − R7, etc.

the names of Novotny, Grimshaw, Plachutta, etc., composers have long been studying a combination of exquisite subtlety which very rarely is offered by the chances of actual play.

We may borrow from Henri Rinck (No. 45) an end-game study in which this combination is magnificently realised, one perhaps well known to many of our readers. Two White Pawns are going on to queen, and the two Black pieces cannot stop them. On his third move White intercepts the two lines on which the Black pieces hope to check the advance, the long White diagonal and the Queen's file. The White Bishop is sacrificed on the "critical square", Q5, and, whichever piece captures it, one Pawn queens.

We have said that this combination-theme does not often offer itself in actual play. But No. 46 is a pleasing example which will bear comparison with the preceding study. The "critical square", where two lines cross, is Q6(3), and a Black Bishop goes thither to intercept the lines, which allows one of the Black Pawns to queen.

The Critical Square

When such a move is played among the complications of the middle game, it reveals uncommon mastery. To dis-cover the critical square, to plant a piece there while all the hostile forces are powerless to prevent the act of aggression, is a manœuvre sufficient to prove what profound re-sources the chess-board offers. No sacrifice could produce greater astonishment.

The Queen here defends Black's QKt2, a Rook defends his QB4. His QB2, therefore, is the critical square on the crossing of rank and file. The White Bishop installs itself there, and suddenly mate cannot be escaped.

What is difficult to realise in a game is precisely this cross-

No. 47
Naples, 1914
3 Amateurs

S. Tarrasch

1 B — B7!, R × B (Q × B; 2 R × P ch, Q × R; 3 Q — Kt7 ch); 2 Q — Kt7 ch, with mate in 2, for if K × P, then 3 R — R2 ch, Q — R5; 4 R × Q mate.

ing of important lines. There is always a critical square, but the reason is not because lines cross there. We must often be content with intercepting one line, and the com-bination may still be very fine. Nevertheless, for him who knows all the possibilities of this theme, our examples may

seem incomplete. We must state again to the idealist that
we are not here in the realm of abstractions. We are on a
battlefield where two confronting forces strive to blow each
other to pieces. The rare beauty, therefore, must be recog-
nised of a few examples which follow.

In No. 48 the Black Queen has two duties, pinning the
White Rook and defending the KBP. White therefore

No. 48
All-Russian Championship,
1924
Rosenthal

G. Lövenfisch
1 P – Q5, and wins.

No. 49
New York Tournament, 1924

E. D. Bogoljuboff

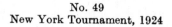

R. Réti
1 B – B7 ch, K – R1; 2 B – K8!, and
wins.

plays 1 P – Q5 to intercept the long white diagonal. If
1 . . Q × P, the rank is abandoned and the KBP is defenceless
against 2 Q – B6 ch. If 1 . . Kt × QP or P × P, White's
Rook is unpinned. It is clear that in this position our idea
of combination is a little simplified. There is only one piece
defending two lines, not two pieces as in the preceding examples. To obtain the ideal interception-theme, we should
have, instead of the Black Queen at QKt2, a Rook at QR2
and a Bishop at R1, Kt2 being then the critical square, to
be occupied by an intercepting piece.

Black's Bishop in No. 49 is defended by King and Rook.
The King can be driven away by B – B7 ch, but how is the
Rook's defence to be got rid of? By interception, on the
eighth rank, between Rook and Bishop. Observe that Black

has not only to protect the Bishop on B1, but also that square itself, since the withdrawal of the Bishop does not guard the mate on it. If, for instance, 2..B×P ch; 3 Q×B, R×B, White still mates. He has two threats against one defence.

Pinning and Unpinning

Among other ways of utilising lines must be mentioned the pinning or unpinning of pieces, which has some resemblances to what we have just been examining.

No. 50
Paris, 1906
X.

E. Chatard
1 R—Kt1, B×Kt; 2 Q×B, R—B7;
3 R—QB1!, and wins.

No. 51
Study by A. Troitsky
Trudovaya Pravda, 1926

White to play and win.
1 P—B6, P—Kt7; 2 P—B7, P—Kt8
(=Q); 3 P—B8(=Q) ch, K—R2;
4 Q—B7 ch, K—R1; 5 B—Kt2 ch,
B—K5; 6 Q—R7!!, and wins.

Black's threat in No. 50 is to win the Queen by pinning her with Rook on the seventh rank. But White allows this and replies with a counter-pin, which wins Rook or Queen. Certainly Black made a mistake in R – B7; but the answer was unexpected, and it is this which constitutes the combination. White's Queen and Black's Rook are both pinned, and Black's Queen and White's Rook are unguarded. In a position of remarkable symmetry White wins.

A magnificent illustration of this battle of line against line, of pin on pin is No. 51. Here we have one piece, the

Black Bishop, under a double pin. The two pieces which attack it are undefended, but, as it can only take one, a prize falls to White—a Queen!

This combination rests on the presence of the Black King behind the pinned piece, unguarded. In its beauty and simplicity it lingers in the memory.

Clearing a Line

In the same order of ideas we may place combinations wherein, by checks or sacrifices, lines are opened to one's

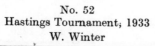

No. 52	No. 53
Hastings Tournament, 1933	New York Tournament, 1889
W. Winter	S. Lipschütz

T. H. Tylor	J. H. Blackburne
1 Q – R7 ch, K – B1; 2 Q – R8 ch, K – K2; 3 Kt – B5 ch, P × Kt; 4 B – B5 dbl. ch, mate.	1 R × P ch, K × R; 2 Kt – R5 ch, R × Kt; 3 Q – B7 ch, and wins.

pieces for decisive action. There is no longer a question here of the interception of lines, but the ideas realised are alike. In the interception of lines one closes lines to the adversary at critical points, while here one opens lines to one's own pieces. The skilled hand deals with the valves on this side and on that.

There is no manœuvre more familiar than that of drawing the Black King to his K2 on the file occupied by White's Rook at K1. But in the example which we now present, No. 52, this line is obstructed by a White Bishop and a

Black Pawn, and White's Rook is pinned. Any halting-time would equalise the positions. It is necessary therefore to proceed by a series of checks. Note with what art the combination develops, so that the King's file opens without interruption and the Bishop comes into play. After the sacrifice of the Knight, this Bishop uncovers the Rook, bringing about a mate by double check, with two pieces *en prise*. A real cabinet-jewel!

The next example (No. 53) is inferior in quality, but is also very pretty. Here it is necessary not only to open to the Queen the diagonal obstructed by the Knight, but also to

No. 54
New York, 1857

P. Morphy

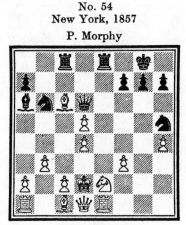

J. W. Schulten

1..R × B; 2 P × R, B × Kt; 3 R × B, Q × P ch; 4 K − K1, Q − Kt8 ch;
5 K − Q2, R − Q1 ch; 6 K − B3, Q − B4 ch; 7 K − Kt2, Kt − R5 ch.
White resigns.

clear the Rook from QB7. A less aggressive first move, like Kt − R5, would be met by R − Kt5, followed by R × R ch. Successive checks are therefore essential.

In Example 54 it is the hostile pieces which obstruct the decisive inroad of the attackers. White must get to his Q5 to break down all resistance. But this square is protected by a Knight and masked by a Pawn, which is protected by a Bishop. There is a regular breastwork to be demolished.

The process is the same as before; opening of a line by a capture of the Bishop, to command Q5, capture of the Knight which defends the square, and finally the arrival at the key of the position.   When the key is secured, when the critical square is reached, it is not difficult to find the correct method of procedure.

We will finish this chapter with a wonderful example of the "Indian Theme" (No. 55).   Black intercepts his own line

No. 55
San Sebastian Tournament, 1912

S. Tarrasch

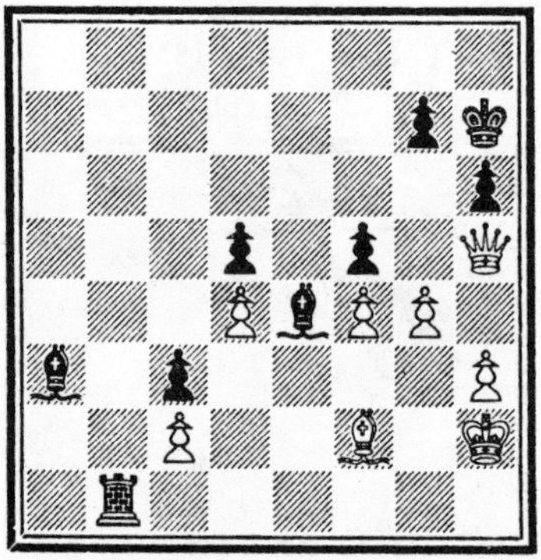

R. Spielmann

1 . . B – B8!; 2 K – Kt3, P – Kt3; 3 Q – R4, B × P ch, and wins.

of attack on the rank, to open it again.   By this manœuvre his KB penetrates into the enemy's camp, whereas 1 . . B – Q3 would not have allowed him to attain this object, the defence by 2 B – K3 being sufficient.

All these combinations confirm what we have said, that geometry is at the base of chess.

Exercises

In the first of these two positions (No. 56) we have a case of interception of a line depriving an important piece of its only defence.   In the second (No. 57) we see a pin, followed by an unpin, a winning manœuvre. The game did not actually go so; it is a variation which might have occurred.

No. 56
Pasadena Tournament, 1932
A. Alekhine

A. J. Fink
Black to play and win.

No. 57
Budapest Tournament, 1926
H. Mattison

E. Znosko-Borovsky
What might happen after
1..Kt−R4?

CHAPTER VI

DISCOVERED CHECK

A Familiar Manœuvre

IT would be superfluous to linger to any extent of time over this type of combination, which is so well known that it constitutes a commonplace trap. Every beginner is put on his guard against checks by discovery and the still more dangerous double checks. There is the less need to dwell on the subject because this elementary idea occurs in very many combinations.

The discovered check generally presents itself in one of two ways. Either a piece, uncovering another which gives check, attacks an important hostile piece and wins it, or the two pieces give check simultaneously, very often with fatal results.

A notable illustration is a famous opening-trap in *Petroff's Defence*: 1 P – K4, P – K4; 2 Kt – KB3, Kt – KB3; 3 Kt × P, Kt × P?; 4 Q – K2, Kt – KB3??. The discovered check by 5 Kt – B6 wins the Queen for a Knight, while 5 Kt – Kt6 dis. ch would win a Rook. The success of this little combination lies in the fact that the Knight at B6 attacks not only the Queen but also the square K7, so that the Queen cannot at once cover the check and save herself. It is necessary to look well whether the piece one wishes to attack can get out of danger.

No. 58 is a very pretty example of such a discovered check. Its special feature is that it is a Pawn which discovers the check—a rather rare occurrence. As the Pawn in so doing captures a hostile piece, and, further, becomes a piece itself, it is easy to grasp the significance of such a check.

Particular point is given to this example by the fact that the Pawn can be promoted to Knight instead of Queen, and so give double check. Would this have been a superfluous touch of beauty? The double check also leads to a quick mate; *e.g.* 6 P × R(= Kt) dbl. ch, K – R3 (K – Kt1; 7 Kt – B6 mate); 7 R – K6 ch, K – R4 (K – Kt4; 8 P – B4 ch and mate next move); 8 P – B4. Now, to avoid mate by 9 B – B3 ch, Black must sacrifice his Queen and a Pawn, thus deferring the end for four moves: 8.. Q – Kt2; 9 B × Q, P – Q4; 10 B × P, R – Kt1; 11 B – B3 ch, R – Kt5; 12 P – KR3 and mate next move. So, instead of mate on

No. 58
Paris Championship, 1930
S. G. Tartakover

J. Cukierman

1 Q – K7 ch, K – Kt1; 2 Q – K8 ch, B – B1; 3 R – K7, B – K3; 4 P × B!, R × Q; 5 P × P ch, K – Kt2; 6 P × R(= Q) dis. ch, K – R3 (B × R; 7 Q × B ch and mate in 2 moves); 7 R × P ch and 8 Q – Kt6 mate.

the 9th move, White achieves it on the 13th; and it was consequently better not to choose the double check on the 6th move—though it is always attractive to under-promote to gain one's end!

Double Check and Discovery

Examples of discovered check complicated by double check abound, especially in the central combinations, which we shall study later. In order not to repeat ourselves, we refer the reader to the examples given in Part III, Chapter VII, in particular to Nos. 146 and 158. In both instances the Bishop's check, discovering a Rook's check, is at once fatal. This shows how dangerous it is to leave the King on a line commanded by a hostile Rook.

It is not unnecessary to say that the same combination may occur without a check; but in that case it is usually less efficacious. Without the King's presence it is no more than a double threat. A piece moves with a threat and uncovers another piece, which also threatens. For instance, a piece attacks a Rook, uncovering another piece's attack upon the Queen; one of the two attacked pieces is therefore lost. There is no discovered check, but the idea is similar, and the result is occasionally equally decisive, for the attacked pieces will be more valuable than the attackers. Nowadays, when it is not the custom to announce check, the similarity is accentuated.

We must never neglect the timely application of the scalpel to the infected organ; keeping in mind that at chess the surgeon's aim is the death of the patient!

Exercises

Example 59 is interesting, not only through the number of checks threatened (two discovered, one double), but also

<table>
<tr><td align="center">No. 59
Chicago, 1899
F. J. Marshall</td><td align="center">No. 60
Club Tournament, London, 1935
W. H. Watts</td></tr>
</table>

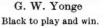

<table>
<tr><td align="center">S. P. Johnston
White to play and win.</td><td align="center">G. W. Yonge
Black to play and win.</td></tr>
</table>

because the checks merely threaten the King. It will be seen that they are none the less dangerous for that.

No. 60 illustrates a very unusual mate, only 5 moves after the position in the diagram. Though White could have made a longer fight, he has already a lost game; but it is far from obvious how the end is going to be brought about by a discovered check.

CHAPTER VII

STALEMATE INTO MATE

The Hunting of the King

THE majority of combinations develop around the opponent's King. It is to reach him that bold sacrifices are made of part of a player's forces. So we have seen the termination of some of the most diverse of combinations to be checkmate.

The King himself may be a theme of combination. When he is in a precarious position we may entertain hopes of not merely gaining material, but registering an immediate victory. If in order to win the Queen we can even sacrifice two Rooks, we can without hesitation let all our pieces go, and all our Pawns but one, provided that we are sure of a mate with this one Pawn.

Therefore in a direct attack against the King everything can be justified to overthrow the enemy's position: daring, temerity, hardihood—any of those synonymous terms by which we designate the fighting quality. But there is a reverse to the medal. If we do not attain mate we are lost.

Stalemate

The most precarious situation of the King is when he is in stalemate, when he has no move at all, for then a check suffices to turn stalemate into a triumphant mate. It is sometimes enough to drive off the pieces that guard the square where the mate can be administered. Very often, however, an involved combination is necessary to attain this end.

The dangerous stalemate position is the object of laborious researches and elegant combinations.

On the other hand, the player with the inferior game must strive after a draw by all means possible, and stalemate is one of them.

It is useless to give here many examples of this type of combination, for they only occur in the end-game, when the poverty of material usually limits imagination and compels us to be satisfied with a simple manœuvre. Most often the occasion is some blunder by our opponent, who falls into an obvious trap. We shall give only two examples.

In an artistic composition (No. 61) White succeeds in the *tour de force* of getting rid of his two pieces and two Pawns to

No. 61
Study by H. Rinck
British Chess Magazine, 1917

No. 62
Liverpool, 1934
X.

1 B − B5 ch, K − R4; 2 Kt − K3, Q × P;
3 Kt − Q5, Q − K4; 4 Kt − B4 ch,
Q × Kt; 5 B − Kt6 ch, K × B;
6 P − R5 ch, K × P. Stalemate.

J. Mieses

1 P − QR3, P − QR3; 2 P − QR4,
P − QR4; 3 P − R3, P − R3; 4 P − R4,
P − R4; 5 P − B5, P × P. Stalemate.

bring about a position where his King, who had three flight-squares, has no longer any. The task is all the more difficult because the Black Queen is in play.

In No. 62 we have an ending obviously lost for White, on account of his doubled Pawns, his isolated and vulnerable KBP, and his *Zugzwang* [1] position. He begins by exhausting the playable moves, and brings about the stalemate by the sacrifice of his last unblocked Pawn. This very simple example has the merit of not depending on any bad move. On the contrary, any effort by Black to avoid the menace of stalemate would probably have cost him the game.

[1] *Zugzwang* : Disagreeable obligation to move—since by so doing the position is weakened.

To give some idea, however, of what a stalemate may be like in the middle game, here is a very fine example, No. 63, where, strange to observe, a Queen and two Rooks fail to force a win against a Knight and a few Pawns. A subtle Queen-sacrifice leads to a position of stalemate which is astonishing on account of the number of White's men without a move.

We come back to combinations where the stalemate position is turned to advantage to effect a mate. The first

No. 63
St. Petersburg, 1902
V. Abkin

A. Bartolitch

1 Q − B6 ch, K − Kt1; 2 Q − Kt7 ch, K × Q; 3 P − R6 ch, K moves. Stalemate.

example (No. 64) is taken from Stamma's famous collection of a hundred end-games. It is the "smothered mate", which we know already and which frequently occurs in practice. To obtain it here it is necessary that Black shall leave his QB2 unguarded and that his QKt1 shall be obstructed, so that the King cannot escape after the disappearance of White's Queen.

White himself is under the threat of immediate mate, and the combination is clearly the only way for him to come out with the honours of war.

It will be right perhaps here to increase our vocabulary with a new term additional to the idea of combination proper. Stalemate, indeed, is not a combinational idea; it only prompts us to elaborate an idea to our advantage. It is a spur to the imagination.

Another example follows from the same famous collection (No. 65). At the first glance there is no stalemate; but White's R – R4, while stopping mate on R2, opens a diagonal for the Queen. The smothered mate would be easy but for the Knight at B6, obstructing the QB file and allowing R × Kt after Kt – B7 ch. The Knight on B6, therefore, is used for a more complex combination. It must clear the QB file by

No. 64
Study by P. Stamma

No. 65
Study by P. Stamma

1 R – K8 ch,   B – Q1;   2 R × B ch, R × R; 3 Kt – B7 ch, K – Kt1; 4 Kt – R6 dbl. ch, K – R1; 5 Q – Kt8 ch, R × Q; 6 Kt – B7 ch.

1 R – R4, Q × R; 2 Q – Kt8 ch, K × Q; 3 Kt – K7 ch, K – R1; 4 Kt – B7 ch, R × Kt; 5 R – B8 ch, R – B1; 6 R × R mate.

checking, *i.e.* after Black's King has moved to Kt1. White's Queen-sacrifice is the logical manœuvre. She cannot be captured by the Rook, since then Kt – B7 gives smothered mate; and if K × Q, then 3 Kt – K7 brings about the stalemate position aimed at, with its double threat of Kt – B7 ch and R – B8 ch.

Mate

Generally speaking, combinations based on the adversary's stalemate position are simple enough. When one is confronted merely with a King in a bad situation, the combinations are more complicated and more interesting. To break down resistance two methods are available: one radical, to mate in the actual position, the other more delicate, when our forces are insufficient, or the hostile King is well guarded, to entice him into the middle of the board, under the converging fire of our pieces. This last policy is always advisable, for it is dangerous for a monarch to lay himself open to the charge of professional vagabondage!

No general rule can be given for taking advantage of the bad situation of the King. All the combinational ideas

No. 66
Match-game, Biarritz, 1912
F. J. Marshall

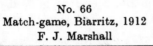

No. 67
New York Tournament, 1857
P. Morphy

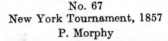

D. Janowski

1..R(K1)–K6; 2 B–Kt4 (2 P×R, R–Kt7 ch; 3 K–B1, R×B dis. ch. Or 2 B–K4, R×B, etc.), R(K6)×P; 3 B–Q1, R–B3. White resigns.

L. Paulsen

1..Q×B!; 2 P×Q, R–Kt3 ch; 3 K–R1, B–R6; 4 R–Q1, B–Kt2 ch; 5 K–Kt1, B×P dis. ch, and wins.

which we have seen can be utilised. Methods differ, for the variety of positions is great. But the object is not to attract the King *anywhere*, only to the spot where our forces can crush him before he regains breath.

We will limit ourselves to a few examples of positions frequently encountered.

The White King's position in No. 66 is so bad that there are several winning solutions. The simplest is obviously 1..R×B; 2 R×R, R–K3, followed by R–Kt3 mate. The line chosen by Marshall, almost as quick, is more elegant. The problem is made easier by the fact that two mates are possible, one on the KKt file, the other on the rank. Though the mating-squares are guarded, we know how to get rid of troublesome pieces, and we shall see elsewhere, in com-

binations directed against a KKtP or the square KKt2, the
strength of a Bishop at KR6.

Marshall's combination recalls Morphy's famous sixth game
against Louis Paulsen (No. 67), where the onlookers, seeing
the Queen-sacrifice, thought that the coming great champion
had suddenly been attacked by mental aberration. The
object of this sacrifice is to break the barrier which protects

No. 68
Carlsbad, 1911
S. G. Tartakover

A. Nimzovitch
1 Q – B6, R – KKt1; 2 B × B ch, R × B;
3 B × P, and wins.

No. 69
Breslau Tournament, 1912
F. J. Marshall

S. Levitzky
1 . . R × B; 2 R – QB5, Q – KKt6!
White resigns.

the White King, and the result is a position somewhat
similar to that which we have just been examining.

In No. 68 everything is protected around Black's King:
K1, K2, B2, and the Bishop in fianchetto. But this Bishop
is weak because, pinned against the King, it cannot move
if attacked by the White Queen. Black's Queen has to
guard both KB2 and a check on Q1, and is an example of
the piece with too much to protect.

We may add that if Black's King were on his Kt1, a
beautiful combination would be possible: 1 Q × P ch, Q × Q;
2 R – K8 ch, B – B1; 3 R × B mate. It is no longer the
Bishop that is pinned, but the Queen, a much more serious
matter.

One of the most paradoxical of finishes was that which
occurred in a tournament-game of Marshall's (No. 69). His

Queen being attacked by 2 R – QB5, he moves her, not into safety but into danger of being captured in three different ways.   Yet there is no danger.   The three captures lead respectively to mate on the move, mate in 2, and (if 3 Q × Q, Kt – K7 ch; 4 K – R1, Kt × Q ch) a speedily won ending. The part played in the combination by Black's Rook on KB1 is curiously unobtrusive, as far as action is concerned, but very powerful.

The Royal Vagabond

The combinations wherein the King is drawn out of his retreat and towards our forces, to find his death among them, are much more interesting, but also more difficult.

No. 70
Wagram, 1913
X.

R. Spielmann

1 . . R – KKt1? (B × Kt was necessary);
2 Q × P ch!,   K × Q;   3 R – R4 ch,
K – Kt3;   4 R – R6 ch,   K – Kt4;
5 P – R4 ch,   K – Kt5;   6 Kt – K3 ch,
K – Kt6; 7 R – B3 mate.

Although the King may be ill-protected behind his barrier, we must sometimes renounce the idea of mating him. It is then that, however impossible it may appear, we must entice him into a well-prepared trap. This plan demands great precision, for in the event of the mate failing, the King in the heart of his enemy's position may become a real fighting piece.

The Black King here has a good enough shelter behind his RP.   White threatens by R – KR4 to mate with the Queen.   But Black has time to parry this menace by bringing his Rook to Kt2 (or Kt3), a defence which seems all the stronger because with Rook on Kt-file he himself threatens mate.   However, on Kt1 the Rook blocks his King's flight.   Hence the combination removing the King's slender barrier.   His forces being insufficient to give mate to Black's King at home, White draws him into his own camp along the only road open to him, the KKt file.

Such combinations may exhibit singular beauty. In the next example, No. 71, the White King's position is bad, but nothing decisive seems in the air. To effect a mate, however, it is sufficient that the King shall be drawn in among Black's pieces. Observe the beauty of the two sacrifices with the one object of a check from the QR, threatening mate by R – R8. For this it was necessary to dislodge

No. 71

Variation from a match-game,
St. Petersburg, 1897

M. Tchigorin

E. Schiffers

1..R – R8 ch;   2 Kt × R, B – R7 ch!;
3 K × B,   R – R1 ch;   4 K – Kt3,
Kt – B5 ch; 5 K – Kt4, R – R5 mate.

No. 72

Study by A. Anderssen

1 Q – B5 ch, K × Q; 2 B – Q4 ch, K × B;
3 Kt – K6 ch, K – K5; 4 P – B3 ch,
K × P;   5 Kt(B7) – Kt5 ch, K – B7;
6 Kt – R3 ch, K – B6; 7 Kt(K6) – Kt5
mate.

White's Knight by the first sacrifice. The Knight having moved, a protection is taken off White's KR1, and the diagonal is opened for Black's KB, which sacrifices itself to allow the QR to come in with check. Unable to return to Kt1, Black's King must leave his asylum, only to fall into another mating-net. But this pretty combination is only a variation which might have occurred, not the actual play.

Sometimes we see a regular excursion by the King across the board. He must be drawn to the fatal square where mate attends him. The positions are often artificial, like No. 72, conceived by the great Anderssen; but they may occur in practical play when the idea is familiar to us. The essential is, as ever in such combinations, to force the King alone to move, without any of his pieces being able to come to his assistance—which might rapidly change the fate of the game.

This was a position in a game at a simultaneous exhibition, and is a striking instance of the King's journey from Kt1 to Kt8. His Majesty dies of indigestion after swallowing all that is offered to him!

No. 73
Dundee, 1930
E. Znosko-Borovsky

X.

1 RP × P, P × P ch; 2 K × P, B – R6 ch; 3 K × B, Kt – Kt5 dis. ch; 4 K × Kt, Q – Q2 ch; 5 K – Kt5, B – K2 ch; 6 K × Kt, R – Kt1 ch; 7 K – R7, B – B3 dis. ch; 8 K × R, Castles, mate.

It is useless to make any deep analysis, for we know that the solitary King, abandoned in front of his forces, is doomed to death. What would have happened if he had refused all the sacrifices? His death would have been slower, but none the less sure.

We may add, merely as a curiosity, a game won by F. C. Spencer (date unknown), in which the King's wanderings began in the very opening. After a number of fantastic moves, by no means forced, he finished up by being mated.

The game was a *Muzio Gambit*: 1 P – K4, P – K4; 2 P – KB4, P × P; 3 Kt – KB3, P – KKt4; 4 B – B4, P – Kt5; 5 B × P ch, K × B; 6 Kt – K5 ch, K – K3; 7 Q × P ch, K × Kt; 8 P – Q4 ch, K × P; 9 P – Kt4, B × P ch; 10 P – B3 ch, B × P ch; 11 Kt × B, K × Kt; 12 B – Kt2 ch, K × B; 13 Q – K2 ch K × R; 14 Castles, mate.

This game resembles a help-mate problem!

Exercises

We give two positions. The first, a very fierce tournament-game, has a marvellous solution. A cluster of combinations ends in an unexpected flight back by the King. This position might serve as an example of several combinations.

In the second, from an off-hand game which obtained no

little publicity, we see a wonderful hunt of Black's King across the board, started by a Queen-sacrifice. It will be noted that there is an improvement upon the "author's solution."

These two combinations elevate the King-chase, usually only a curiosity, to the rank of a work of art.

No. 74
Moscow Tournament, 1935
V. A. Chekhover

No. 75
London, 1912
Sir George Thomas

M. Botwinnik
White to play and win.

Edward Lasker
White to play and mate in 7 moves.

CHAPTER VIII

THE UNPROTECTED PIECE

The Tactical Opportunity offered by an Unprotected Piece

O NE of the reasons why we strive, from the earliest stages of the game, to bring our pieces into touch with one another and to have them all guarded is that an unprotected piece or one insufficiently protected is a weakness which may suggest an idea for a manœuvre, perhaps even a combination, by our opponent. As one tempo is enough to free a piece from its tiresome predicament, it will not be a question of the elaboration of a strategical plan, merely of a simple tactical manœuvre. But it is otherwise with a Pawn, whose weakness often constitutes the basis of a general strategical plan.

The opportunity must never be missed that is offered by a defenceless piece. If we simply attack it, it may be retired or defended, and the result will only be a tempo gained. To obtain more substantial advantage and give scope for a combination, the menace against the unprotected piece must be reinforced by another, or others, as in one of our preceding examples. However slight each of these menaces may be, they acquire strength by their co-ordination. Under the united pressure the adversary must give ground somewhere. For instance, when Black's KRP is only guarded by his King at KKt1, and his QR on its own square is without support, if you (White) have a Bishop at Q3 you can sacrifice it by 1 B × P ch, and if K × B, then 2 Q – K4 ch and 3 Q × R, provided that the long diagonal is free. This only wins the Exchange; but 1 Q – K4 wins a whole Rook, as it threatens mate. An example of the superiority of a simultaneous double threat over two consecutive threats, and of the simple game, frequently, over the combination.

When the unprotected piece is the Queen, it is obviously not necessary that she shall have *no* protection, for if she can be won by a Bishop-sacrifice, advantage is assured. The more important the unguarded piece, the greater the facility of the combination.

The mechanism of this type of combination is clearly illustrated here. If White were to attack the unprotected Bishop directly, it would retreat, and that would be all. The unguarded Rook at KR1 permits a second threat. How are the two threats to be combined? If 1 Q – QB3, B – B4; 2 P – K6, Castles QR would save Black; the reason being that White uses the two threats successively and not simultaneously. He must therefore begin with 1 P – K6, with the double threat of Q – QB3. A threat, it is often said, is stronger than its execution. It looks as if after 1 P – K6 Black has only to retire his Bishop and there is no more double threat. But by not moving his Queen

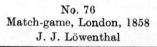

No. 76
Match-game, London, 1858
J. J. Löwenthal

P. Morphy

1 P – K6!, B – B4;   2 Kt × B, P × Kt;
3 P × P ch, K × P;   4 Q – KR3, Q – B3;
5 QR – K1,   KR – K1;   6 R – K5,
K – Kt3 (obviously not R × R; 7 P × R);
7 KR – K1, R × R; 8 R × R, and White
won by his K-side superiority.

White has gained a tempo, and, what is more important, the Queen at K3 prevents Queen-side castling (for then Q – R7) and forces Black's King to his own disorganised wing. Note that after 1 P – K6, B – R5 would lose by 2 Q – Q4; and if 1.. Castles KR, 2 P – B5, threatening Q × P, would demolish Black's position. Note also that Morphy had sacrificed his QBP, foreseeing his gain by it.

The Double Threat

This very instructive example enables us to see what too often passes unnoticed. There is here the combination with the double threat. The ordinary player usually prefers the direct threat, which appears to him stronger. But that is a mistake. The indirect or distant threat promises much

more, and the double threat more still.   Lastly, the order
of the moves has an importance which is too little recog-
nised.

Morphy clearly could not see all the possible consequences
of his Pawn-sacrifice on QB2; but the idea of combination
supplied the gaps in reasoning.   People often bring against
deep study of chess the reproach of spoiling inspiration, and
reducing all to pure reason.   For our part, while we cannot
cease to insist that simple analysis is not enough, and that
one cannot penetrate into the mysteries of combination
when one is lacking in imagination, still we claim that, as
everything is visible on the chess-board, all that happens on
it is subject to principles, which can be discovered, to the
great profit of the most modest amateur.

At any moment of the game the presence of an undefended piece may give rise to a combination.   In the openings it is all a matter of traps.   The classical example is
Légal's Mate, wherein Black's undefended Bishop at KKt5
is the pivot of the combination.   White's KB is sacrificed
at KB7, and the piece is won back with the gain of a Pawn,
thanks to the double threat against the King and the Bishop.
This combination may occur in slightly different positions,
introducing with them variations.   Sometimes the Queen
is sacrificed, sometimes not.   Here the Bishop is sacrificed
first, followed by a Knight-check, there the Knight's move
comes first, threatening Black's KBP and, through the
Queen, Black's Bishop.   But always it is this Bishop's lack
of defence which inspires the combination.

The famous Monticelli trap, based also on an undefended
Bishop, is more interesting (No. 77).   Black's QR is loose,
which allows White to multiply his sacrifices, beginning
with a Knight and continuing with the other Knight and a
Bishop.   How are so many sacrifices to be recompensed?
This combination is played on two long diagonals which
cross at White's K4, Bishop and Rook being on one of them,
a mating-threat on the other.   Such are the elements of a
sufficiently complicated combination.

No. 78 is a clearer example.   The action again takes place
on the two wings; a strategic manœuvre to the right, a
tactical diversion to the left.   The initial Bishop-sacrifice

is plainly visible to all. But the mate on Kt6 is held up by a Bishop, which bars the way for the Queen. Merely to retire this Bishop would be to give precious time to the defence. Then comes in the idea of the unprotected piece, the Queen on her R3. We know that an unprotected Queen may be attacked with impunity by a minor piece. After the first Bishop-sacrifice the second Bishop can also be

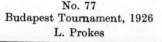

No. 77
Budapest Tournament, 1926
L. Prokes

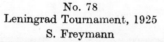

No. 78
Leningrad Tournament, 1925
S. Freymann

M. Monticelli

G. Lövenfisch

1 Q – B2!,   Kt × Kt?;   2 Kt – Kt5!,
Kt – K5;   3 B × Kt, B × B;   4 Q × B,
Q × Kt; 5 Q × R, etc.

1 B × P, P × B;   2 R × P ch, K – Kt2;
3 B – Kt7!, K × R; 4 B × Q, and wins.

offered up, since thus arises the threat of mate. Black has to surrender his Queen, and White wins with Queen and two Pawns against Rook and Bishop. Had the Queen been defended, the result would be problematical, with Queen and two Pawns against Rook and two Bishops.

Again we have to pay attention to the order of the moves, and to note the moment when the second Bishop is sacrificed. 2 B – Kt7 would lose, for then Q × B ; 3 R × P ch, B – R2, and all is saved.

The Black Queen at QR6 makes possible the attack on KR6; but if White had not noticed this his attack on the solid King's position would have been in vain. It is highly unreasonable to play with one's eyes fixed on one part of the board regardless of what passes elsewhere. The Black

Queen's position looks unimportant; but it is vital to the result.

No. 79 is a similar position, with White action against the King on one side, the Queen on the other.   The combination rests on the unsupported Queen, and the decisive sacrifice resembles a discovered check.   We must add that the moves given were only the main variation.   Actually Black

No. 79
Chicago Tournament, 1926
A. Kupchik

No. 80
Moscow Tournament, 1935
E. Rabinovitch

F. J. Marshall

1 R × P, if K × R;   2 Q − Kt3 ch,
followed by 3 Kt checks, winning the
Queen.

P. Romanovsky

1 R − R4,   Kt × Kt;   2 B − Kt5!, and
wins, for if Q × B, then 3 R × P ch,
K × R; 4 Q − R5, and mate next move.
Actually Black declined the Bishop-
sacrifice, playing B − R3, and after
3 B × Q lost in a few moves.

realised the threat well enough, and the continuation was: 1..Q − Q1; 2 R − Kt3, P × P; 3 Kt − Kt6 ch, etc.

In No. 80 is yet another example of the same kind. White's Queen is intent on going to KR5, with a mate, but her way is blocked by the Bishop.   The latter, as before, removes itself, attacking Black's Queen.   Note that White had already given up a Knight before offering the Bishop. If he had continued 2 P × Kt, then Q × P defends Black's KRP.   Note also how the combination is assisted by the Black King's stalemate position.

All these examples demonstrate the opening of lines obstructed not by hostile pieces but by those of the player making the combination.   Lines may be opened with or without a check; and the line may be diagonal or vertical, or even, conceivably, horizontal.

No. 81, based on the same idea, presents a special case. Although again we have an unprotected piece on one side of the board and an attack on the other, two pieces are finally attacked at once, in such a way that the Rook cannot go to the defence of the Knight. A very characteristic

No. 81
Baden-Baden Tournament, 1925
A. Alekhine

R. Réti

1.. Kt × R; 2 B × R, Kt − Q5; 3 R − K3, Kt × B ch; 4 R × Kt, B − Q4, and wins.

instance of this type of combination, for the White Knight's position at QKt7 seems mere chance. As a matter of fact, the Knight has captured a Pawn there, and it is reasonable that a piece so distant from its own forces should not only be in danger but should be the cause of loss of the game. We may recall No. 76, where the Bishop's capture of the QBP serves as a lure for the decisive attack.

Detailed analysis of such combinations, with their sacrifices which are only justified after a series of moves, is very difficult, but becomes much easier when one is familiar with the idea that is the live-wire in them.

We must not be afraid of dwelling on this fundamental point, that combinations, like tactical manœuvres, must be inspired by an idea. Otherwise one becomes lost in a labyrinth of variations.

Exercises

Two examples follow. In the first almost all the Black pieces, especially the two Rooks, are in bad positions, which permits numerous sacrifices. In the other we have an almost perpetual discovered check, followed by the gain of an unprotected piece.

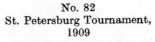

No. 82
St. Petersburg Tournament,
1909
E. Znosko-Borovsky

No. 83
Moscow Tournament, 1925

Dr. Emanuel Lasker

O. S. Bernstein
White to play and win.

C. Torre
White to play and win.

CHAPTER IX

THE OVERWORKED PROTECTING PIECE

Economy and Security

Not only the unprotected piece but also the piece with too much to protect may furnish the material for a combination.

The judicious assignment of their duties to our forces is a very important question. In principle, the greater part should be devoted to the active battle; only the barest minimum must be saved for the defence, without, of course, exercising economy to the pitch of niggardliness, which would be dangerous. But there are often vulnerable points which call for especial precautions. It is better to condemn one piece too many to the defence than to speculate recklessly in attack.

It is easier to formulate such general precepts than to apply them in the heat of action. All excess being an error, one sins sometimes through excess of caution, sometimes through excess of daring. It is not enough to declare, in principle, that every square of more or less importance, or every piece, should be defended at least once to protect oneself against defeat. If one's forces are scattered, the enemy may, Napoleon-like, deliver a heavy blow against some vulnerable point in the position.

When a defending piece is driven off by our attack, or exchanged, the square which it defended becomes weak, and we can get control of it. We must manœuvre in such a fashion that our opponent has no time to bring up a new piece to the menaced point. It is a matter for combination when this point is important enough to warrant a sacrifice to eliminate the defending piece. Such a combination may be simple; but it grows complex when the defender commands a line, and may consequently move along it without abandoning its defence. This work of piece-hunting gives

scope for combinations which are as curious as they are
brilliant.

In No. 84 Black's Queen has to protect the KR, under
doubled attack, and may herself be attacked, to draw her
off the defence. So long as she can stay on the open diagonal
starting from her K1 she is safe. Since it is not a question
merely of winning a Rook, but of mate, White may sacrifice

No. 84
New Orleans, 1920
C. Torre

No. 85
Study by A. Troitsky
Novoe Vremya, 1898

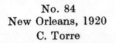

Adams

1 Q—KKt4!, Q—Kt4;   2 Q—QB4!,
Q—Q2; 3 Q—B7!, Q—Kt4; 4 P—QR4,
Q×RP; 5 R—K4, Q—Kt4; 6 Q×KtP,
and wins.

1 P—R4 ch, K—Kt5 (forced); 2 K—Kt2
(threatening Kt—K3 mate), Q—QB4;
3 R—R5!, Q—R2;   4 R×P, Q—B4;
5 R—R5, Q—Q5; 6 P—B3, Q—Q7;
7 R—R2, Q—B8; 8 R—B2, and wins.

all, even his Queen, to prevent her stay on this diagonal.
We see White's Queen offer herself at B4 and B7 simultaneously to Queen and Rook; though it is obvious that the
Rook can no more abandon the rank than the Queen the
diagonal. The two pieces engaged here in the defence of a
single piece and a single square are inadequate.

Such a chase of Queen by Queen over the chess-board is
one of those dramatic situations that astonish the novice and
make our game so attractive. The combination, difficult
as it is to elaborate, is executed with more simplicity and
clearness, without a White Queen, in the following study.

In the beautiful example No. 85 it is the square K6(3) that
Black has to guard, his Queen being unable to leave the bent
line QR2 – K6 – QB8 without allowing a mate by the Knight.

White drives her off it by offering the sacrifice of his Rook, until on move 8 it can no longer be refused.

Steinitz's famous game, which gained him a brilliancy prize in the first great tournament at Hastings, is another presentation of the same idea.

Here again, as in No. 84, Black's Queen has to defend a Rook on the rank. She cannot therefore take the White Rook, which persistently offers itself on the 7th row. If 1..K × R, then mate in a few moves by 2 R – K1 ch, K – Q3; 3 Q – Kt4 ch, K – B2; 4 Kt – K6 ch, K – Kt1; 5 Q – B4 ch, etc. Note the complication introduced by the mate that threatens White at his QB1, which prevents him from capturing the Queen otherwise than with a check. Hence the charming combination, which ends precisely with this capture.

If we compare the two positions 84 and 86 with the study

No. 86
Hastings Tournament, 1895
C. von Bardeleben

W. Steinitz

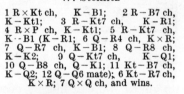

1 R × Kt ch,   K – B1;   2 R – B7 ch, K – Kt1;   3 R – Kt7 ch,   K – R1; 4 R × P ch, K – Kt1; 5 R – Kt7 ch, K--B1 (K – R1; 6 Q – R4 ch, K × R; 7 Q – R7 ch, K – B1; 8 Q – R8 ch, K – K2;   9 Q – Kt7 ch,   K – Q1; 10 Q – B8 ch, Q – K1; 11 Kt – B7 ch, K – Q2; 12 Q – Q6 mate); 6 Kt – R7 ch, K × R; 7 Q × Q ch, and wins.

85, we are inclined to consider that, despite the purity and economy of Troitsky's masterly production, the actual games are richer in ideas and more brilliant. So we cannot agree with the judgement which makes games the "prose" of chess while artificial compositions are its "poetry". What we can admit is that compositions resemble classical poetry, say like Racine's, whereas games are like the Shakespearean dramas with their infinite variety. Everyone to his taste !

The Overtaxed Defender

In the foregoing examples a piece had only to defend a single square, a single piece, and there was material for a combination. The combination based on a piece overtaxed by calls upon its defensive powers is far commoner.   In the first case it is difficult to conceive other than a simple manœuvre, while the overtaxed defender offers many more opportunities that must not be missed.   We can capture it with a superior piece, thus opening at least two squares to our attack.   Then, as the defender cannot quit its post without abandoning the defence of one of the squares under

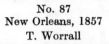

No. 87
New Orleans, 1857
T. Worrall

No. 88
New York Tournament, 1927
F. J. Marshall

P. Morphy
1 R − B8 ch, Q × R; 2 R × Q ch, R × R;
3 Q × P mate.

A. Nimzovitch
1 R − K8, Q × R; 2 Q × Kt ch, K − Kt1;
3 B − R6, and wins.

its guard, we can merely occupy one of those squares; for after the capture of our occupying piece the other square, perhaps more important, is left without protection.

In short, when a piece defends a single square it is the normal situation, and one is usually content to use normal methods against it; but when the piece's defensive power is overtaxed the situation is abnormal, and then the combination, with or without sacrifice, must upset the whole position.

In No. 87 Black's Queen has to defend KB1 and KKt3. The former square being also defended by a Rook, it is the latter that is the aim of a manœuvre with which we are familiar, a checking sacrifice on the rank to draw off the Queen; and then follows what the French call the *épaulettes* mate, at Kt 6.

It is to be noted that in this position White is already a

piece down, Morphy having conceded the odds of QKt. The certainty of mate allowed him to sacrifice two more pieces. (As a matter of fact, he only announced it, and Black resigned.) What does it matter how much wood one throws on the flames of a triumphal bonfire?

Our last example began with a "brutal" check. In No. 88 we see more elegant procedure. But the idea is still the same, to drive off the defending Queen. A Rook is sacrificed at K8 so as to win Black's Knight. It is not yet mate; but after 3 B – R6 Black's Queen, having to defend B1 and Kt2, has too much to do at B2, and 4 Q – Q8 ch forces mate.

The two stages of this combination constitute its charm. There is another subtlety about it. The White Queen and Bishop operate upon the squares KB6, Kt7, R6, and B8, and to do so comfortably want the Black Queen on white squares such as her K1 and KB2. All this is quite simple, but it calls for perspicacity on White's part.

No. 89
London, 1858
P. Morphy

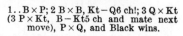

T. W. Barnes

1..B × P; 2 B × B, Kt – Q6 ch!; 3 Q × Kt (3 P × Kt, B – Kt5 ch and mate next move), P × Q, and Black wins.

We will now look at a more complicated example, with more than two steps in the combination. As it is necessary to reach several squares, the pieces which defend them must be dislodged one by one. Thus the desired object is attained, which is to command the most important of the squares.

This example teaches us to appreciate correctly the value of the squares concerned. The White King is in stalemate. It is enough therefore to put him in check. But White has defences where needed; at QB2 by Kt, at Q3 by B and BP. This BP also prevents a mate by B – Kt5, and must therefore be diverted by White. If 1..Kt – Q6 ch, White replies 2 B × Kt, not P × Kt. Therefore Black must begin by diverting the Bishop; and note here how simple and logical Morphy's brilliant combination now seems, when we observe its two special features, the square protected by two pieces and the stalemate-position of the King. The most brilliant combinations, we see, may be based on the simplest ideas.

To conclude this study of a very fertile idea, we present a very beautiful and involved combination.

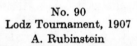

No. 90
Lodz Tournament, 1907
A. Rubinstein

S. Rotlevy

1..R×Kt;   2 P×Q, R—Q7;   3 Q×R, B×B ch;   4 Q—Kt2, R—R6, and wins.

Here a whole system of White pieces defends a multitude of weak squares and pieces; Q at K2 defending KB and KRP, Kt defending KB, etc. First, the Knight must be eliminated, at the price of the Queen. Then White's Queen is attacked, to drive her from the defence of the KB. When Black has secured this Bishop, the attack shifts to White's KRP, protected only by the Queen, without possibility of intervention by another piece. This is a fresh example of the great importance attaching to the order of the moves.

We are far from expecting that, after having studied these combinational masterpieces, our readers will be ready to achieve the like; but we do believe that, after having been initiated into the mechanism of all these stratagems, and having grasped their governing ideas, they will have a full appreciation of the masterpieces of chess, and will have the courage to venture occasionally upon adventures that may be brilliant. After all, when we are artists, are not the finest works of art our own? Why not, when we are chess players, the most brilliant combinations?

Exercises

The reader anyhow, after what he has seen, should not find much difficulty in the solution of the two examples

below; in the first by eliminating the defences of Black's
KKtP, and in the second by cutting the White Queen off
from her K3, where the vision of an *épaulettes*-mate is
hovering.

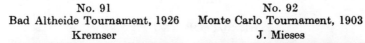

No. 91	No. 92
Bad Altheide Tournament, 1926	Monte Carlo Tournament, 1903
Kremser	J. Mieses

 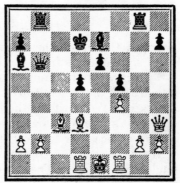

Giertz	A. Reggio
White to play and win.	Black to play and win.

CHAPTER X

THE SUPPORTING PAWN

The Weak Square

THE theory of chess teaches that the weakness of a square arises from the fact that it is not guarded by a Pawn and cannot be so guarded. A square guarded by a Pawn, on the contrary, is strong and cannot easily be attacked. We must try therefore to settle ourselves on our opponent's weak squares, and to make strong squares for our own pieces; for so we shall have a sure advantage.

We have seen the course of action against a square defended by a piece. The piece may be dislodged by attack with a minor piece or a Pawn. We may exchange it off, intercept its line of defence, or, finally, make a sacrifice, which in this case is never very large.

When the square is defended by a Pawn, however, what is the course of action? It would be useless to attack a Pawn with a piece, and as for a sacrifice, this would be heavy where a piece is given up for a Pawn. Still, we know that the beauty of a sacrifice often depends on its heaviness.

In accordance with theory, we must attack a protecting Pawn, not a Pawn that is protected; the root, not the stem. But combinations are exceptional cases, which often break this rule. First, however, let us look at the general rule, leaving the exceptions on one side.

Demolishing the Defence

Black in No. 93 is attacking the KKtP, and if he wins this Pawn threatens mate on White's Kt2. As the KKtP is defended by KRP, it is against the latter that the attack is first directed; but no time can be lost over preparations, for by R – Q2 White would defend both the KRP and KKt2.

94

So the opening sacrifice explains itself. It is in order to check with the QR on the KR file and then play Q × P ch. As the QR cannot at once give check, the second quiet move of R – B3 must be played, though in a combination a quiet move is always risky as giving precious time to the defence.

This is a simple case. But note that Black is obliged

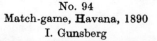

No. 93
Berlin Tournament, 1907
W. Cohn

D. Przepiórka

1 . . R(R3) × P; 2 K × R, R – B3,
and wins.

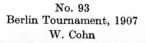

No. 94
Match-game, Havana, 1890
I. Gunsberg

M. Tchigorin

1 R – K6, P – Kt6; 2 B × Kt, Q – Q2;
3 B – B3, P – KB3; 4 QB × P, R × B;
5 R × R, P × B; 6 R × P ch, K – B1;
7 R – B6 ch, K – K2; 8 Q – Kt6, and
wins.

first to sacrifice one Rook and then quietly to bring up the other. And remember, too, that a sacrifice is only an exchange: material against time and space.

In Example 94 the process is less crude, more subtle. Black's KKtP is defended by his KBP, but if the White Queen can get to KKt6 a mate, after B × Kt, will be inevitable. So Tchigorin conceived the following plan: to offer his Rook at K6, when, if it is taken, the KKtP falls, and if it is refused the Knight is lost. A very simple but interesting combination by virtue of its sequel. By 3 B – B3 White takes up again the same attack on the KKtP, and now it is a direct attack. Black has to abandon the natural defence of the KKtP by the advance P – KB3; an example of the weakening of a strong square. Lastly, when White after

6 R × P ch seizes the "critical square" with his Queen, White has nothing to do but to give up.

We may now look at one of the most complicated examples that could be imagined (No. 95). Here again the attack is directed against the KKtP, protected by a secure KBP. Black therefore employs the same method as in the previous example. He attacks the KKtP with R – K6, as the Rook

No. 95
Baden-Baden Tournament, 1925
A. Alekhine

R. Réti

1 .. R – K6; 2 Kt – B3, P × P; 3 Q × P, Kt – B6 ; 4 Q × P, Q × Q; 5 Kt × Q,
Kt × P ch, and wins.

can only be taken at the price of unguarding the KKtP. White's sole defence is to block his third rank with a piece at KB3. The combination is a long one, and we have already shown the finish in No. 81. White succeeds in stopping the break-through at KKt3, but only by weakening his position.

Cutting a Way through

A Pawn may not only protect an important square but also obstruct a line and bar the way to a square of which possession will decide the fate of the game. The attack on such a Pawn is no less difficult, but it often succeeds in splendid combinations, wherein care must be taken to note whether the opening of a line or the attainment of a square is the object.

In No. 96 the mate on White's Kt2 is guarded by his Knight,

which cannot be disturbed. The long white diagonal is open to Black's QB as far as the 8th square, where also a mate is possible. As White KKtP is attacked three times and only defended twice, a start might be made with 1..P × P; but then 2 BP × P brings White's Queen into play. For that reason Black begins with the capture of the KRP,

No. 96
Warsaw, 1917
A. Rubinstein

Belsitzmann

1..Q × RP ch; 2 K × Q, P × P dbl. ch;
3 K − Kt1, R − R8 mate.

No. 97
Magdeburg Tournament, 1927
R. L'Hermet

R. Spielmann

1 Q × P!, P × Q; 2 P × P dis. ch, K − B1;
3 R − Kt8 ch!, K × R;   4 P − R7 ch,
K − B1; 5 P − R8(= Q) mate.

a procedure with which we are acquainted. After White's forced reply the capture of the KtP follows with a double check, leading to mate. It is not, therefore, so much to capture the KKtP that Black attacks the KRP, but to open a road to R8.

This attractive idea, which is akin to that of the opening of lines, is rich in beautiful combinations. They may be classed apart, without confusing them with the cases of the opening of lines closed by pieces.

The marvel of Example No. 97 never ceases. After the first sacrifice of the Queen White gives a succession of checks, to leave his opponent no time to secure his defence. The Queen-sacrifice is not enough. A Rook must be sacrificed also, still with the object of reaching the square KR8 without a pause in the checks.

The combination in No. 98 rests on the same idea, to reach KR8 with a check on the rank. The KRP is an obstacle that must be removed, so the Queen is sacrificed. White cannot continue 2 R – R3 ch, for then Q – R3 would prolong the struggle. He plays first P – B6, closing the 6th rank. If 2..Q × B, then 3 R – R3 ch and mate next move.

No. 98
Barmen Tournament, 1869
J. H. Zukertort

No. 99
Lwow, 1926
Tannenbaum

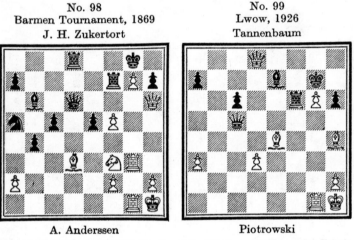

A. Anderssen

Piotrowski

1 Q × P ch!, K × Q;   2 P – B6 dis. ch,
K – Kt1;   3 B – R7 ch!, K × B;
4 R – R3 ch, K – Kt1; 5 R – R8 mate.

1 Q – R8 ch,   K × Q;   2 P – Kt7 ch,
K – Kt1; 3 B – R7 ch, K × B; 4 P – Kt8
(= Q) mate.

The third check, and second sacrifice, with the Bishop, secures the control of the Rook's file without loss of time.

Without loss of time—that is of vast importance. The least respite would allow Black's KR to move and give a flight-square to the King. By a double sacrifice on his R7 White gains the time necessary for the mate on R8. The first sacrifice crushes the resistance of the Pawn, with a gain in space, the second secures a gain in time.

Too much attention cannot be paid to this double sacrifice. Many players quick at a combination would hesitate at the second, which would seem to them too costly; but it is often the second which justifies the first.

In No. 99 there is no question of a Pawn-obstacle. The White Queen is already in the enemy's camp. She is sacrificed not for the KRP but to allow her KtP to advance.

The combination therefore resembles the last. And there is another resemblance, in the Bishop's sacrifice on R7. But now it is not a matter of gaining time. Since it is the King that obstructs the Pawn, he is dislodged first from Kt2 and then from Kt1, by the two sacrifices, allowing the Pawn to continue its glorious advance and to prove the weakness of an obstructive King.

This example differs somewhat from the others, but in comparing all these combinations we see always the same idea, the same processes; a clear appreciation of the critical square to be reached, especially when it is guarded by hostile Pawns, and then sacrifices so as to occupy a line by eliminating these Pawns and to cut our way through to our final objective. If possible we proceed by continuous checks, allowing the adversary neither time nor space for escape.

Exercises

In the first of these two examples a way is cut for the advanced Pawn, with attention to the time-gaining checks. In the second Black must clear the rank on which his Rook is from the Pawn-obstructions, in order to give play to that Rook.

No. 100	No. 101
Pistyan Tournament, 1928	New York Tournament, 1889
F. J. Marshall	M. Tchigorin

K. Sterk	W. H. K. Pollock
White to play and win.	Black to play and win.

PART III

COMBINATIONS DEPENDING ON POSITION

CHAPTER I

COMBINATION IN RELATION TO POSITION

Ideas and Positions

THE "pure ideas" of combination, with which we have just been dealing, obviously have not exhausted our subject. We now come to combination as conditioned by position.

It may be objected that *all* combinations depend on the position. True; but there are some which may arise at any point on the board, while others are met only in certain parts of it, under various conditions. We must not confuse these very distinct types.

However that may be, we shall again come across combinations we have already seen, for the precise reason that they may arise anywhere. But we shall see some that have not yet been examined and that cannot be classed among pure ideas because of their limited possibilities.

We shall begin by analysing the relations of ideas with positions rather than the ideas themselves. We shall see first in what circumstances a certain combination is correct, and shall then enquire to what type of position a certain kind of combination corresponds. For there are types of positions and types of combinations, so that there is a correspondence between them.

Given a position, we should know, by analysis, with what combination it corresponds, every other combination being thereby excluded. Reciprocally, if we are preparing a combination of a certain kind, we should know what position should be brought about, in all its details, to make that combination correct. Of course, in every case there are unforeseeable peculiarities, which may upset everything; but the indispensable conditions must be fulfilled. Without these, there is "nothing doing".

Greater ease of play should result from our studies so far.

We shall not lose ourselves in the maze of combinations. We shall know what ought to be done. Avoiding disillusions, we shall strike judiciously at the enemy's weak point. We shall not fall through ignorance into ingenious—and ingenuous—traps.

So, having examined combinational ideas, we now turn to positions in order to recognise combinations under their double aspect. After that it will only remain to profit by this study and adorn our play with the most dazzling fantasy!

The Centre and the Wings

The diversity of positions is as large as that of combinations, and we cannot therefore examine them all. We must pass over all secondary and superfluous examples, and limit ourselves to what is of general importance.

Central positions differ greatly from positions on the wings, and the resulting combinations are not the same. All is changed, the end to aim at and the method of procedure. As we push our examination further, we discover that on the wings, too, distinctions must be drawn. We have to give there minute attention to the various types of position. The weakness of a certain point, the presence of a certain piece, may have a great influence on the combination. So, too, in the centre we must recognise that various combinations depend on certain positional weaknesses.

We will start from one side of the board, to come later to the centre. It would be useless to go to the other side, for we find there almost the same combinations, and what differences there are are not of such a nature as to call for our attention in this necessarily limited examination. We leave these subtleties to the writers who come after us. On the day when all combinations are known and classified the question may be reconsidered more exhaustively. That day is still far distant. Should we add, Thank heaven?

CHAPTER II

THE KING'S ROOK'S PAWN

Castling

THE object of castling is not only to put the King into safety, but to give greater freedom to the pieces which, after this precautionary move, have no longer to defend the King. The King himself is not inactive after it. He protects the Pawns which, in front of him, protect him. He has to dispense with the protection of the pieces, permitting even his Rook to go to the centre of the board.

It is generally only, among the pieces, the Knight at KB3, or the Bishop, if played in fianchetto, at KKt2, that defends him. But one often sees them go, leaving him alone behind his Pawns. The latter are therefore more or less weak, and, on account of their protective duty, have great importance and are the target of dangerous attacks. The Queen's wing Pawns (we are not considering the cases of Castles Q), without the King and without pieces to support them, are obviously weaker; but an attack directed against them is much less effective than one against the other wing. The spoils of the King's wing may often decide the issue. It is for this reason that the King-side Pawns are so often brilliantly attacked. On this side the heaviest sacrifices are frequently justified, whereas on the other strict economy of sacrifice is necessary.

We will begin with combination against the KRP at R2(7).

Three Attacking Pieces

Usually the attack is conducted by three pieces, Bishop, Knight, and Queen. The Bishop occupies the diagonal QR1 – KB6, the Knight commands KKt5, and the Queen plants herself at KR5, or sometimes KKt4. This triple force is normally sufficient to assure the success of the attack.

But, when the Knight goes to Kt5, to reinforce the attack
of the Bishop along the diagonal, Black can play P – KKt3
or P – KR3 to avert the storm. It is to prevent this parry
that the Bishop is often sacrificed at KR7, leading to
Kt – Kt5 ch, Q – R5, and mate on R7. In his analysis of
this combination White must bear in mind, after Kt – Kt5 ch,
the King's two flight-squares, his Kt1 *and* Kt3.

In the first case the Queen goes to R5, and if Black has a
Rook at KB1 the threat is of mate on KR7. If Black's KB1
is vacant, the check on KR7 is reinforced by the threat of
one on KB7. In this case, with two Pawns for the Bishop
sacrificed and a strong attack on the hostile King, the combination is generally crowned by success. Matters may be
quite different when Black's KBP is defended otherwise than
by a Rook on its KB1; and here is a first difficulty.

In the second case, when Black plays K – Kt3, a check
on the diagonal QKt – KR7 seldom leads to gain, because
the Knight on Kt5 is *en prisé*, and Black has several ways
of parrying this check, for instance by P – KB4. Without
the Queen, however, the attack cannot succeed. Where
then shall the Queen go? Q – R5 is impossible, and White
must be content with Q – Kt4, threatening a discovered
check by moving his Knight—a very dangerous check, because it may cut off the retreat K – B3, or from K6 may
menace not only the KKtP but also an important piece, such
as the Queen on Q1 or a Rook on KB1, more than compensating for the sacrifice. When none of these threats is
realisable the combination is doomed to failure; but it is
rarely that discovered checks are innocuous.

Against this menace Black has usually but one defence,
P – KB4, attacking the Queen and opening a new escape
for the King. In this variation White, though having the
resource of Q – Kt3, must make no error in his analysis, for
the Queen may be harassed by P – B5. She has then to
return to KKt4, where a Bishop on Black's QB1 may attack
her after P(at K3) – K4. That Pawn-move is less dangerous
before P – KB4, for then Kt – K6 dis. ch covers the Queen.

Generally Black's KRP is defended not only by the King
but also by a Knight at KB3. To make the combination
possible, therefore, White must dislodge this Knight, or

capture it if it is not defended by the other Knight, for
instance at Q2. The result is normally achieved by
(1) P – K5; (2) the pin B – Kt5; or (3) Kt – K4 or Kt4. The
most effective method is the advance of the KP, but it
is all a matter of circumstances.   Black's Knight at KB3
being always liable to such attacks, it may be asked whether
it would not be better posted at KB1; but there its role is

No. 102
Hamburg Team Tournament, 1930
V. Marin

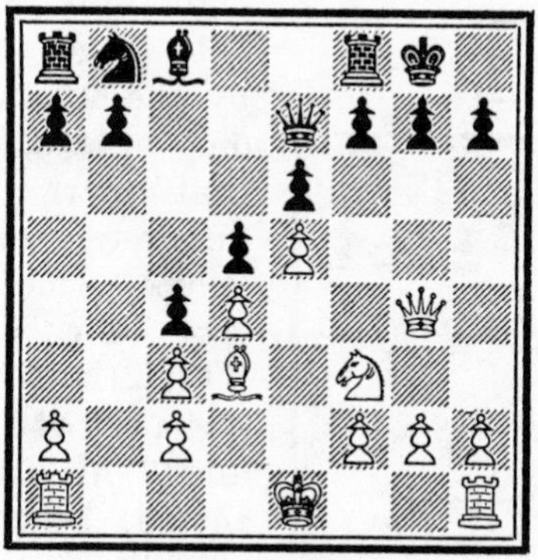

F. D. Yates
1 B × P ch, Black resigns.

too passive, while at B3 it threatens, by Kt – K5, to cut
White's diagonal QKt1 – KR7, which is so important in the
attack that we are studying.   Besides, it prevents Q – R5
unless White sacrifices his QB.   It must be noted that when
eliminating the Black Knight on B3 White must keep a
Knight himself.   It is necessary for the attack and must be
able to deliver check from Kt5.   If that square is guarded,
notably by a Black Bishop, the Knight must be replaceable
by another or else the combination must be abandoned.

The Bishop-sacrifice

Let us take a few examples of this combination, for a
general view and a consideration of its features.

The position in No. 102 shows the matter very simply.
The three necessary pieces are present.   But Black's KRP is

only defended by the King; there is no Knight on KB3, nor a Bishop on K2 to guard against Kt – Kt5. White's Queen forbids Black's escape by K – Kt3. So there is really but one variation, 1..K × B; 2 Q – R5 ch, K – Kt1, under the worst conditions, KB1 being occupied by a Rook and K2 by the Queen. Obviously 1..K – R1 is useless, 2 Q – R5 still forcing mate.

We pass now to a more complicated example.

Here again Black's King-side is insufficiently protected. The three White pieces are well posted to execute their

No. 103
Nice Tournament, 1930
J. J. O'Hanlon

E. Colle

manœuvre, the Knight being able to go to Kt5, guarded by the QB, while Black has only his Queen commanding that square. There are some differences to be noted: (1) White's Queen not being at Kt4, Black's King can go to Kt3; (2) his KB1 being vacant, he has also that flight-square; and (3) his KBP being unprotected, Black has to guard against both Q – R7 and Q – B7.

Careful analysis proves that White wins in all variations. Success is easy against 2..K – Kt1, because of the double threat just mentioned. We see the valuable lesson for White that in such a case the sacrifice may be made without hesitation, and for Black that he must foresee the sacrifice and parry the menace. In the present position Black's

1 B × P ch, K × B; 2 Kt – Kt5 ch, K – Kt3 (K – Kt1; 3 Q – R5, Kt – B3; 4 Q × P ch, K – R1; 5 R – K4. Or 3..Q – B3; 4 Q – R7 ch, K – B1; 5 Kt – K4); 3 P – KR4, R – R1 (P – B4; 4 P – R5 ch, K – B3; 5 Q × P ch); 4 R × P ch, Kt – B3 (P × R; 5 P – R5 ch, R × P; 6 Q – Q3 ch, K – B3; 7 Q – B3 ch, B – B5; 8 Q × B ch); 5 P – R5 ch, K – R3 (R × P; 6 Q – Q3 ch, K – R3; 7 Q – R7 mate); 6 R × B, Q – R4 (to stop the threat 7 R × Kt ch, P × R; 8 Kt – K6 ch, K – R2; 9 Q – Q3 ch, K – Kt1; 10 Q – Kt3 ch and mate next move); 7 Kt × P ch, K – R2; 8 Kt – Kt5 ch, K – Kt1; 9 Q – Kt3 ch, Black resigns.

previous move was QBP × P—a grave blunder, for a defensive move, such as Kt – B3, would have removed all danger.

Generally the King's flight to Kt3 is not advisable, for there he is too exposed to attacks. In our example Black

has a somewhat favourable position, in that the attack by
Q – Kt4 is stopped by Kt – B3 or P – B4, the retreat Q – Kt3
being unavailable. We see then that this attack is only
possible when White's KKt3 is neither blocked nor menaced.
Nevertheless here White wins by 3 P – KR4, with the threat
of P – R5 ch. Note that this threat should be accompanied
by another, such as, in this case, Q – Q3 ch, made possible
by the sacrifice 4 R × P, stopping P – B4. We see also that
Black has not any longer the defence of Kt – B3, because
of Q – Q3 ch and Kt × BP, winning. The weakness of his
KBP weighs terribly on Black, and whenever his King has
to go to R3 he is lost. White's Queen supplies the place
of the sacrificed Bishop on the White diagonal.

The attacked King's position here is so unfavourable that
there is a triple solution of the problem at move 6; the
actual one, 6 Kt × P dbl. ch, and the very subtle 6 Q – Q3.
From the beginning of the combination it stands out
that with K – R3 the game is lost for Black. A new point
to be noted.

The Move P – KR4

All these general considerations are of importance. They
can easily be taken into account before the combination
begins, and thus we avoid long analyses, with multiple variations leading to mate. We must remember especially the
part played by White's KRP. In our last example it had
only to support the Knight at Kt5 and to threaten P – R5 ch,
but it is often used for other purposes. When White's
KKt5 is covered by Black, so that it is not a safe place for
a Knight, nevertheless Kt – Kt5 in conjunction with P – KR4
may justify a Knight-sacrifice to open the KR file. The
Rook then, if still at KR1, replaces the Knight in the attack.
In our example, as the Rook was at K1 there would have
been no object in opening the file, and moveover White's
KKt5 was not threatened.

In the next example (No. 104), with a still longer com-
bination attached to it, White's KKt5 is commanded by
Black's KB. His KR must therefore intervene; so 2 P – KR4.
The reply P – QB4 does not suffice, though it is true that

there is no satisfactory move; not P – KR3 because of the attack P – KKt4 – Kt5, nor P – KKt3 because of P – R5, nor yet Kt – Q2 because it does not stop the Bishop-sacrifice. Black's KBP being unprotected and his K2 blocked, he is compelled to capture the Knight, letting White's Rook into the attack. This consideration justifies the first sacrifice of the Bishop.

No. 104
Rejkjavik, 1931
A. Asgiersson

A. Alekhine

1 P – K5, B – K2; 2 P – KR4, P – QB4; 3 B × P ch,   K × B;   4 Kt – Kt5 ch, B × Kt;   5 P × B dis. ch,   K – Kt1; 6 Q – R5, K – B1; 7 Castles Q, P – R3; 8 P – Kt6, K – K2;   9 P × P, R – B1; 10 P × P, Kt – Q2; 11 R × P, Q – R4; 12 Q – Kt5 ch,   K × P;   13 R – R7, R – KKt1;   14 R – Q4,   Q × BP; 15 R × Kt ch,   B × R;   16 Kt – K4, Q – Kt5;   17 Kt – Q6 ch,   K – B1; 18 Q – B6 ch, P × Q; 19 R – B7 mate.

It is impossible to analyse all the variations here, or even the principal one, comprising as it does no less than 19 moves. It is plain, too, that White could not imagine all the tactical combinations which sprang out of the main combination. The essential point is to have so favourable a position that without a clear vision of the result a bold sacrifice is justified. How, indeed, should one not win when one has all one's pieces in play, while the adversary's are not and his King will be at K2?

Many amateurs, though so appreciative of daring where the masters are concerned, never launch out on a combination or indulge in a sacrifice unless a mate is staring them in the face, or at least some great gain in material is within their grasp. That is wrong, because such a prize rarely offers itself. To act boldly it is enough to see the position clearly, and not to misjudge the hostile chances, either of defence or of counter-attack.

In our example the Bishop-sacrifice is justified because the essential conditions which we have laid down are fulfilled. There is nothing to fear. The quantity of combinations which this sacrifice gives rise to, with the numerous, yet sufficiently similar, variations, proves that success is not due to luck, but that we have an instance of a law by which advantage must result from great positional disequilibrium.

Another example of the same kind follows, White's position being identical and Black's differing in one move only.

Black's predicament here is still worse, for his Rook at KB1 prevents his King from escaping mate if he returns to Kt1. He must therefore go to Kt3, which, as we know, leads to disaster. Still, after this sortie, there is nothing to be feared from the usual attack by 5 Q – Kt4, for then B × Kt; 6 P × B, Q × P. The attack is repulsed, thanks to the Black Queen's entry. But the precarious situation of the King at Kt3 gives scope for the attack, which comprises some pretty sacrifices.

Once more, the combination is made feasible by Black's errors. Why did he not reply to 1 P – KR4 with a defensive move? His move, too, previous to the diagrammed position, P – QKt3 instead of P – B4, was equally

No. 105
Nuremberg Tournament, 1883
J. Mason

A. Fritz

1 P – KR4, B – Kt2; 2 P – K5, B – K2; 3 B × P ch,   K × B;   4 Kt – Kt5 ch, K – Kt3 (K – R3; 5 Q – Q2); 5 Kt – K2, B × Kt;   6 P × B, P – KB4 (Q × P or R – R1; 7 Kt – B4 ch); 7 KtP × P i.p., R – R1 (P × P; 8 Q – Q3 ch); 8 Kt – B4 ch;   K – B2;   9 Q – Kt4, R × R ch; 10 K – Q2,   P × P;   11 Q – Kt6 ch, K – K2;   12 Q – Kt7 ch,   K – K1; 13 Q – Kt8 ch,   K – K2;   14 Q × P ch, K – B1; 15 R × R, B – B1; 16 R – R8 ch, K – Kt2;   17 R – R7 ch,   K × R; 18 Q – B7 ch,   K – R1;   19 Kt – Kt6 mate.

lacking in defence. Perhaps it seems inconceivable in a player like Mason. Of course, one relies on one's analysis and thinks always to escape from danger by masterly tactics, by some ingenious device. But, since nothing can fight against the necessity of circumstances, it is best (and particularly so for the ordinary player) to restrict oneself to general reasoning. A real champion may allow himself to make exceptions and to go contrary to the natural order of things—it is perhaps his mission, but it is not the average amateur's!

Rook replaces Knight

We see that the Rook on KR1 can play an active part when its file is open. It may then replace the Knight sacrificed at KKt5. So we must always bear in mind the move P – KR4 in this type of combination. Whenever a Knight, or a Bishop, plants itself at Kt5 for the attack, P – R4 is an admirable support, and after a capture of the piece the Pawn is excellently posted at Kt5, attacking the important squares R6 and B6. With the aid of the Queen at R5 the result is often a mate. If Black does not capture the piece, it remains menacing. When P – R4 has been played, moreover, White is ready to launch a Pawn-assault, and every advance of the hostile Pawns merely gives more scope for a bold attack.

In this example we find the necessary conditions for the combination against Black's KR2. But Black has two pieces on the diagonal leading from his Q1. So there is not yet for White the opportunity of Kt – KKt5. He begins therefore with P – KR4, though it allows Black a tempo to prepare against the imminent sacrifice.

No. 106
Vienna Tournament, 1894
S. R. Wolf

C. Schlechter

1 P – KR4, P – KB3; 2 Kt – Kt5!, P × Kt; 3 B × P ch, K × B; 4 P × P dis. ch, K – Kt1; 5 R – R8 ch!, K – B2 (K × R; 6 Q – R5 ch and 7 P – Kt6, etc.); 6 Q – R5 ch, P – Kt3; 7 Q – R7 ch, K – K1; 8 Q × P mate.

Black has a serious problem before him. How is he to prevent the sacrifice on his KR2 *and* White's Kt – KKt5? If 1..P – KR3, then threaten 2 P – KKt4 and a further Pawn-advance. If 1..P – KKt3, 2 Kt – KKt5, with the threat of Kt × RP and P – R5. Finally, if 1..P – KB4, there is open to White P – KKt4. Black chooses, instead of these, 1..P – KB3, to stop not only Kt – KKt5 but also Q – R5; for after 2 Kt – KKt5, P × Kt; 3 P × P, there will be time for 3..P – KKt3.

But, in spite of Black's reasoning, the storm bursts upon him; two sacrifices, blow upon blow, shattering his position. First White gives up the Knight, to open the file for his KR, which is not enough in itself.   Therefore comes in the second sacrifice B × P ch, gaining several tempos; for now 4 P × P discovers check and the Queen goes to R5 with a threat of mate.

Yet a third sacrifice, of remarkable beauty, is offered, 5 R – R8 ch.   Once more a gain of time; for, if K × R, 6 Q – R5 ch forces mate, and, if Black does not capture, the Rook takes part in the final combination, in front of the Queen.

It is to be noted that, preceding the diagrammed position, Black had committed an error by B – Q2, losing time for defence and allowing his opponent the indispensable move, P – KR4, which made the sacrifices possible.   Kt – Q2 or P – KB4 was much better.

When the sacrifice crashes on us we know that it is late in the day to try to save ourselves.   Forewarned is fore-armed, in chess as in other things.   We must have foresight of the combination, examine the circumstances of its occur-rence, and provide for the defence.   Often a simple pre-ventive move suffices to cause the adversary to abandon his dashing enterprise.   It is not to be supposed that any player is of such aesthetic susceptibility as actually to invite his opponent to illuminate the sky with a brilliant firework-display!

The number of examples which we have seen of combina-tions arising from a mere error on the opponent's part should not cause surprise.   Why do very strong players commit such errors?   Do they fail altogether to foresee the possible combination, and the sacrifice which they have often made themselves?   What is probably often the explanation is that these players, over-confident of having an exceptional case to deal with, devote their attention to tactical details and the elaboration of some recondite defence which may bring safety and even advantage.   So they come to neglect general principles, which take their stern revenge. Nothing could prove better than the examples which we have seen the necessity of basing one's play on the general ideas that are inspired by the sound reasoning-out of a position.

Let us look at another defence against P – KR4. There is here the same combinational threat as we have had. But Black's position is more satisfactory. The Bishop at KB3 is not obstructing the flight-square K2, and the move P – KKt3 will cut off two threats, B × P ch and Q – R5.

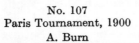

No. 107
Paris Tournament, 1900
A. Burn

F. J. Marshall

1 P – KR4, P – KKt3; 2 P – R5, R – K1;
3 P × P, RP × P;   4 Q – B2, B – Kt2?;
5 B × P, P × B;   6 Q × P, Kt – Q2;
7 Kt – KKt5, Q – B3;   8 R – R8 ch,
Black resigns.

Also, if White plays 2 P – R5, which is logical, he can no longer play Kt – KKt5. Although one might prefer for Black 2..Kt – Q2, in place of R – K1, intending Kt – B1 or B3, there is no harm done yet. White, having opened the Rook's file, but unable to play Q – R5, plays instead Q – B3, preparing to sacrifice the Bishop on Kt6. And now Black makes his decisive error. He should have defended his KtP with K – Kt2. All the requisites for the success of the combination are here, Queen, Rook, and Knight, the last being now able to occupy Kt5. The inadequacy of Black's second move is to be noted. His Rook at K1 becomes on the 6th move *en prise*, thus preventing Q – B3. If Black's Knight were already at Q2 the attack could be repulsed by Kt – B3, followed later by Q – K1. White's final Rook-sacrifice on the 8th rank is beginning to become familiar to us.

Our last examples show that the idea of the sacrifice by B × P ch, followed by Kt – Kt5 and Q – R5, may undergo modifications. The Bishop may be sacrificed on Kt6 or the Knight on Kt5. Other sacrifices may be introduced without changing the basic idea; for instance, of the Rook at R5 (after P – R4 and the capture of this Pawn by Black), to open the Bishop's diagonal to KR7.

Below we have the sacrifice of a Knight instead of a Bishop at KR7. Why? White's task is made easier by the presence of a second Knight at K4, to add to the previous trio of pieces. One Knight may therefore be sacrificed without modifying the essential conditions of this combination. But the second Knight is pinned, because of the mate threatened on White's KKt2, and so can only move with a check.

Black cannot accept the offer of the Knight because of this last fact; 2 Kt – B6 dis. ch would win the Queen. As for Black's actual move, it is quietly met by the Knight's withdrawal, leaving Black's position extremely weak. He is threatened now with Q – R5, to which there is no longer the answer P – R3, and further by B – B4, followed by B × P ch. If 2 . . P × Kt, simply 3 B × KP and White wins easily.

No. 108
Carlsbad Tournament, 1929
A. Becker

J. R. Capablanca
1 Kt × RP, P – KB4; 2 Kt(R7) – Kt5,
Black resigns.

As no general rule can be formulated for all these cases, the variations should be carefully analysed. Success is assured, however, when we have made certain of the presence of the essential conditions. Without them the most brilliant stratagems are but vain attempts.

What happens when the pieces are not posted as indicated to be necessary for the success of our combination? Defeat; that is to say, unless we can find new variations on the same theme.

In No. 109, for instance, the Knight at K5, instead of KKt5, changes the aspect of the combination, there being no mate on KR7 through Queen and Knight. Still, the Knight at K5 threatens the unprotected KBP, and also gives the possibility of a perpetual check by Q – R5 – B7. White has also a second Knight at QB3, which can support the attack from K4 and so reach Kt5, where precisely a Knight is wanted. The combination materialises again, and may achieve success. But the loss of time resulting from altered circumstances does not allow hopes of victory if Black finds the best defence. If he had played 3..K – R1 (instead of R2) White's Knight could not have gone to Kt5 with a check, and there was only a draw to be had.

It is, by the way, very strange that in a tournament at Prague in 1931 the same position occurred between

No. 109
New York Tournament, 1916
O. Chajes

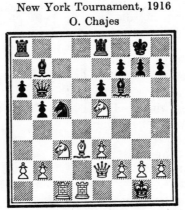

D. Janowski

1 B × P ch, K × B;   2 Q – R5 ch, K – Kt1;   3 Q × P ch, K – R2?;   4 Kt – Q7, Kt × Kt;   5 R × Kt, B – B3;   6 Kt – K4, B × P; 7 Kt – Kt5 ch, K – R3; 8 P – KKt4, P – Kt3; 9 P – KR4, R – R1; 10 Q – R7 ch, R × Q; 11 R × R mate.

V. Mikenas and I. Kashdan, who (not knowing the previous game, though it won Janowski a brilliancy prize in the Rice Memorial Tournament at New York) agreed to a draw —and that when Black had again made the wrong move of 3..K – R2!

When Black plays K – Kt3

We must now retrace our steps and look again at the dangers which may befall the Black King on flight to Kt3. Without going back to the advance of P – KR4 (and in consequence without bringing in the KR) we will return to the first form of our attack with Queen, Knight, and the Bishop sacrificed on KR7. Black's King, forbidden Kt1, because his flight-squares are blocked, escapes to Kt3. We

will take one of the most favourable examples for Black and
see what comes of it.

In the position of No. 110 a sally by the White Queen to
KKt4 does not seem decisive, for she can be attacked from
various quarters. Black is at fault in playing 4 . . K – R3. He
should continue the attacks on the Queen, with P – KB5;
and if 5 Q – Kt4, then P – K4, or if 5 P × P, then Kt – B4;

No. 110
Buenos Aires, 1911
J. Molina

J. R. Capablanca

1 B × P ch, K × B; 2 Kt – Kt5 ch, K – Kt3; 3 Q – Kt4, P – B4 (P – K4
4 Kt – K6 dis. ch, K – B3; 5 P – B4 and White's KR comes into play)
4 Q – Kt3, K – R3 (better was P – B5; 5 Q – Kt4, P – K4); 5 Q – R4 ch
K – Kt3; 6 Q – R7 ch, K – B3 (K × Kt; 7 Q × KtP ch); 7 P – K4, Kt – Kt3
8 P × P, P × P; 9 QR – Q1, Kt – Q6; 10 Q – R3, Kt(Q6) – B5; 11 Q – Kt3
Q – B2; 12 KR – K1, and wins.

6 Q – Kt4, Kt – R3, when a repetition of moves would lead
to a draw. Perhaps, however, White can maintain the
attack. *E.g.* 4 . . P – B5; 5 Q – Kt4, P – K4; 6 Kt – K6 ch,
K – B3; 7 QR – Q1, Q – K1 (Kt – Q6; 8 Kt – K4 ch);
8 R – Q6, with manifold threats.

In this case it was necessary to evolve fresh combinations
in order to force a win. It seems that it is the entry of
White's QR that decides the day; just as in the variation
beginning with 3 . . P – K4 it is his KR. In all cases new
strategy has become necessary to make the attack successful.

Our conclusion is that the sortie of the King to Kt3 is
usually bad. It is a policy of despair unless White's Queen
can be attacked on Kt4 and Kt3. Then a defence is possible;

and it is necessary to graft new manœuvres on to the stock of the original combination—which is true for both White and Black.

The problem of the attack on the KRP becomes clearer and clearer. In pulling it to pieces as we have done, we gradually see its rich possibilities. But whatever be the tactical variations, the general idea remains at the base of them, with the general principles which are the condition of victory or defeat.

Exercises

We give two illustrative exercises. In the first it will be found that the KR enters the game decisively by the KB file instead of, as generally, its own. In the other the QR, having in White's last two moves arrived from its original square, comes in to supplement the attack by Q, Kt, and B (here the QB). Only Q and R menace Black's KRP, which indeed in the main variation escapes capture after its protection by P – KKt3. White's Queen-moves are pretty.

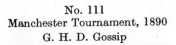

No. 111
Manchester Tournament, 1890
G. H. D. Gossip

No. 112
Berlin, 1932
Dr. Schober

E. Schallopp
White to play and win.

K. Richter
White to play and win.

CHAPTER III

THE SACRIFICE OF THE TWO BISHOPS

The Hostile KRP and KKtP

WE have seen that for the success of the combination against Black's KRP three pieces are required, Queen, Bishop, and Knight, of which the last may be replaced by a Rook. Without these pieces there is nothing to be done; nor is there unless all of them can bear upon KR7. After the sacrifice, to get rid of Black's Pawn, two pieces are necessary for mate or an important gain. And there is the further condition that no Black piece must be able to come to the rescue.

It goes without saying that we can lavish our sacrifices if we have a surplus of other forces. Such cases are not interesting. Other combinations call for our attention, namely those in which, the attack on a single Pawn (KRP or KKtP) being insufficient, success can only be attained by a combination against the two.

Let us look at the following case. Suppose that we are a piece short for attack on the KRP, or that one of our pieces is badly posted. The combination is held up. But if we have another piece bearing upon another Pawn, or if our badly-placed piece, so far as the attack upon the KRP is concerned, threatens the KKtP, a double combination becomes possible.

Naturally, after the sacrifices made for these two Pawns, we must still have two pieces to deliver mate. But which pieces? Evidently Queen and Rook; for after the disappearance of the two Black Pawns we need to command the two open files. Note that in these combinations the Knight is absent. If it were present it could join its action to one or the other Bishop's against one Pawn, when the attack on the two Pawns would become useless. As the two Bishops sacrifice themselves to shatter the enemy's castled position, it is plain that there remains only the Rook's aid for the Queen to secure mate. This Rook must be in a state to intervene in affairs at once, before the enemy has time to defend himself.

To sum up, the necessary pieces for this combination are the Queen, the two Bishops bearing upon KKt7 and KR7, and a Rook upon a more or less free line. The Knight is not indispensable, except to eliminate a piece protecting the hostile King's position. As we have not enough available force to overcome more obstacles, it must not be the case that our opponent has more than one piece defending that position.

The Double Bishop-sacrifice

The example to which we now come may serve as a model for all combinations of this type. If the White Knight were at KB3 we should have a pattern case of the combination against the KRP. At KKt3 it is of no use in a combination of the kind. On the other hand, it is very useful in an attack on the KKtP, for it can at once get rid of the hostile Knight, the only piece protecting the castled King.

We have, therefore, all the pieces necessary for our combination: the two Bishops bearing upon the Pawns in question, the Queen with easy access to the King's wing, and lastly, the Rook on a semi-open file. If this Rook were already at KB3, the sacrifice of the KB alone would suffice, for then Queen and Rook would achieve mate on KR7. The Rook would, in the manner we know, replace the Knight. As time must be lost in its development to a threatening post, the enemy can profit by it to make a move useful in

No. 113
Amsterdam Tournament, 1889
J. H. Bauer

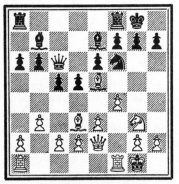

Dr. Emanuel Lasker

1 Kt—R5, Kt×Kt; 2 B×P ch, K×B;
3 Q×Kt ch, K—Kt1; 4 B×P, K×B;
5 Q—Kt4 ch, K—R2; 6 R—B3, and
wins.

defence, such as P – B4 or P – Kt3.   This is the reason for
the second sacrifice, to crush resistance without loss of time.

It is somewhat astonishing that White, having neither
time nor strength to carry the combination through with
his first sacrifice, arrives directly at success with a second.
The remedy for poverty is more expense!

This lesson is good for many players, often quite gifted,
who, after deciding to make a sacrifice, are pulled up on the
way by a lack of courage.   A second sacrifice? they ask; a
further diminution of already insufficient forces?   They do
not enquire of themselves whether the reduced forces will
be strong enough against the enemy's dismantled position.

In comparing the two combinations, one against the KRP
and the other against KRP and KKtP, we must note the
different parts played by the pieces.   In the first the lead
is entrusted to Queen and Knight, the Rook only serving to
replace the latter; as for the Bishops, one is sacrificed on
KR7, the other may merely support the Knight on Kt5.
In the second combination, where the Knight is often missing, it is the Rook which takes a share in the mate, the
Bishops sacrificing themselves in the cause of ultimate
success.

In conclusion, there is an important distinction, depen-
dent on the pieces employed in them, that the first combination is carried out on squares, the second on lines.   We
have already stressed the importance in our analysis of
combinations based on the opening of lines.

We must make sure in what circumstances we should
contemplate the sacrifice of the two Bishops, what positions
our storm-troops should take up, and what pieces are
essential to us.   If we cannot satisfy the necessary conditions, we must renounce the sacrifices.   Our opponent, for
his part, is called upon to foresee what combination is threatening him: of two Bishops, or of one at his KR2.   He must
at all costs take the necessary precautions to bring our
plans to naught.

In No. 114 are all the elements of the combination with
the double Bishop-sacrifice.   The Black King cannot escape
from the two right-hand files, his K2 being blocked by his
Queen.   Black has no defensive piece on the wing, which

relieves White of the necessity of another piece to eliminate Black's. The Rook being ready to give check, the combination offers itself very favourably to White—who, it may be added, had cunningly induced his opponent to bare his King's side.

It may perhaps be asked whether Black was forced to accept the second sacrifice, whether he could not have got

No. 114
Southsea Tournament, 1923

J. A. J. Drewitt

A. Alekhine

1 B × P ch, K × B; 2 R − R3 ch, K − Kt1;
3 B × P, K × B; 4 Q − Kt4 ch, resigns.

No. 115
St. Petersburg Tournament.
1914

S. Tarrasch

A. Nimzovitch

1 . . P − Q5; 2 P × P, B × P ch; 3 K × B,
Q − R5 ch; 4 K − Kt1, B × P; 5 P − B3
(5 K × B, Q − Kt5 ch; 6 K − R2, R − Q4;
7 Q × P, R − R4 ch; 8 Q × R, Q × Q ch;
9 K − Kt2, Q − Kt4 ch, etc.), KR − K1;
6 Kt − K4, Q − R8 ch; 7 K − B2, B × R;
8 P − Q5. P − B4; 9 Q − B3, Q − Kt7 ch;
10 K − K3, R × Kt ch;   11 P × R,
P − B5 ch, and wins.

out of trouble by taking the first Bishop and refusing the second. The old argument comes up: Black has a piece in hand. Let us see.

After 3 B × P the threat is 4 Q − Kt4 and 5 R − R8 ch. If 3 . . P − B4, then 4 Q − R5, Q × B; 5 R − Kt3. Or White may prefer 4 B − R6, threatening Q − R5. Besides, what can be expected in such a position? The Black King has one piece to defend him, his Pawns have fallen, and he is attacked by all the White pieces.

The lesson to be learnt from this example is that in a

position of the kind the combination must be accepted or refused as a whole.   You must accept or refuse both sacrifices, not one alone.

No. 115 is one more position of the same type, with Black as the attacking party for a change.   Black has all the elements necessary for the combination, so that White would do well to avoid it by playing 2 P – K4, closing one Bishop's diagonal.   But actually White accepts the first sacrifice and refuses the second.

Another important question arises, here as in No. 114. Cannot White, after accepting all that is offered, counter-sacrifice the Queen to remain with Rook and two Bishops against Black's Queen?   This eventuality must always be kept in mind, for the fate of the game may depend on it. In the earlier example, after 6 . . P – K4;   7 R – R3 ch, Q – R3; 8 R × Q ch, K × R, White wins a Bishop by 9 Q – Q7. Can we not do the same here?   Obviously with 9 . . Q – Kt4 Black wins the Knight.

Here then are the three phases of the combination: the essential conditions and the combinational idea; the refusal of the second sacrifice; and, lastly, acceptance of all, with a counter-sacrifice in reply.

We must now hope, after studying all the details of this brilliant combination, that we may be able to prove its effectiveness against a disorganised opponent.

Exercises

In No. 116 the presence of two Bishops prompts us at once to look for a combination aimed at Black's KKtP and KR2, while the position of our Queen and one Rook invites us to sacrifice.   But after P – KR4 on both sides the Bishop-sacrifices are without profit.   How is the game to be ended brilliantly?

The attack on the two Pawns is not necessarily conducted by the double sacrifice of the Bishops only.   The much rarer sacrifice of the two Knights is illustrated in No. 117. The absence of a Bishop at Q3 does not allow the forcing of the attack by B × P ch.   On the other hand, the presence of a Bishop at QKt2, with the eventual intermediary Pawn

at KB6, invites concentration on Black's KKtP.   But here
we certainly have a case where the defender is ill advised
to accept the second sacrifice.

No. 116
Marienbad Tournament, 1926
F. Sämisch

No. 117
London League Match, 1899
R. C. Griffith

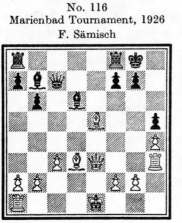

D. Janowski
White to play and win.

P. W. Sergeant
White to play and win.

CHAPTER IV

THE PAWN AT KKt7 AND THE KKt FILE

Combinations against KKt7 and KR7 Compared

EVERYTHING seems to prove that it is better to direct
an attack at the KKtP rather than the KRP. To
begin with, it is more decisive: mate on Kt7 instead of
check on R7. Next, it is easier, the KtP having usually no
defender but the King, while the RP may be defended by
a Knight, which must be dislodged. Lastly, if we succeed
in forcing our opponent to play P – KKt3, we produce two
weaknesses, at his KB3 and KR3, which allow us to attack
by P – KR4, without disturbing our pieces. After P – KR3,
on the other hand, Black has no really weak square, and the
attack by P – KKt4 – Kt5 is much more difficult to drive
home, because we must displace our pieces directed against
KR7 and divert them against KKt7.

We might, therefore, suppose that combinations against
KKtP are commoner than those against KKt7. In reality
there is nothing in it. We must look for the reason of this
apparent anomaly.

All comes down, without a doubt, to the varying difficulty
in marshalling the pieces against the respective squares.
When attacking KR2 we plant our Knight at Kt5, which
is always easy from B3. Then the KB may be posted at
Q3, or even further from KR7, without being obliged to
approach nearer to the square aimed at, the diagonal
QKt1 – KR7 being open, or easy to clear. But in the
attack against Black's KKtP the long black diagonal is
often obstructed by a hostile Pawn, obliging our QB to post
itself very near the centre of attack, and often to sacrifice
itself on KB6 or KR6. It is really difficult in a normal
opening, when the Bishop is developed, for instance, at K3,
to make it change its direction *via* Kt5 towards B6. Only
the "ultra-modern" openings with the fianchetto allow us to

keep the long diagonal free; but then the adverse KB may be at KKt2(7), which is an excellent defence against the attack we are examining. In such a case Black's P – KKt3 loses much of its weakness, for his Bishop defends KB3 and KR3.

So too with the Knight. At KR5 this may be attacked by a Black Knight at KB3; and KB5 is often barred by a Black Pawn at K3, or by the QB. The Knight of which we are speaking is not the KKt from B3, but the QKt, which has had a long journey to KKt3 to join in the attack.

The conclusion is that there is great difficulty in grouping our pieces suitably and rapidly for an attack which, in itself, is easy and decisive.

Yet the combination occurs frequently enough. We shall see that it is very interesting. In conducting an attack against the KKtP we should not prevent its advance to Kt3. On the contrary, it is often useful to provoke it, for it weakens the Black King's position and opens squares for our pieces at KB6 and KR6. This is another difference in the two attacks. Black's P – KR3 does not sensibly weaken his castled King's position. After it the direction of our attack must be changed, whereas after P – KKt3 there is nothing to modify, except that our KR should act upon its file, opened by means of P – KR4 – R5. Although our QB is easy to dislodge, it can, for the purposes of the combination, be posted at KB6, where it threatens mate by R – R8. Normally, however, it should go to R6, threatening to win at least the Exchange.

Still another very sharp difference is to be remarked between these combinations. White has no interest in the advance of a Pawn to KKt6, since its capture by Black's RP involves no inconvenience for him except the partial opening of the KR file. Quite other is a capture by Black's KKtP, for in either direction it shatters his castled position. White has therefore great interest in advancing a Pawn, even to sacrifice it on KR6; which explains why both sides strive, from the very beginning, to reach the squares B6 or R6, where they may double the opposing Pawns.

The outcome of this examination is that we see the attack conducted against the KRP from a distance, against the

KKtP from near, with the assistance, it may be added, of a Rook on the KKt file. The presence of Black's Rook on KB1 is only a trouble to him, blocking the square for his Bishop, which would be of great defensive value there. The absence of that Bishop, indeed, is an essential condition for the success of the attack, whereas the presence of the Rook on KB1 is already a guarantee of victory.

The Black King's Bishop

Let us look at some positions of this type. They will familiarise us with the combination and impress on us the necessary conditions of success.

We must never forget that it is our QB that must play the principal, if not decisive, part in the attack.

Black's KKtP in No. 118 is defended by Kt at K3; but the defence is ineffective, because KB × Kt is threatened. As for Black's other Knight, it is threatened by the QB, which can thus break up Black's castled position. The Rook on B1 is shut in by the Queen, and itself shuts in the King. Lastly, White has a Knight at B5, which threatens Black's KKt2; and White has Kt4 for his Queen, threatening a fatal check on the 3rd move.

We have thus the combination in all its purity, with the best possible conditions for White. If Black plays

No. 118
Budapest Tournament, 1926
A. Rubinstein

F. D. Yates
1 QB × Kt, P × B; 2 B × Kt, and wins.

2 . . P × B; 3 Q – Kt4 ch, Q – Kt3 to stop mate; 4 Kt – K7 ch wins the Queen. This, however, is only a secondary detail, which does not embellish a combination lacking in sacrifices.

The order of the exchanges must be observed. First QB × Kt and then (K)B × Kt. It is only logical to break up Black's castled position without revealing our intentions. If KB × Kt first, Black answers Q × B or P × B, in both cases protecting the KKt, and in the second threatening White's Knight.

It is the absence from the scene of Black's KB that makes the combination decisive.   We shall have nearly always to remark this: Black's KB is the best piece for the defence of his KKtP.   When it is on the spot, or can come to that Pawn's protection, the attack is very difficult.   When it is

No. 119
Magdeburg Tournament, 1927
A. Preusse

A. Brinckmann
1 Kt × P ch, P × Kt; 2 B × Kt, Q − B4; 3 Q − B3, and wins.

missing or is too far away, the attack is almost always successful.

No. 119 is a similar example.   The Bishop at Kt5 and Knight at B5 are important features to be noted.   These are perhaps at their best posts in this type of combination, for all Black's vulnerable squares are thus under their threat—KKt2, KB3, KR3.   It is not the Bishop but the Knight that is sacrificed.   We know that the former must play the leading part in the mate aimed at.   No Black piece defends nor can even go to defend the KtP, and therefore the two White pieces, with the Queen, are sufficient to win the game.   The Black Queen can, indeed, stop her rival from mating; for which reason White proposes an exchange, to open the Kt file and allow the KR to replace the Queen. Note, lastly, the strength of the Bishop on B6, cutting off

Black's King from K2 and preparing for an eventual mate by R – R8.

These last two combinations are so simple that the reader may be inclined to dispute their claim to be called by such a name. The next example, at any rate, much more complicated and very pretty, is a combination in the full sense of the term.

First observe that White's Knight is not on B5. Now we know that at B3 this Knight cannot participate in the attack on the KtP. As the only material here consists of Queen, Rook, and Bishop, it is not yet very clear how these pieces are to unite their action against the KKtP. But if, moreover, the Rook is pinned against the Queen, the attack is facilitated by the absence of Black pieces from the King's side.

To assemble the attacking forces against the KKtP, several combinational ideas arise, for the position offers various tactical possibilities. Firstly, Black's Queen at QR3, unprotected, allows the proffered Bishop-sacrifice at

No. 120

Budapest Tournament, 1921

K. Sterk

A. Alekhine

1 B – B6!, KR – B1; 2 Q – K5, R – B4;
3 Q – Kt3, P – Kt3; 4 R × Kt, Q – Q6;
5 R – KB1, Q – B4; 6 Q – B4, Q – B7;
7 Q – R6, Black resigns.

B6, with the threat of R – Kt4 ch, winning the Queen. Therefore this QB can with impunity plant itself on the most important square. There is another undefended piece, Black's Knight, which the unpinning of White's Rook will give him. Lastly, there is a Knight-combination, which might occur in this variation: 1 B – B6, KR – B1; 2 Q – K5, Q × R; 3 Q – KKt5, K – B1; 4 Q × P ch, K – K1; 5 Q – Kt8 ch, K – Q2; 6 Kt – K5 ch, K – B2; 7 Q × P ch, followed by 8 Kt × Q.

It may be seen from this example how a combination is built up piece by piece; but one has to admit that it requires some imagination to be an "ace" in the combinational sphere!

It is very useful, no doubt, to possess the ideas of combination, it is indeed the primary condition of success in the brilliant game. But one has to know, also, how to co-ordinate combinations. Here is a magnificent puzzle to put together, with, as the final picture, the death of one's opponent.

The student must not be discouraged, for when he knows how to apply separately certain simple ideas he has already made a great step towards the art of combination, and by assiduous practice he may perhaps one day aspire to mastery.

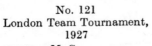

No. 121
London Team Tournament,
1927

M. Censer

F. D. Yates

1 B × Kt, Kt × B; 2 B − R6!, Kt × Kt;
3 P × Kt, R − Q1; 4 Q − Kt4, P − Kt3;
5 Q − KB4, P − QB4; 6 Kt − B6 ch,
K − R1; 7 Q − KR4, Black resigns.

One thing that must be admired in this last example is the skill with which White has managed to draw all the Black pieces to the Queen's wing. Was it to be suspected that a storm was brewing on the other side? The thunderclap resounds, and all comes crashing down.

In the preceding positions we have seen a Bishop close to its field of action. When it is remote the form of the combination changes, for the decisive menace of B − KB6 is not there.

White's situation appears much less favourable in No. 121 than in the foregoing examples, with his KR not in play and with the Black KB present for defence. But he has his two Knights well placed, one on the important square KR5. Action, concentrated about the three squares, Black's KKt2, KR3, and KB3, begins with the offer of the QB. This cannot be taken, for then 3 Q − Kt4 ch, B − Kt4; 4 Kt × Kt, Q × Kt; 5 Kt − B6 ch. White has thus for the attack three pieces against Black's one, his KB. We know that this advantage is enough for success. Although the KR takes care to get out of the way, Black's King's escape

is hampered by his Bishop on K2.   White's manœuvre with
his Queen is especially admirable.   To reach one of the
vital squares, B6 or R6, she makes an astonishing *glissade*
along the fourth rank.   All the concern is with the black
squares.   The Knight on B6 threatens a mate additional
to that on Kt7, as is usual in this combination.

Though the position is somewhat uncommon, with
Knight at R5 instead of B5 and Bishop at R6 instead of B6,
this example may be considered one of the purest of its type,
for its various phases are linked up closely; convergent action
of the pieces against the KKtP, forcing the weakening move
P – Kt3, then the seizure of the weak squares R6 and B6,
and finally the manœuvre for mate on either Kt7 or R7.

There is another type of attack, which instead of provok-
ing the KtP's advance sacrifices a piece for it, as in the combinations against the KRP.   If there is no tactical possibility to stimulate the attack, an additional piece is needed,
and recourse must be had to the Rook.   This is a combination based on the opening of a line, which cannot as a rule
succeed without the prevention by minor pieces of a chal-
lenge by Rook against Rook on the file.

No. 122 illustrates a rather exceptional case, for success
is due to an attack on the QP, which is not part of our
present combination, and partly also to the insufficiency of
the defence.   We must not be surprised, however, at this
tactical diversion, seeing that the attack has only two pieces
immediately engaged against superior enemy forces.

No. 123 is a more characteristic case.   The double sacrifice, of Knight on Kt7 and of Bishop on R6, reminds us of
the double Bishop-sacrifices on R7 and Kt7.   It can be seen
at a glance that if both sacrifices are accepted the White
King cannot escape over K3, while if he goes to R4 he is
mated.   And Black has a KB to cut off the squares Kt3
and B2.

The two combinational themes which meet in this example
make it especially notable.   Once more the King, on the
extreme files of the board, finds himself in so disastrous a
situation that in spite of the presence of almost all his forces
he cannot escape mate.   Attention must also be called to
Black's 3rd move, which has two objects; to advance the

King-side Pawns, and to prevent White from occupying K5 or KKt5, which would break the attack. We have already said that these quiet moves are the most difficult parts of

No. 122	No. 123
Breslau, 1874	London Tournament, 1899
Pfeifer	Dr. Emanuel Lasker

Riemann

1 B×P, K×B; 2 P—KKt4, K—B2;
3 P×P, P×P; 4 Kt—K5 ch, followed
by 5 R×P, and wins.

W. Steinitz

1..Kt×P; 2 K×Kt, B×P ch;
3 K—B2 (3 K×B, Q—B4 ch), P—KB3;
4 R—KKt1, P—KKt4; 5 B×P, P×B;
6 R×P, Q—K3; 7 Q—Q3, B—B5;
8 R—R1, B×R; 9 Kt×B, Q—B3 ch;
10 B—B3, B—B4; 11 Kt×P, Q—KKt3,
and wins.

an attack, for they convey no immediate threat and give the enemy time for defence. One has therefore to be very sure of oneself not to meet with some unforeseen reply.

The Pawn at KKt3

We will now look at the case where the KKtP is already at its 3rd, thus making two weaknesses, at KB3 and KR3, of which advantage may be taken.

We have already given an instance of this weakening move being played under the stress of an attack. When it is made before the attack other combinations become possible. No. 124 is a typical case. Though defended by Bishop and Queen, Black's Knight is obviously weak. To put it under a genuine pin it is necessary to get rid of Black's KB. When we know about the inspiring ideas, how simple these sacrifices appear! When the Bishop has gone, White must concentrate upon the Knight all possible attacks. Hence the second sacrifice, which justifies the first.   A sad consequence for Black of the weakening of his castled posi-

No. 124
Vienna Tournament, 1930
Wahle

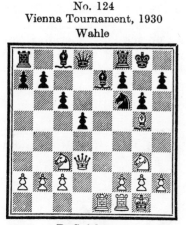

R. Spielmann

1 R × B, Q × R; 2 Q − B3, K − Kt2; 3 KKt − K4, P × Kt; 4 Kt × P, and wins.

tion.   Every undefended or indefensible square creates a weakness on the chess-board.

But, it may be said, White has sacrificed a whole Rook, and the win of the Knight will give him no advantage.   It will; for the final position is that which White wants for his threat of mate upon Kt7.   Owing to his Rook on KB1, it takes Black two moves to escape it.   White must profit by this fact to play Q − K3 − R6.   Thus after White's 4 Kt × P, if K − Kt1, there may follow 5 B × Kt, Q − Kt5; 6 P − QB3 (driving the Queen off the diagonal), Q × KtP; 7 Q − K3 and 8 Q − R6, Black having no defence against the deadly threat.

It is precisely on account of this threat that our example is so appropriate here; for it is not merely a matter of inducing Black to unguard his KB3 by the advance of P − Kt3 (of which we had an instance when dealing with Knight-combinations), but also of the attack on the square KKt7(2).   And in this combination we find again our essential conditions; the presence on White's side of Queen,

Bishop, and Knight, and the absence on Black's of his KB. The combination before us, therefore, is one of two stages, which makes its beauty more subtle.

Another way of profiting by the weakening move P – KKt3 is to attack the Pawn at its 3rd. We have already seen some examples of this. No. 125 is more especially related to cases of attack on the Pawn's original square.

Generally speaking, an attack against Pawn at KKt6(3) should be prepared for by the advance P – KR4 – R5, in

No. 125
German-Austrian Match, Dresden, 1926
C. Carls

A. Becker

1 R × P ch, P × R; 2 Q × P ch, B – Kt2; 3 B – K6 ch, R × B; 4 Q × R ch,
K – R1; 5 B – R6, and wins.

order to get rid of a defender with P × P, P × P and so considerably weaken it. We have had illustrations of the destruction of a barrier to get at a square so laid open. Here the square in question is KKt7(2). But Black's Bishop defends it and can cover a vertical check. In such circumstances the attack became more difficult, and another piece is required to bring it to success. Here it is the KB, with a check at K6 and a new mating-threat. In most cases of the kind it is B – KR6 which is the decisive stroke; but the right time for it must be chosen. For instance, here, 3 B – R6, R – K2; 4 B – B5, K – B1 is not a clear case.

The disappearance of his Pawn-barrier forces the defender to erect another barrier of pieces, which proves insufficient when White has at his disposal three pieces bearing on two squares, two on each square.

Once again we reach conclusions of a general nature, which should rid the ordinary player of his early impression that combinations do not lend themselves to general considerations.

Exercises

In No. 126 we have an exceptional case, which exhibits striking beauty. Though Black's KKtP cannot be attacked its advance has so much weakened his King's position that the White QB exercises a terrible pressure on Kt7 and B8. No. 127 is also exceptional. White has more than the regulation number of pieces bearing down on the castled King, who is only directly guarded by one piece. Yet analysis extending over many years since the actual game was played has failed to prove that White should have won. It is as an exception that this example is particularly interesting.

No. 126
Moscow Tournament, 1925
B. Verlinsky

No. 127
Berlin Tournament, 1897
A. Burn

C. Torre
White to play and win.

R. Charousek
White to play. What result?

CHAPTER V

KING'S BISHOP'S PAWN AND CASTLED KING

The Weakness of the KBP

IT is a familiar fact that in the initial position of the game the KBP is the most vulnerable of the Pawns. It is the only Pawn, too, which is protected solely by the King. How many games are lost on account of its weakness, and how many combinations are directed against it! In the very opening we must think of it, for the slightest carelessness in its regard may be fatal. Danger hovers over it so long as the King has not sought safety in castling. Even when the storm of a combination is not raging we cannot feel at ease. Defence is more difficult than attack. Look at the famous "*Fegatello*" trap in the *Two Knights' Defence*: 1 P – K4, P – K4; 2 Kt – KB3, Kt – QB3; 3 B – B4, Kt – B3; 4 Kt – Kt5, P – Q4; 5 P × P, Kt × P?; 6 *Kt × BP*. Look also at the *Allgaier Gambit*: 1 P – K4, P – K4; 2 P – KB4, P × P; 3 Kt – KB3, P – KKt4; 4 P – KR4, P – Kt5; 5 Kt – Kt5, P – KR3; 6 *Kt × P*. By the insertion of Kt – QB3 as 2nd move on each side we have another illustration in the *Hamppe-Allgaier Gambit*.

We may see then that anxiety to castle is due not merely to the desire to place the King in safety, but to the wish also to protect the KBP with Rook.

With the KBP we are nearer the centre, and many of the manœuvres concerned with this Pawn are central combinations, which we shall study later. For the present we shall only consider those combinations against the KBP that have a relation with the castling-position or with manœuvres against the other Pawns on the King's side. In the latter case the Pawns at KR2 and KB2 are often faced by the hostile Knight at Kt5 and Queen on R5. We have had some illustrations of this attack, which belongs rather to combinations against the KRP.

To be correct the combination against the KBP should rather be central; otherwise it is nearly always inadequate and easily refuted. It is of a type which can only succeed exceptionally, in certain tactical circumstances.

A very Effective Bishop

The most frequent case is that of the sacrifice of a Knight at B7, with a Bishop on the diagonal QR2 – KKt8. The

No. 128
Tenby (Major Open) Tournament, 1928
E. Znosko-Borovsky

C. Mansfield

1 Kt × P, Kt × KBP; 2 B × P ch, K × B; 3 Q – R5 ch, K – Kt1.   Black wins.

object of this sacrifice is not to get Rook and Pawn for two minor pieces, but to disorganise the Pawn-barrier protecting the King. It is then that the KB plays the decisive part. Its importance is shown in the next example.

Both players in No. 128 make the same sacrifice. Though Black makes it second, he wins the game precisely because his KB is on the diagonal QR2 – KKt8, allowing a conclusive discovered check. White is lost before he can execute his own threat.

The presence of the KB on the diagonal of attack is enough to inspire us with this combination against the KBP. Though the Knight-sacrifice enters into our plan, there is need for great caution. Only in special circumstances, again, can we thus attain success.

We have here another combination that goes astray, despite its ingenuity, because the necessary Bishop is not where it should be. And, once more, Black finds himself obliged to turn to the KRP, with a sacrifice to break the Pawn-barrier. But so his forces become scattered, and the battery of Q + B + Kt, which would be enough attack against one of the Pawns, is insufficient against the two.

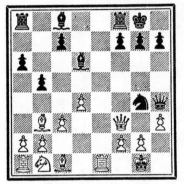

No. 129
New York Tournament, 1918
F. J. Marshall

J. R. Capablanca

1..Kt×P;   2 R−K2! (2 Q×Kt?,
B−R7 ch;   3 K−B1,   B−Kt6),
B−KKt5; 3 P×B, B−R7 ch; 4 K−B1,
B−Kt6; 5 R×Kt, Q−R8 ch; 6 K−K2,
B×R; 7 B−Q2, B−R5; 8 Q−R3, and
wins.

It is to be noted that White has no Knight in action to sacrifice for the opposing KBP, against which there is not even an attack fore-shadowed. In one variation, however, there is a possibility of offering a Queen-sacrifice for it, *viz.* if 2 Q × Kt?, B − Kt6?; 3 Q × P ch. White's well-posted KB is the tactical circumstance that is needed for the success of this attack.

The Tactical Possibility

The majority of examples which we might adduce prove the ill-success of this combination; and when it succeeds there is a better defence possible for the loser. The least tactical possibility is enough to change the outcome of the combination.

No. 130 demonstrates a possibility well grasped. The Black KBP was doubly attacked, but doubly defended, and White's KB, though on the right diagonal, is held off from attack on the Pawn by the solid barrier of two Knights. But the opportunity comes. In the diagrammed position Black had just moved P − KKt3, to which the answer made

appears to lose the Exchange, but in reality aims at giving
up Queen and a Rook for the two Knights, and so clearing
the diagonal for the KB.

A characteristic instance is No. 131. The point of difference from the preceding examples is that here the KBP is
not guarded by a Rook. In general, the policy is to draw
out the King, when we enter upon central combinations,

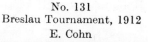

No. 130
Kassa, 1894
M. Engländer

No. 131
Breslau Tournament, 1912
E. Cohn

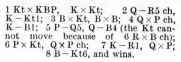

R. Charousek

1 Q – Kt4!,   Kt – K6;   2 Q × Kt!,
Kt × R ch; 3 R × Kt, P × Q; 4 B × P ch,
R – B2;   5 R × R,   Q – K1 (best);
6 R – B6 dis. ch,   K – Kt2;   7 R – B4
dis. ch, K – R3; 8 R – R4 ch, K – Kt4;
9 R – Kt4 ch,   K – R3;   10 Kt – B5 ch,
    and White mated in 6 more moves.

A. Burn

1 Kt × KBP,   K × Kt;   2 Q – R5 ch,
K – Kt1;   3 B × Kt, B × B;   4 Q × P ch,
K – B1;   5 P – Q5, Q – B4 (the Kt cannot   move   because   of   6 R × B ch);
6 P × Kt,   Q × P ch;   7 K – R1,   Q × P;
          8 B – Kt6, and wins.

with manœuvres exploiting the King's exposed situation.
We shall deal with this in the next chapter.

In the present example the King retired to Kt1, so that
the combination is one of those directed against the castling-
position. Nevertheless, thanks to the pin on the open KB
file, White's Queen gets to R5 with a check and plants herself at R7; which facilitates the task but does not yet secure
victory. But now there tacks itself on a tactical combination of a special character. The Black Queen at QB2 is
guarded only by a Knight, which 5 P – Q5 removes. This
is another illustration showing that in this type of combina-

tion it is necessary to see clearly all the new themes which may arise.

The essential point in No. 131 is the presence of White's KB on the diagonal QKt1 – KR7, not QR2 – KKt8, transforming the combination into an attack upon the KRP. For attack on the KBP we know that the Bishop's presence is essential on the latter diagonal; and the combination must especially engage our attention when the KB7 is protected by Rook or any other piece save King.

Pawns on KB2 and K3

When the KP is diagonally in front of the KPB, the combination grows more complex, and the attack, at first

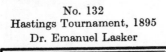

No. 132
Hastings Tournament, 1895
Dr. Emanuel Lasker

A. Burn

1..Kt×P; 2 R×Kt, R×P; 3 Kt—B5?, R×Kt; 4 P×R, B×Kt; 5 B×B, Q–Kt4 ch; 6 B–Kt4, P–KR4; 7 Q–Q2, B–K6. White resigns.

sight, seems less likely to succeed. That, however, is wrong. Although the KP bars the attacking KB's line, the possibility of winning it considerably simplifies the combination. There will be *two* Pawns for the sacrificed piece, or Rook and *two* Pawns for two pieces, even if the attack does not succeed.

In spite of all, an attack conducted under these conditions seldom leads to advantage.

We have now a picturesque instance of this type of combination. First, it is not the Bishop which captures the KP, to pin White's KR, but a Rook. The pin is still there, however, as the KR cannot move without allowing a terrible discovered check. 2..B×P would have merely pinned, whereas R×P brings with it additional menaces—against the pinned Knight, against the KB, etc.—and it threatens P–Q5.

Nevertheless, all these possibilities do not prevent us asking how Black would have won if White had played 3 B – K2. The attack would have remained strong (*e.g.* Q – Kt3; 4 Kt – Q4, B × B; 5 Kt (Kt3) × B, QR – K1), but a win would have been far off.

Nevertheless, the simple 1..Kt × P; 2 R × Kt, B × P would have secured Rook and two Pawns for two minor pieces, which, with an attack, is advantageous; but when the attack comes to an end it is generally found that there is not enough for a win.

How remote we are from the atmosphere of combinations against KRP and KKtP! There the crushing victory was in sight. Here recourse must be had to supplementary combinations, or account must be taken of the material to be gained. So although the KBP may be the weakest on the board, we have to be careful with our combinations against it.

Exercises

In No. 133 we see a new aspect of the same combination. In the first place, there is not a sacrifice of a piece for the

No. 133
Stockholm-Berlin Match, 1928
E. Post

G. Nyholm
White to play and win.

KBP, but a manœuvre based on the pinning of this Pawn. We often have, in practical play, cases of this kind, which allow the planting of a piece or a Pawn at KKt6. In our present example other more complex ideas supplement this simple one. White wins in spite of the limited number of his attacking pieces. The reason is because the hostile King is shut in, and we can direct an attack against the whole castled position, particularly against the "companion squares", KB7 and KR7.

No. 134, though rather complicated, is very pretty. Several combinations are linked together, but the attack is directed against the KBP and the castled position. This example recalls No. 131, the KB file being open, and Black's KKt consequently pinned. The KRP advanced to the 3rd lends a new attraction to the combination, which contains no less than four sacrifices.

No. 134
St. Petersburg Tournament, 1909
C. Schlechter

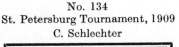

S. G. Tartakover
White to play and win.

CHAPTER VI

THE ATTACK ON KB7 AND K6, WITH THE KNIGHT-COMBINATION

From the Castled Position to the Centre

W<small>E</small> have already remarked that combinations against the KBP sometimes develop in the centre, sometimes on the King's side. All that has been said in the preceding chapter of cases where the KBP is defended by a Rook applies also to another type of combination, which we are about to examine, where the KBP is only defended by the King, and where there is an additional weakness at K3(6) or in a Pawn on it. In these last combinations the action in the centre is more pronounced, because the sacrifice of a piece at KB7 draws Black's King towards the centre.

The attack in No. 135 extends over the whole castled position, though aiming in the first place at the squares KB7 and K6, the sacrifice taking place on the latter square.

White's QB plays a preponderant part. The two terminations emphasise the double

No. 135
Cheltenham (Major Open)
Tournament, 1929
D. Noteboom

E. Znosko-Borovsky

1 Kt×P, P×Kt;   2 Q×P ch, K−B1;
3 Kt−Q5, B×Kt; 4 KP×B, Kt−Kt1;
5 R−Q3, P−Kt3;   6 R−KR3,
Kt−Kt2; 7 R×P, Kt×Q; 8 R−R8 ch,
            K−B2;   9 P×Kt mate.
An alternative line for White is—
7 B×Kt ch, K×B; 8 R×P ch, K×R;
9 Q−B7 ch, K−R1;   10 R−K3, etc.

nature of the combination. In one the King is mated on his KB2 by White's KP, in the other on KR1 by White's KR.

After this rather exceptional example of the attack against the castled King we pass to cases of central combinations.

King Mated, Queen in Stalemate

There are two variations, one where the Black King is brought to his K3 to be mated, the other where a White Knight is planted at K6 to win the Queen. Black has therefore to choose between mate and loss of Queen, an evil choice; but the attacking party has necessarily to give

No. 136
Vienna, 1899

X.

No. 137
From a simultaneous exhibition,
Frankfurt, 1912
S. Tarrasch

Hamlisch

W. von Holzhausen

1 B×P ch,   K×B;   2 Kt−Kt5 ch,
Black resigns, because, if K−B3,
3 Q−B3 mate, and if K−K1 or B1,
3 Kt−K6 in either case wins the Queen.

1 B×P ch, K×B; 2 Kt−K6, and wins.

his whole attention to force it. The Queen may be shut in on her own square either by her King on K1 or by the Rook which has gone thither after castling.

Let us look at some examples.

In No. 136 the four moves that brought about the diagrammed position can easily be gathered, and we may readily grasp the combination which presented itself to White. The Queen is shut in, the KBP unprotected, and the square K3(6) undefended by a piece. As a Knight planted at K6 is sufficient to win the Queen, a start must be made with the suppression of the KBP, the only hindrance.

We have here a familiar Knight-combination. After sacrifice we require a Knight to strike the decisive blow. The difference is plain between this and the combinations in the last chapter. Instead of the Knight being sacrificed and the Bishop kept, the reverse is the case.

The combinations to which we now proceed are much commoner, and more effective, but do not show great diversity.

We see in No. 137 the same combination, with still greater precision. There is a feature which we shall find in several other examples. The Knight is offered at K6; but, if K × Kt, then 3 Q – Q5 ch and 4 Q – B5 mate.

We must admit that such a situation can only occur after a gross blunder by Black; here Kt – Q2, shutting off from K3 the protection of the QB. It may be added that Dr. Tarrasch was playing Black in a game conducted with a number of others simultaneously, which excuses the lapse.

The next example is from a famous blindfold game won by the late World Champion at a time when a war-wound kept him in a military hospital in 1916 (No. 138).

The Black Queen not being shut in here, the object of the first move is not to win her. It is only a gain of time by the threat, but is necessary to allow Q – K6. The sacrifice must be accepted, and so Black's King is drawn into a mating-net.

No. 138
Tarnopol, 1916
M. Feldt

A. Alekhine

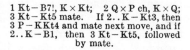

1 Kt – B7!, K × Kt; 2 Q × P ch, K × Q;
3 Kt – Kt5 mate. If 2 . . K – Kt3, then
3 P – KKt4 and mate next move, and if
2 . . K – B1, then 3 Kt – Kt5, followed
by mate.

These examples show us that the secret of this Knight-combination lies in the intimate relation between the squares KB2(7) and K3(6). But each example has its peculiar features. In the last a Knight is sacrificed to allow the entry of the other Knight. Further, as the Black Queen is not shut in, White must aim solely at mate.   The combination is simplified, but not easy of realisation because the fewness of the threats lessens the chances of success.

No. 139 greatly resembles what we have just seen, with the Black Queen not blocked, the successive Knight- and

No. 139
Zürich Tournament, 1934
G. Stahlberg

O. S. Bernstein

The threat is   1 Kt×P,   K×Kt;
2 Q×P ch,   K×Q;   3 Kt−Kt5 mate.
But it was actually Black's move.

No. 140
Hastings Tournament, 1929
G. Koltanowski

T. H. Tylor

1 B×P ch,   K×B;   2 Kt−K6, K×Kt;
3 Q−B4 ch,   P−Q4;   4 P×P ch,
K−B2;   5 P−Q6 dis. ch,   Kt−Q4;
6 P×B,   R×P;   7 Kt×Kt,   Kt−K4;
8 Q−B4 ch, K−Kt1; 9 Kt×R ch, and
wins.

Queen-sacrifices, and finally the second Knight's mating check at Kt5.   But Black has a parry to White's last move of Kt(from Q2) − B3, in Kt × Kt.

It is in cases like this that weak players allow themselves to be caught in combinations that are capable of being refuted and let their opponents beat them elegantly.   How is one to foresee all the threats which are hatching at so many points?   Only by steeping oneself in the study of the various kinds of combinations.   Then one scents their presence and can provide for defence against them.   The combinational themes are so often similar, the very structure of positions is so often alike, the methods of execution vary so little!

This particular combination is more complicated when, after the sacrifice at K6 or KB7, our Queen cannot go to

K6.   The mate-threat is cut out, and the King must then be compelled to advance by closing his retreat to B2.   For this it is enough to dominate the diagonal QR2 – KKt8 or to plant the Queen at KKt6.   In both cases the King's position at his K3 can give the attacker victory if he has open lines and pieces at his disposal for attack.

No. 140 takes us back to the first positions examined, in which there were two successive sacrifices on KB7 and K6. The beauty and complexity of this combination compel us to admire, with its King's advance and retreat to death. White's Queen, being unable to reach K6, acts along the diagonal QR2 – KKt8 and does not suffer the King to get safe home.   By what sacrifices might he not succeed in escaping from the hornets' nest if his Queen could only move—for after 5 P – Q 6 White threatened to win by 7 P × P. The Queen's "stalemate" here added itself as a terror to the danger of mate to the King.   This threat compels Black to give back the sacrificed material with so great a positional loss that he must quickly succumb.

This example, among many others, shows us how dangerous is the situation of a King at K3.   The combination comes with fatal force and the task is much simplified when the Queen is in danger.

In No. 141 we see the second method of taking advantage of the Black King's bad position at K3.   The Queen at Kt6 cuts off his retreat to B2.   A very interesting combination.   The King is not threatened with mate, and the Queen is not shut in.   And yet White can sacrifice two pieces. Whether the Bishop be accepted or refused, the reply Q – Kt6 now threatens mate, either with the Queen or with the Rook upon the open King's file.

The almost identical position of the Black pieces in these examples is noteworthy; Q on Q1, R on K1, B on K2, Kts at Q2 and KB3.   This is almost essential for the purposes of a threat against K6(3).   There is a similar likeness in the White position; Kt at K5 or KKt5, another at KB3 in case the first is sacrificed, KB on the QR2 – KKt8 diagonal, QB pointing to Q6 when Black's King is brought to his K3, and lastly Q on one of the diagonals QR2 – KKt8 or QKt1 – KR7. The other pieces and the Pawns change their places to take advantage of the tactical possibilities which may arise in the course of the combination.

Now let us look specially at the case of Black's Queen. We have already seen that she should be shut in, the ideal position being Q on Q1, K on K1, B's on K2 and QB1, Kt on Q2, P on QB2. Success is not assured if the Queen can escape.

In No. 142, however, the Queen has ready escapes along two diagonals. Can there be a question of catching her?

No. 141
Wiener Schachzeitung Corre-
spondence Tournament, 1928
H. Heeren

No. 142
Hamburg, 1912

X.

R. Hochmair

1 Kt×P, K×Kt; 2 B×P ch, K×B;
3 Q−Kt6, and wins.

P. S. Leonhardt

1 P−QR4, B−K2?; 2 B×P ch,
Kt×B; 3 Kt−K6, Q−Kt3 (Q−R4 ch;
4 B−Q2); 4 P−R5, Q−Kt5 ch;
5 P−B3, Q−B5; 6 Kt−B7 ch, K−Q1;
7 P−QKt3, Black resigns.

1..B−K2, which looks a logical move, obstructs one of her diagonals, leaving the other open. Kt−K6 bars one square on this, leaving two. This justifies White's first move, P−QR4. By his B−K2 Black falls into the trap.

So, if the Queen is not shut in, we must begin by asking ourselves whether there is not a way of catching her. The combination then passes from the King's to the Queen's wing, but its character is unaltered; the squares KB7(2) and K6(3) are its bases.

When what we have now explained is fully understood,

has a player an excuse for not seeing and not knowing how to meet such combinations?

Exercises

In the first of these we have the same combination against KBP and K3, leading to complete demolition of Black's castled position.   Attention must be paid to White's QB on the long diagonal, as in No. 135, commanding the Black squares.   As for the Queen, she acts on the White squares, with the aid of a Knight, not a Rook as in No. 135.

The astonishing similarity (as regards the pieces' identity) of No. 144 to No. 138 will be noted at once, though they arose from different openings (*Caro-Kann* and *French Defences*) and in the former the position came about after 12, in the latter after 14 moves, while in one case there is an initial capture, in the other not.   The winner of the latter game humorously noted that he "plagiarised" from the Champion.   He had learnt!   But there is a flaw; Black's Queen has a flight-square.

No. 143
Berlin Tournament, 1926
E. Grünfeld

No. 144
Vienna, 1935
E. Fischer

E. Colle
White to play and win.

A. Gerschenkron
White to play and win.

CHAPTER VII

COMBINATIONS IN THE CENTRE

Central and Lateral Combinations

WE come now to the centre of the board, and all is changed, both in the character of the combinations and in the use of the forces. In combinations on the wings we have seen the minor pieces acting in the same direction; in those in the centre attacks often come from both sides, in the guise of development. There is another difference. Many lateral combinations do not make use of the Rooks. In central combinations, on the contrary, it is often the Rooks that play the principal part, seizing the middle vertical lines in order to penetrate into the enemy's camp.

Moreover, in the lateral attacks we have examined the defender generally had for sole protection a Knight at B3 and a Pawn-barrier on the second row, which had to be broken. All combinations came down to this work of demolition. In the centre the two Pawns are nearly always advanced from the opening of the game. Frequently one disappears, while the other maintains itself on its 4th square. We can almost say that no barrier exists, so easy is it to break. On the other hand, the King is protected by a number of pieces.

When the King is no longer in the middle of the board central combinations lose in interest. The main object and the principal spoil are lacking. When the King has not moved the combinations present remarkable features. The most common is the entry of the Rooks on open files. Also we find a very advanced Pawn in their place, to prevent the King escaping and his pieces covering him.

Castling Hindered

Under the central attack directed against him the King can seek escape by castling. Then our plans are upset.

The storm troops have to be regrouped, since a wing-attack is conducted on quite different lines. Our first aim, therefore, must be to keep the King in the centre, where he is very vulnerable.

In No. 145 we have illustrated a very common device to keep the King in the centre. It is not, however, particularly characteristic of this type of combination, for after Black's initial error a mate on KB7 supplements the central combination, merely through the opening of the KB file.

No. 145
Berlin, 1864
E. Schallopp

No. 146
Mannheim Tournament, 1914
A. Flamberg

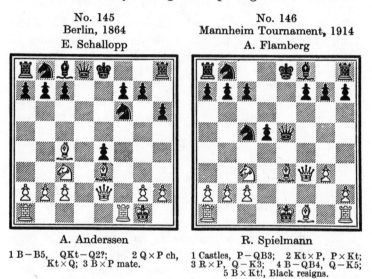

A. Anderssen

R. Spielmann

1 B−B5, QKt−Q2?;   2 Q×P ch,
      Kt×Q; 3 B×P mate.

1 Castles, P−QB3;   2 Kt×P, P×Kt;
3 R×P, Q−K3;   4 B−QB4, Q−K5;
      5 B×Kt!, Black resigns.

This example is a connecting link between two main types of combinations, for it comes under those of the centre by reason of the two open files and the threats of QR − Q1 and Kt × P. Although the Bishops have often a preponderant action in central combinations, the manœuvre with them, rather exceptionally displayed here, may be considered as a subsidiary variation.

No. 146 is a much more characteristic example, as the two Rooks play an important part on the two open files. In order to control one of these files the Knight is sacrificed. The Bishops' action is subdued, but still necessary, one going to QB5, as in the last example, not here to stop castling but

B – K2, which it renders an inadequate defensive move. The opening of the KB file is not made use of here. Analysis of this combination reveals certain essential features which we shall come across again generally. Why is the Queen sacrificed on move 5? Because, after Q × Q, White would have the following: 6 KR – K1 ch, B – K2; 7 R × B ch, K – B1; 9 R – Q8 mate.

The King separated from his Rooks

The mate by Rook at Q8, which is the end of the last combination, is new to us. It is only possible through Black's complete abandonment of this square, his Rook being cut off from defence of the King. Sometimes, to prevent the King's escape by castling, it is necessary that there should be no connection between him and both Rooks. An important point, which stands out still more clearly in the next example.

No. 147 is a really typical example of this kind of combination. Of the two middle files one is strongly occupied by White's first move. Black's King is separated from both his Rooks, as is necessary to allow the mate on Q8 after K – B2 or K1. One Rook could defend the square if the 8th row were not obstructed. Black's KB preventing castling, we get the indispensable requisites for the combination. We shall find them throughout.

No. 148 is made especially interesting in that the combination is displayed on the two open files. Preceding analyses have established that a mate is possible at Q8 or K8 when the two Black Bishops separate the King from his Rooks. Firstly, as the heavy artillery is already concentrated on the Q file, it is the mate on Q8 which is aimed at. Now the Knight here defends that square, but is insufficient because it can be taken at once. On the other hand, this Knight by leaving Kt1 no longer protects Q2, allowing the menace of another mate there. If the Knight stays at home it fails to defend one square, if it comes out it abandons the defence of the other—a point which will be useful for us to remember in future analyses.

We must note also that, as Black's KB prevents his

castling, it is not necessary to play B – B5, which on the contrary would give Black valuable time, if not to prepare for castling, at least to protect his Q1 by B – K3. White therefore plays instead B – B6, reinforcing the attack on Q8 by clearing the file and attacking the vital square a third time.

The first solution we give of No. 148, with Q8 as its object, is the shorter. The more artistic solution, Nimzovitch's

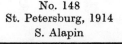

No. 147
Vienna, 1910
S. G. Tartakover

No. 148
St. Petersburg, 1914
S. Alapin

R. Réti

1 Castles, Kt × Kt?; 2 Q – Q8 ch, K × Q;
3 B – Kt5 dbl. ch, and Black resigns,
being threatened with mate by R or B
at Q8.

A. Nimzovitch

1 B – B6, Q × B; 2 B × Kt ch, P × B;
3 KR – K ch, and wins, mate by Q – Q8
or Q7 being unavoidable.
A second solution (that which actually occurred) is 2 KR – K1 ch, B – K2;
3 B × Kt ch, K – B1; 4 Q – Q8 ch,
B × Q; 5 R – K8 mate.

actual line, ends with a mate on K8. There is a particu-larly pretty variation: 3..B – Q2; 4 Q × B ch, K – B1; 5 Q – Q8 ch, R × Q; 6 R × R ch, B × R; 7 R – K8 mate. White has only two pieces, Bishop and Rook, the bare requisite for the mate.

Morphy's unforgettable game in the box at the Opera in Paris gives a famous example of mate on Q8 (No. 149). White has only the Q-file for his attack. His task seems the more difficult in that Black's QR, in touch with the King after its 2nd move, defends Q1. But the KB prevents castling and any other escape by the King.

The difficulty is solved by the entry of White's KR after his QR has annihilated the defence of Black's QR.   To clear the road blocked by Black's QKt the Queen is sacrificed; a secondary idea, not modifying the essential combinational idea, which is still the manœuvre concerned with the two squares Q7 and Q8, especially the latter.   This sacrifice demonstrates the importance of the *end* in central combinations, where an immediate mate is in question.   It is in this type of combination that we see the heaviest sacrifices.

No. 149
Paris, 1858
Duke of Brunswick and
Count Isouard

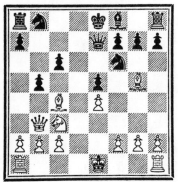

P. Morphy

1 Kt×P!,   P×Kt;   2 B×KtP ch,
QKt−Q2; 3 Castles Q, R−Q1; 4 R×Kt,
R×R;   5 R−Q1, Q−K3; 6 B×R ch,
Kt×B; 7 Q−Kt8 ch, Kt×Q; 8 R−Q8
mate.

It is a strange fact that a similar combination may occur after the opponent's Queen-side castling.   But in this case his QR finds itself in the centre, and an exchange of Rooks often brings the King back.   What is necessary for the combination is that the King shall be separated from his KR in particular.

To sum up, central combinations are only made possible by a backward development on the adversary's part, Bishop or Knight cutting the connection between King and Rook.   It is well, as always, to have both central files open, to permit mate on K8 or Q8; but one file, with only one mate in view, may suffice.

In No. 150 we have the same combination with Black castled on his Queen's wing.   His KKt separates his KR from the scene of action.   The two White Rooks on open files make the defence by a single Rook inadequate.   The manœuvre is interesting.   First comes an attack on the Queen by the sacrifice of a Bishop, which doubles the menace against Black's QR—recalling the move 1 B – B6 in No. 148.   The following Queen-sacrifice is designed only to force the opposing Queen to abandon the defence of the QR; an idea which is familiar to us.

White's position is so strong that there are other possible solutions, *e.g.* by 1 R × R ch, K × R; 2 B – Kt5 ch.   There is nothing astonishing in this, when we consider that Black

No. 150
Breslau, 1859
Hillel

A. Anderssen

1 B – Kt5, Q × B; 2 Q – B5 ch, Q × Q; 3 R × R ch, K × R; 4 R – K8 mate.

is three moves behind in his development and has two pieces on their original squares, while all White's pieces are in action.

The Advanced Pawn

We come now to the other type of central combination, in which a far advanced Pawn plays the decisive role. This Pawn comes in, obviously, because some element is lacking for the successful execution of our scheme; either our offensive force is inadequate or the defensive force is too strong. For instance, the Pawn may be necessary to prevent the hostile King escaping on his second rank.   When the King is in touch with his Rooks, and a mate on the back rank is impossible, a Pawn at its 6th may make mate possible on the 7th.   On the other hand, if the Rooks are off, or if we have only a single Rook, the advanced Pawn may be a convenient substitute.   An advanced Pawn, with minor pieces to support it, may effectively intervene in such cases. It allows combinations which could not be imagined without it, and lessens the number of pieces indispensable for a central combination.

Without yet dealing with the nature of these combinations, we may analyse a few positions, beginning with some familiar examples.

White's two Rooks have power of action on the two open files. But Black's QP shelters the King, who is also in touch with his two Rooks and close to his minor pieces. So it is to White's Pawn at KB6 that is to fall one of the principal parts, serving as a basis for the manœuvres of the White pieces to prevent the King's escape.

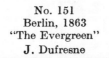

No. 151
Berlin, 1863
"The Evergreen"
J. Dufresne

A. Anderssen

1 QR—Q1,   Q × Kt;   2 R × Kt ch,
Kt × R (K—Q1;   3 R × P ch, K—B1;
4 R—Q8 ch);   3 Q × P ch,   K × Q;
4 B—B5 dbl. ch, K—K1; 5 B—Q7 ch,
    K moves; 6 B × Kt mate.

Black's Knight on K2 is obviously the most vulnerable piece. Defended as it is by the other Knight and the King, it is attacked by Rook, Bishop, and Pawn, which are enough to break down this defence. After Black's K2 it is his Q2 which is blown up by a bomb! The double check, by discovery, from Bishop and Rook, brings the struggle to a successful end for White.

The King, however, on the back row, is mated not by Rook on that, but by the two Bishops on the next. The example, which is very like the preceding ones, illustrates the peculiarities of this new type of combination. Given the impossibility of mating on the 8th rank, White uses his advanced Pawn to effect it on the 7th. The Black King is imprisoned by this Pawn on the side of the board, and cannot escape to a corner on account of the obstacle on the horizontal line.

The game in which this position occurred was called "the blossom in Anderssen's wreath of laurel", and is also commonly known as "The Evergreen".

No. 152 is given as a curiosity.   It shows a combination belonging to the first group, but with the aid of an advanced KP.   The mate on Q8 is familiar, and the move P – K6 allows us to put this example with the combinations which we are now studying.   How did the strange position arise? From a *Two Knights' Defence*, with 5. . Kt × P?;   6 Kt × BP —the *Fegatello*.   After a short excursion the King returns

No. 152
From a simultaneous display,
Paris, 1932
X.

E. Znosko-Borovsky

1 Kt × Kt, P × Kt;   2 B × P ch,   Q × B;
3 Q × Q ch,   K – K2;   4 B – Kt5 ch,
K – K1;   5 P – K6, B – K2;   6 Q – Q8 ch,
B × Q;   7 R × B mate.

No. 153
Hastings Tournament,
1934–5
J. R. Capablanca

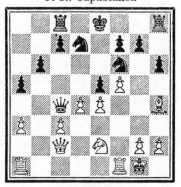

A. Lilienthal

1 P × P,   Q × KP;   2 P × Kt!,   Q × Q;
3 P × P, R – KKt1;   4 Kt – Q4, Q – K5;
5 QR – K1, Kt – B4; 6 R × Q ch, Kt × R;
7 R – K1, R × P;   8 R × Kt ch,   Black
resigns.

home, and there, cut off from his Rooks and without a flight-square on the next rank, he falls victim to the mate on Q8.

The charming example, No. 153, shows the complications which may rise out of a simple idea.   We have a central combination, with the Black King in the middle of the board.   The Queen-sacrifice stops castling and leads to a mating-net after 2 P × Kt and 3 P × P, opening the Bishop's diagonal.

Black's King not being cut off from his Rooks, White cannot mate on the 8th rank, while the 7th is sufficiently protected.   But, as the King has no escape, it is enough for

White to seize the two centre-files to secure a mate.   There are some pretty variations ; *e.g.* if 4..Q – Q6, to keep the Queen,   5 KR – K1 ch,   Kt – K4;   6 R × Kt ch,   K – Q2; 7 R – Q5 ch, K – K1; 8 R – K1 ch, and mate next move. Or, if 4..Q × QBP, there enters a Knight-combination: 5 KR – K1 ch, Kt – K4; 6 R × Kt ch, K – Q2; 7 R – K7 ch, K – Q3; 8 Kt – Kt5 ch, winning the Queen.

An extraordinary point about this combination is that, after White's first move, the most important K-file is thrice blocked.   It is opened, nevertheless, and White's Rooks can then begin their work of destruction, with the valuable aid of the Bishop and the Knight, which at the right moment bars the Black King's flight to QB3.

The Double Rook-sacrifice

We have said that one of the peculiarities of this combination is the absence of Rooks sacrificing themselves to break down resistance.   Decisive action by the minor pieces supplies the place of this.   We must not forget, therefore, that in combinations of the type—and it is one of the reasons of their beauty—the Rooks, being useless, may be sacrificed without fear.

In No. 154 Black's position is cut in two by White's Pawn at K6.   The King can neither castle nor escape to the wings. By Queen-side castling White could win merely on his superior position.   Black strives to save himself by a gain in material compensating for his positional inferiority.

The second White move is particularly beautiful.   The Knight-sacrifice cannot be accepted, for after 2..P × Kt; 3 B × P ch, K – Q1; 4 R – Q1 ch wins easily.   But if this Knight is not taken it still wins the game, being the piece that was lacking to secure the mate with the aid of the advanced KP.   In the offer of the Knight was involved a double Rook-sacrifice, with a magnificent victory to follow.

It seems a very simple combination; but it must not be forgotten that the win required the sacrifice of both Rooks —a new combinational feature for us.

In brief, we have seen the double Bishop-sacrifice (on KKt7 and KR7), and the double Knight-sacrifice (usually on KB7 and K6); and now we have the double Rook-sacrifice (on their own squares). Each kind of sacrifice has a different aspect and takes place in different quarters of the board. The Rooks alone, it is to be noted, are sacrificed without taking a share in the attack. So negative a sacrifice cannot be considered a combinational idea, and it might occur in many varying circumstances. Neverthe-

No. 154
St. Petersburg Tournament, 1912
G. Lövenfisch

A. Alekhine

1 Q – K2, Q × P; 2 Kt – Kt5!, Q × R ch; 3 K – B2, Q × R; 4 Kt – B7 ch, K – Q1; 5 Q – Q2 ch, B – Q2; 6 P × B, Black resigns.

less, we meet with it especially in central combinations. It is certainly very curious that in the first group of these the combinations can only be elaborated with the help of the Rooks, while in the second these Rooks are surrendered as perfectly useless.

Although it has played a leading part in the foregoing examples, the advanced Pawn is not always indispensable. It can sometimes be replaced by a piece, especially a Bishop, barring the King's moves in two directions; but the Pawn has a strength based on its stability and its power of breaking down the defence of the pieces, and even of the opposing Pawns.

In the famous game of which No. 155 illustrates a position, White's B – Q6 was played to block Black's QP, so keeping closed the diagonal of his QB and shutting off his King's escape. The White Bishop plays the same role as the advanced Pawn in the last example. Here the Knights share in the attack, one threatening the square QB7 and the other KKt7, while both command the critical square K7. The object of White's 3rd move is to cut the long black diagonal, so that Black's Queen cannot defend her KKt2, a manœuvre which we have already seen.

Black's King, thus threatened from two sides, at QB2 and KKt2, has no escape but over white squares.   P – B3

No. 155
London Tournament, 1851—"The Immortal Game"
L. Kieseritzky

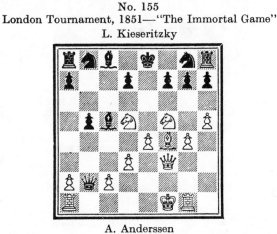

A. Anderssen

1 B – Q6, Q × R ch; 2 K – K2, B × R; 3 P – K5, Kt – QR3; 4 Kt × P ch, K – Q1; 5 Q – B6 ch, Kt × Q; 6 B – K7 mate.

avails him nothing, for after Kt × P ch his KBP is insufficiently guarded. His best course, therefore, would be to make for the other side, to QB1, playing, instead of 3..Kt – QR3 (which only, unnecessarily, protects the square QB2), 3..B – R3, leaving B1 open for the King. The mate would then be averted, but not the loss of the game.

As the whole combination evolves on White's 7th rank, the Rooks do not come into the game and may be sacrificed to gain time. The assault is carried out by the Queen and minor pieces.

In No. 156 one Rook is sacrificed, the other remains out of play. The Queen works in their place on an open file. There is no advanced Pawn; but Black's King is separated from his Rooks.   This example is intermediate between the two types of combination which we are studying.   The absence of an advanced White Pawn is compensated for by the Black Pawns' position, which hems in their King. There is no way, however, for White to reach the 8th rank;

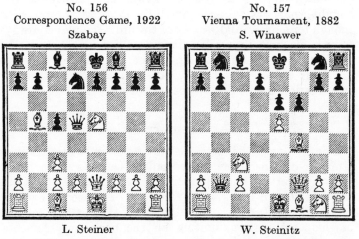

No. 156
Correspondence Game, 1922
Szabay

L. Steiner

1..Q×KtP?;   2 Q−Q3,   Q×R ch;
3 K−K2, P−K3; 4 B×Kt ch, K−K2;
5 B×B, R×B; 6 Q−Q7 ch, K−B3;
7 Q×P ch, and wins.

No. 157
Vienna Tournament, 1882
S. Winawer

W. Steinitz

1 K−Q2, Q×R; 2 Kt−Kt5, Kt−QR3;
3 Kt−Q6 ch, K−B1; 4 B×Kt, P×B;
5 Q−B5, Kt−K2;   6 Kt−K2, Q×R;
7 P×P, P×P; 8 B−R6 ch—and does
              not win!

it is on the 7th that the fate of the game must be decided. Black has already a Knight pinned on Q2; and at this the attack must be aimed.

Black did wrong to take his Queen away from the centre, which makes the example an exceptional case.

No. 157 is more characteristic.   Two Rooks are sacrificed in a very difficult position.   All the Black pieces except the Queen are in their original squares, but the King is sheltered behind a strong Pawn-barrier.   White has no Pawn on the 6th rank, and lacks forces for the attack.   Lastly, Black's King has an escape towards the corner, and a certain freedom of action on his 2nd rank.

Some elements are missing, therefore, for the success of White's combination, so that his best course was to make sure of a draw.

We must insist on this point, that, despite the complexity of the combination, without involving oneself in analysis, it is enough here to ask oneself the question whether the essential conditions of success are here united. No tactical device can remedy the defects of White's position. It was the Pawn-sacrifice at QKt2, leaving *en prise* Rook and Knight, that was wrong. But, in spite of all, it was good enough for a draw; and we advise the ordinary player always to risk his luck in similar situations, for he must not be afraid to put his imagination to the test—which develops it. It is better to suffer defeat by the miscarriage of a combination than to be incapable of conceiving one.

Exercises

Our first exercise illustrates the attack on the central files after the opponent has castled on the Queen's side. There is a very pretty intermediate move. It is not easy to divine on what square Black will be mated. The second exercise recalls No. 147, with a variation less. It is a typical case of this combination, uniting all the necessary elements. The solution is not hard to discover.

No. 158
Leipzig Tournament, 1877

E. Schallopp

K. Göring
Black to play and win.

No. 159
From a blindfold simultaneous
display, Antwerp, 1931

X.

G. Koltanowski
White to play and win.

CHAPTER VIII

THE ADVANCED KING'S BISHOP'S PAWN

Advanced Pawns

E
VERY advanced Pawn, when it does not present an obvious weakness, is a powerful weapon, which often decides the fate of the game. Imagination can weave wonderful schemes around it. As an outpost it may establish itself within the enemy's lines and ultimately shatter them. On account of the two squares that it always attacks diagonally, its intrusion makes defence difficult. Moreover, the support which it offers to pieces allows them to settle themselves firmly in the heart of hostile territory.

Whatever its file be, a Pawn reaching its 6th square becomes a trump in our hand. In the centre it cuts the opposing position in two; on the wings it either menaces the King's safety at home or paves the way for a final rout.

From the strategic and tactical standpoints, advanced Pawns create surprising possibilities, and the advantage conferred by them may result in victory, either through positional manœuvres or through brilliant combinations.

Steinitz said that after playing Kt – K6 he could sleep peacefully, for the Knight would win for him; and Tarrasch declared that one must never allow one's opponent to establish a Pawn at its 6th, especially on the Rook's files.

We could give a large number of examples of the profit accruing from an advanced Pawn at various points on the board; but this profit is usually gained by simple positional manœuvres. We have even seen some magnificent combinations springing mainly from a weakening of the opponent's castled position by the advance of the KBP. Those which we are about to examine, however, may serve as examples of other Pawn-advances in like circumstances. First we will take two cases of passed Pawns on other than the KB file, to show their strength.

In No. 160 the Pawn, arriving at Q6, acts as a support

for the Knight at K7, and prevents the King's escape. It also offers support for the Queen (at K7 again). And finally it can deliver mate (from the same square), in event of 6..KR – Kt1; 7 Q – K7 ch, Q × Q.

This Pawn, therefore, may be said to yield its full value. In No. 161 a Pawn advances to KR6 to attack the

No. 160
Budapest Tournament, 1926
H. Mattison

No. 161
The Hague Tournament, 1921
A. Rubinstein

E. Znosko-Borovsky

A. Alekhine

1 P × P, P × P; 2 P – Q6, Q – Q2;
3 Kt – K7 ch, K – Kt2; 4 Q × P ch,
K – B1; 5 Kt – B5, Kt – K1; 6 R – R1,
and wins.

1 P – KR4, B – Q3; 2 P – R5, KKt – K2;
3 P – R6, P – Kt3; 4 B – Kt5.
5 B – B6, P – QKt; 6 P – K3, B – Q2;
7 B – Q3, etc.

castling-position. The black squares become weak, and White's QB seizes on them with notably increased powers.

There is no immediate combination in this position. As a matter of fact, the game was prolonged over fifty moves. On the 24th the Exchange was won for a Bishop, and on the 45th the Pawn fell, in order to secure a threat of mate in two moves.

In the previous example the advanced Pawn was passed, so that it was not advancing to break up the opposing Pawns. Here, on the contrary, the Pawn advances to weaken the castled position. Had Black played P – R3, there would have followed P – KKt4 – Kt5. If 3..P × P, then Black's doubled RP's are isolated and very weak. And after the actual move, 3..P – Kt3, there are two "holes" left in Black's defence.

It must not be supposed, from what has been said of the Pawn on the 6th, that it means a forced win. All that one can assert is that, as a rule, it wins when there are still a number of pieces on the board, and the Pawn may thus become the pivot of an attack. It wins also when, in the end-game, it is safe from attack, for then it immobilises in

No. 162
World Championship Match, 1927
A. Alekhine

J. R. Capablanca
1 Kt − B 6 ch, B × Kt; 2 P × B, R × R ch; 3 R × R, B − B3, etc.

its neighbourhood the adverse King or some other piece. But otherwise it may become weak, and its threats are not very dangerous.

White in No. 162 establishes a Pawn at KB6, with a threat of mate on Kt7. But he has not enough pieces for the attack. Black, on the other hand, has practically a Pawn to the good, owing to White's doubled Pawns; and his QBP is more menacing than White's advanced KBP.

This game might have ended in a draw, but in fact was won by Black. In spite of his advanced Pawn on B6, White never had the possibility of winning.

The Advanced KBP

A Pawn is already threatening at KB5. The advance to B6 is always in view, and at B7 the prospect of victory is bright.

We will begin our examination with the most frequently occurring position, the Pawn at KB6. It is the threat of mate on Kt7 that mainly gives it its importance. Then there is the break-up of the castled King's Pawns; next the attack on K7, closing a flight-square to the King and preventing a defensive move by a piece; and, finally, the possibility of P – B7.

In No. 163 the Queens have been exchanged, a fact which should, logically, weaken White's attack. But in reality

No. 163
Hanover, 1926
D. Duhm

A. Nimzovitch

1 R × P ch, Kt × R ; 2 Kt × P ch, K – Kt1 ; 3 R × R ch, K – R2 ; 4 Kt – Kt5 ch, and wins.

this does not count here, for the advanced Pawn, preventing the Black King's escape, brings all defence to naught.

We note that the combinational ideas here—the removal of Black's KBP, which protects his KP, and the Knight's manœuvre—are merely instruments in securing the triumph of the advanced Pawn. So now we have a first lesson, that when we have a Pawn at KB6 we must think out some combination in its connection. The Pawn, although it cannot be regarded as assuring success, at least serves as a basis for the elaboration of a profitable combination.

The same case is demonstrated in No. 164. Black's castled position is weakened by White's advanced KBP, and the combination arrives with a crash. The King is

driven into the corner, mate is threatened on Kt7, and the
RP comes on—all made possible by the Pawn at KB6.

White sweeps away the KKtP and KRP to advance his
own, to open a file for his Rook, but above all to allow the
raid by his Queen into the enemy's camp.

We see that the present class of combinations, differing
so much from the last, are marked by the presence of a

No. 164
Hamburg Tournament, 1910
R. Spielmann

P. S. Leonhardt

1 Kt×P, P×Kt;   2 Q×P ch, K−R1;
  3 P−R6, and wins.

No. 165
? Vienna, 1910
R. Réti

A. Albin

1 Kt×Kt, R×Q; 2 R−R3 ch, K−Kt1;
  3 Kt−K7 ch, and wins.

Pawn on KB6.   In No. 163 we had the Rook's action on the
rank.   In No. 164 it was the Pawns that acted, the Rook
not entering the game except in a variation.

We may now look at this intervention of the Rook upon
the file.

White wins in No. 165 by sacrificing his Queen and
thereby gaining command of the KR file.   The combination,
it will be noted, is based on the "matable" situation of
Black's King, prevented from escaping by White's KBP,
which here again has the principal role.   This type of combination is only possible with the King on the side of the
board, nearly always after castling KR.   A Pawn at KR6,
KKt6, or K6 would not offer a mating-threat comparable
with that from KB6.   But, were the King otherwise cir-
cumstanced, after castling QR or not having castled at all,

the Pawn at KB6 would clearly not have the same force. It would simply be a Pawn like the others.

No. 166 presents a new kind of combination, though still with the action of the KBP against the castled King. Mate at Kt2 is threatened. The Knight plays the leading part.

If, instead of 3 R × B, 3 K – Kt1, then 4 Kt – R6 mate. In the variation chosen by White, the Knight performs its

No. 166
Correspondence game, 1908–9
A. Alekhine

K. Vygodchikoff

No. 167
Carlsbad Tournament, 1929
E. Grünfeld

F. Sämisch

1..Kt–B5;   2 R×Q,   B–Kt7 ch;
3 R×B,   P×R ch;   4 K–Kt1,
Kt–K7 ch;   5 K×P, Kt×Q. White
resigns.

1 R–K7, R–B2;   2 R×R, K×R;
3 Kt–K5 ch, Black resigns.

duty by winning the Queen. Note that the Pawn at B6 not only prevents K – Kt2, but acts as a support for pieces threatening mate.

In No. 167 we have an example of artistic beauty. All White's three pieces are attacked. But, after 1 R – K7, Kt × Q is impossible because of mate on Kt7; P × Kt is impossible because of mate on R7; and if Kt × R, then 2 P × Kt, etc. Black's actual reply therefore is forced. White has a good reason for not playing 3 Q × P ch, for after K × P his best offensive weapon is gone. But after 3 Kt – K5 Black has no satisfactory square for his King. If K – B1, 4 Q × P threatens two mates, and the KBP of course cannot be taken.

Yet another Knight-combination! Though we cannot say that it is the only possible combination in such circumstances, it presents itself with such frequency that we can say this: the Knight-combination is so closely bound up with the Pawn at B6 that it is in consequence the most decisive in the circumstances. We do not guarantee, however, that it will always succeed!

In No. 168 the KBP accomplishes its work of destruction, either by advancing to B7, or by staying where it is with

No. 168
Correspondence game, 1908
A. Alekhine

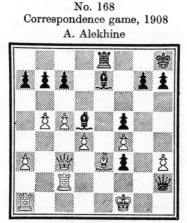

A. Viakhireff

1..Q−R8 ch; 2 B−Kt1, B−R5; 3 R−KR2, Q−Kt7 ch; 4 R×Q, P×R mate.

two objects: to prevent the King's escape and to support its pieces in their attack, especially on Kt7. The squares B7 and Kt7 are its particular field, and we have already seen examples where the pieces supported by this Pawn planted themselves at Kt7 with threats of mate. In this new instance, which recalls Nos. 160 and 166, it is the Pawn that gives mate, after having supported one piece, the Queen, on the vital square.

Such a mate, obviously, can only come about in the final struggle when the opponent's King is immobilised in a disastrous situation; and we know already what sacrifices can be made to get at the King in a stalemate-position. The Pawn in such a case is equivalent to a Queen. It is to be noted, however, that a combination of this type is more difficult of realisation than the simple advance to B7, for it is necessary that a piece shall command the square Kt7, to which the Pawn is going. As it has also to be protected on B6, this task of guarding it is best performed by a Bishop or a Knight, while for the advance to B7 sufficient support is given by a distant Rook.

No. 169 demonstrates strikingly the power of a Pawn at KB7. Apart from its prevention of K – Kt1, the advanced

No. 169
Berlin Tournament, 1928
A. Rubinstein

A. Nimzovitch

1 Q – Kt6, R × R ch; 2 K – Kt2, R – Q7 ch; 3 K – R3, and Black can only
postpone for one move Q × RP mate.

Pawn deprives Black of all defence. We see how limited are White's attacking pieces, Queen and Bishop; yet they are enough to finish the business on the black squares while the Pawn commands the one white.

The already noted strength of Pawn at KB6 is thus increased when it reaches B7, for if the hostile King is present on the edge of the board he is in a position of mate, and brilliant sacrifices are possible. A difference is to be remarked. At B6 the Pawn plays the active part of an attacking piece, at B7 it is passive, its role being to keep the King in the corner and hold off all defence. Otherwise the attack is concentrated on the same squares, especially Kt7, as if the Pawn were at B6. The question always arises, therefore, as to which is the surest way of winning, to keep the

Pawn on B6, for the attack on Kt7, or to push on to B7 and cut off a lateral defence.

In No. 170 two Pawns have reached their 5th rank, Black's KRP and KBP. Neither is blocked. We see them therefore advance to create a mating-threat on Kt7, and

No. 170
Match game, Moscow, 1908
A. Alekhine

B. Blumenfeld

1..P—R6; 2 Q—K6, P×P; 3 K×P, P—B6 ch; 4 K—Kt1, Q×R ch
and mate next move.

then at B6 the BP cuts off the King's escape. So here is the combination. It is enough to draw the King to B1 by a sacrifice for a mate on the rank.

It is not a Knight, but a Rook, which here administers the death-blow, on the rank, as in No. 160.

The Blocked Pawn

In their rich variety, combinations based on an advanced Pawn constantly raise the important question of blockade. To block a Pawn, to stop its advance, is not an easy matter. It is by guarding B3(6) that a Pawn is prevented from reaching that square, and here once more we meet with the over-taxed defending piece, which must be dislodged or exchanged off, if necessary at the cost of a piece of higher value. When the block is an important piece combinations arise as a natural result.

No. 171 shows an earlier stage of the game from which No. 166 was taken.

The attack on a blocking piece exerts its full force when the advanced Pawn can pursue its way, as here.   Nothing is easier than to dislodge the piece; when it is a Queen,

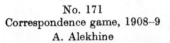

No. 171	No. 172
Correspondence game, 1908–9	Match game, 1909
A. Alekhine	F. J. Marshall

K. Vygodchikoff	J. R. Capablanca

1 . . P – Q4; 2 Kt × R, Kt – R5; 3 Q – B3, P – B6;   4 R – K5,   B × R;   5 P × B, Kt × P, etc.

1 R × Kt,   P × R;   2 B × P ch,   K – K2; 3 Q – R7 ch,   K – K1;   4 Q × Kt ch, K – Q2; 5 Q – R7 ch, Q – K2; 6 B – B8, Black resigns.

attack by a lesser piece is enough.   But it is not a question merely of removing the obstruction; the Pawn must be advanced at once.   So, as we know all the threats that may arise from a Pawn on its 6th rank, we feel no astonishment at the heavy sacrifices made to reach the desired result.

Any piece, especially an important one, is a bad blocker. There should be a Pawn at B3.   But here is another "snag". The castled position would then be much weakened.   There is a target on KKt3(6), and if the attacker can get there success is· in sight.

Such is the case in No. 172.   Under the threat of a White advance of P – B6, Black has played P – KB3, and his consequently unguarded KKt3 has been effectively occupied by White, who threatens now the three adjacent black squares.

We will look at another method of deriving profit from

an advanced KBP. In No. 173 this Pawn is got rid of in order to open the KB file, and as the diagonal QR2 – KKt8 is already open the converging attack on Black's KB2 becomes decisive. White's KBP was merely a support for a

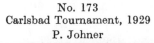

No. 173	No. 174
Carlsbad Tournament, 1929	San Remo Tournament, 1930
P. Johner	K. Ahues

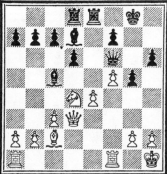

E. Canal   E. D. Bogoljuboff

1 Kt–K6, P×Kt (B×Kt; 2 P×B, Q×KP; 3 B–Kt3. Or 1..R–QB1; 2 Kt×B, etc.); 2 P×P, if Q×KP; 3 B–Kt3, and wins.

1..Kt×P; 2 BP×Kt(Kt4), B×P; 3 Kt×P, P×Kt; 4 B×Kt, B×P ch; 5 Kt×B, Q×Kt ch, and wins.

piece on K6. We see once more the strength of such a Pawn; the shield under protection of which assault is made upon the enemy's lines.

No. 174 demonstrates again the opening of a file against a weakened position and the inroad of pieces massed for the attack. Black's KBP is advanced to its 5th, but the KKt file is not open. The opposing Pawn-barrier, which is much less strong here than on the 2nd rank, must be broken. Another example of a brilliant combination inspired by positional weakness. White's KKt3 is the square to be aimed at, with the aid of the KBP. Thanks to the Knight on K5, a mate in the corner can be seen, the Rook on KR file coming in after White's KRP has disappeared.

To sum up, the advance of the defending Pawns to forestall a hostile Pawn-assault inevitably creates weaknesses from which the adversary may derive great benefit, especially when he has an advanced KBP.

Exercises

The first of these shows the power of the Pawn at KB6, as soon as it is unblocked, to pursue its advance.   In the second we see a Pawn at KB5 threatening to push on.

No. 175
Vienna, 1918
M. Vidmar

No. 176
Hamburg, 1930
H. Rodatz

L. Asztalos
White to play and win.

W. Schönmann
White to play and win.

PART IV

THE LIFE AND DEATH OF A
COMBINATION

CHAPTER I

PREPARING THE COMBINATION

Examination of the Opposing Forces

IT has been stated that a characteristic mark of a combination is surprise; surprise for the defender, not for the assailant, since otherwise the combination will probably be unsound. How often do we not have to abandon brilliant combinations because the preparation has been insufficient to make sure of a win! The theorists who uphold the "spontaneous generation" of combinational ideas are imposing on us with their losing positions suddenly transfigured by a stroke of genius introducing the saving combination. This certainly *may* happen, but it only proves that the play has been bad; for the losing position has not been foreseen with its additional feature of a winning combination. The odds are heavy that a combination imagined under such conditions will be disastrous. Correct play is a very different matter, involving gradual preparation of a favourable position.

This preparation does not demand calculations so exact and profound as does the execution. If that were the case, we could not demand of the average player the requisite foresight. An examination of all the lines of a combination is sufficient work for him. Really, in preparation, it is unnecessary to see and verify clearly all that *might* happen. It is enough to grasp the idea of a combinational possibility and to take in the essential conditions of its success. Then we must try to bring about the position which will make the contemplated manœuvre sound.

In No. 177 even the inexperienced player would have a notion of the sacrifice B × P ch. But this sacrifice at once would be unsound, for two reasons. Black's King can go to Kt3, for after Q – Kt4 would follow P – B4; and also Black's KBP is protected by his Queen, enabling K – Kt1 – B1 when his KR has moved.

White must therefore prepare his combination.   He gains
a tempo by attacking the QBP.   From B4 the Queen can
check at R4 before Kt – Kt5, which will prevent Black's
K – Kt3.   But as yet there is nothing clear against his
K – Kt1.   It is necessary then, on the 2nd move, to reinforce the attack with another piece.   A Rook at KB3 would
threaten the KBP.

If Black parries with P – KKt3 or P – KR3 the 2nd move
will still be useful for a gradual attack, with R – KKt3 or

No. 177
Vienna, 1914
R. Réti

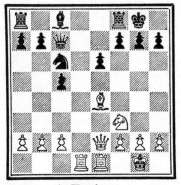

A. Kaufmann

1 Q – B4, P – QKt3; 2 R – Q3, B – Kt2?; 3 B × P ch, and wins.

R3, P – Kt4 – Kt5 or P – KR4 – R5, or a possible doubling
of the Rooks on the only open file.

Why has White, after 2 . . B – Kt2, no longer any hesitation
in sacrificing his Bishop?   Can Black's move have weakened
his King's position?   Yes; for now, his KP being no more
protected by the Bishop, there is the possibility of R × P,
P × R and a series of Queen-checks, culminating in a mate
by Queen, supported, at KB7.   We have here a new
variant of our combination, which is only made feasible by
2 . . B – Kt2.   Through not seeing this Black was over-
whelmed by the storm.

This is certainly a good example of a combination ren-
dered possible by an error on the opponent's part.   It has

its charm, for it is not within everyone's range to conceive a mating attack after two successive sacrifices. A player who wins thus, by taking splendid advantage of an error, has more satisfaction than in winning by picking up a piece accidentally left lying loose.

This example also demonstrates the necessity of considering the position not only of our own pieces but of the enemy's too. That is perhaps the most difficult phase in the preparation of a combination, and to tackle it, if our

No. 178
Baden-Baden Tournament, 1925
A. Alekhine

R. Réti

1..B−R6; 2 B−B3, B−Kt5; 3 B−Kt2, B−R6; 4 B−B3, B−Kt5; 5 B−R1, P−KR4; 6 P−Kt4, P−R3; 7 R−QB1, P−R5; 8 P−R4, P×P; 9 RP×P, Q−B2; 10 P−Kt5, RP×P; 11 P×P, R−K6, etc. (see No. 95).

opponent is not so kind as to contribute towards a "help-mate", it is often more necessary to use artifice than force.

In the next example, No. 178, we see the very complicated position which led up to that illustrated in No. 95. We might suppose from Black's first moves that he had no combination in view and was content with a draw by repetition of moves. But the advance 5..P−KR4 shows that at this moment he foresaw the decisive combination directed against White's KKtP. Defended as it is by two Pawns, it must be attacked at least thrice: by the RP, by the Queen at B2, and by the Rook, which goes to K6 for the purpose.

Could Black at the moment analyse all the variations of his combination? Obviously not; but he knew that it could not be realised with White's Bishop at B3, for that piece obstructed the rank, not allowing Black's Rook to get to Kt6, nor with the Bishop at Kt2, where it parries a check at Kt6. The attack is therefore only possible with the Bishop at R1. When it has gone thither, Black seizes the opportunity with a Rook-sacrifice, which calls for a clear vision of all the variations, whereas the preparatory work does not demand so much.

There is no question here of an error by White, for we cannot so designate a move which leads to a sacrifice 6 moves later and does not result in loss until after 20 moves. Perhaps there was even a means of saving the game at some point. However that may be, our readers, with their interest in the combinational art, cannot reproach Réti for avoiding a draw in this position, where he had a visible advantage. What would they have said, on the contrary, if he had resigned himself to the repetition of moves?

This example, like its predecessor, shows how important it is to examine the position of the opposing forces when we are preparing a combination. The smallest detail may sometimes have momentous consequences.

Examination of our own Forces

The position of our own forces is of no less importance. Among a great number the following is one of the most convincing instances.

The Knight in No. 179 is only sacrificed provisionally, for after two moves White could regain it. He prefers, however, to marshal his pieces for another combination. His 4th and 6th moves are edifying. The Queen goes to K2 for the check on R5, and the Rook to K1 for the check on K4. At this point Alekhine had already conceived his combination, foreseeing all the variations, or almost all. It was a question here of mate, so it was essential to dispose of every piece with absolute precision; but, as a rule, we place them according to the general exigencies of the combination, of which only the *idea* seems quite plain to us.

Concealment of Intentions

All is for the best in the best of all possible chess worlds when our combination is so forceful, or our opponent's position so weak, that we have only to go ahead without fear or concealment.   More frequently we have to disguise our intentions, to lull our opponent to sleep, or even entice him into error.   It is often necessary that he should not suspect

No. 179
Paris, 1913
M. Prat

A. Alekhine

1 Kt × KBP, K × Kt;   2 P − K5, QKt − Kt1;   3 B − Q6, Q − B1;   4 Q − K2, P − QKt4; 5 B − Kt3, P − QR4; 6 QR − K1, P − R5;
White announced mate in 10:—
7 Q − R5 ch, Kt × Q;   8 P × P dbl. ch, K − Kt3;   9 B − B2 ch, K − Kt4; 10 R − B5 ch, K − Kt3; 11 R − B6 dbl. ch, K − Kt4; 12 R − Kt6 ch, K − R5; 13 R − K4 ch, Kt − B5; 14 R × Kt ch, K − R4; 15 P − Kt3, and 16 R − R4 mate.

our plans, so that he may be betrayed into the faulty manœuvres which alone will make our ideas capable of being realised.   It is rarely that the attack can be carried out openly to success when the enemy sees what we want to do to break down his resistance.   Most often we are content not to reveal too much of our plans.   But the real art consists in creating the belief, logically, that our intentions are otherwise than as they seem; which sometimes leads to a game of traps, based on the possible errors of an adversary whose head is beginning to whirl.

In No. 180 White's demonstration on the Queen's wing is very interesting. Its object is to disarm the other player, who has no suspicion of what is in store for him on the King's side. One move is enough to disclose the plan. The action passes from left to right, and Black's position crumples up. White had disposed all his forces for the winning attack, which we have shown in No. 120.

Again in No. 181 there is nothing to indicate that White is about to make an attack on the King's side. Action is

No. 180
Budapest Tournament, 1921
K. Sterk

No. 181
Triberg Tournament, 1921
E. D. Bogoljuboff

A. Alekhine

1 KR − B1, Kt × P;   2 B × Kt, B × B;
3 Q × B, Kt − B4;   4 Q − K2, B − R4;
5 QR − Kt1,   Q − R3;   6 R − B4!,
Kt − R5;   7 B − B6 (for continuation
see No. 120).

A. Alekhine

1 Kt × Kt, P × Kt;   2 R × P, Kt − Kt5;
3 B − K4, P − B4;   4 B × P, and wins.

engaged in the centre, and the pieces do not seem ready for an assault towards the right. But suddenly the scene changes, and an irresistible attack is launched, with multiple sacrifices. The combination had been foreseen, with all its ramifications, but it had been necessary to hide the intention carefully, in view of the limited number of pieces which White had available for his scheme. Particularly to be admired is White's 2nd move, apparently so rash, which takes the enemy by surprise, and of which the object is to allow B − K4. The Rook acts as a buffer, as well as a supplementary piece in the attack. In this dazzling exploitation of the weakness of Black's KRP, see what a pretty win results from 3..P – KR3!

The story is told, as illustrating the height (or depth) of craft, how a player, not wishing to reveal his intentions by moving his King, made an impossible move.   His opponent, enforcing the penalty, exacted a move by the King, not noticing that it was just that which caused him to fall into a carefully prepared trap.   We do not commend this player's

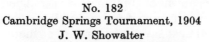

No. 182
Cambridge Springs Tournament, 1904
J. W. Showalter

Dr. Emanuel Lasker

1 R – Q3, R – Kt7; 2 B – Kt1, Q – R8; 3 B – B2, R – Kt8; 4 Kt – B6, R – R8;
5 Q – Kt7, Kt – Kt2; 6 Q – KB7, R – Kt8 ch; 7 K – B3, Black resigns.

example; for there are more honest ways of concealing our plans, in spite of the board set up before the eyes, with all the moves open to be seen.   But we must, nevertheless, use artifice if possible, to throw our opponent off the track.

No. 182 is an example.   White has a much inferior position. His only resource is a stratagem.   How is he to bring it off without arousing suspicion and putting his opponent on his guard?   Only by lulling his suspicions, and making him believe that White is in the depths of despair, without an object in view.   Black, accordingly, abandons protection of his King and presses his attack vigorously—up to the moment when he is caught on the hook, and has nothing to do but give up the game.

CHAPTER II

THE MECHANISM OF COMBINATIONS

Combinational Dynamics

THE mechanism of combinations is of such variety that it is very difficult, if not impossible, to study it. One might almost say that there are as many special cases as there are problems. The mechanism is similar, but the workings are never the same. It is not even possible to state how a combination arises. Sometimes it is a logical reasoning, enlightened by profound analysis of the position, which allows us to discover the adversary's vulnerable point. Sometimes it is intuition, which suddenly makes clear the road by which we must travel. In one case our task is to prepare with the closest care for the decisive attack, while in the other our attention is aroused by a careless move of our adversary's which opens up to us unexpected possibilities. The most flagrant traps enter into combinations as much as the long series of moves, of which the subtlety only gives us hope of distant and not always certain success.

Our study, however, shows that the combination should be regarded as a victory for lively intelligence over inert matter, for quality over quantity. The number of the pieces loses its importance, some of them being merely dead weight, as they do not take part in the combination. They are cheerfully sacrificed for a gain in time or space. Space is limited; what is concerned is a small portion of the chess-board, on which only the decisive squares are of importance. Time is more important, for it is a matter of getting ahead of all measures for defence. Brute force is not what is required. Dynamics come into play.

So, then, combination, with its tactical possibilities, transforms the static positional game, the game in space, into a dynamic game in time. We see that, on this point, the combinational game of the Nineteenth Century is related to the "ultra-modern" game of today.

The time-question now calls for special examination.

The Order of the Moves

We have several times already emphasised the importance in combinations of the order of the moves. The game of threats (which is the essence of combinational play) calls

No. 183
Berlin, 1923
F. Sämisch

A. Alekhine

1 P × P, B × Q; 2 P × P ch, K − R1; 3 Kt − Q5!, Black resigns.

for great precision in their succession. No general rule can be outlined; sometimes it is the distant, sometimes the immediate threat that has the preference. So with direct and indirect, principal and secondary threats. The issue being an outright win, it is decided by analysis with its clear-cut variations, not by vague general considerations.

We will give a few additional examples to illustrate the importance of the order of the moves.

In No. 183 it looks as though the right move were 3 Kt − K6, attacking Queen and Rook, and then, after 3 . . Q − Kt1, 4 Kt − Q5. But look at the difference. White by playing Kt − Q5 first reserves the option of following with Kt − K6 or QB6, according to the move of Black's Queen; e.g., if Q − Kt1 or R2, 4 Kt − QB6, but if Q − Kt2 or B4, then 4 Kt – K6.   The inversion of the Knight-moves might have cost the game, and would in any case have delayed the win.

White's advantage in No. 184 is obvious.   His pressure on the diagonal QR2 – KKt8 is very dangerous to Black. It is clear also that the win will be gained in the centre. But how?   In what order must the moves come to bring

No. 184
Semmering Tournament, 1926
E. Grünfeld

A. Alekhine

1 P – K5, P × P; 2 B – Q3, P – K5; 3 Kt × KP, Kt × Kt; 4 B × Kt, Kt – B3;
5 P × P ch, R × P; 6 B – Kt6 ch, K – K2; 7 B × P, P – Kt5; 8 B – B5, R – K7;
9 KR – K1, Black resigns.

about a prompt decision?   There is another diagonal for action, QKt1 – KR7, but it requires opening and occupying.

Note the precision with which the attack is conducted. First P – K5 to open, with a direct threat, the diagonal just mentioned.   If instead 1 B – Q3, Black would reply with P – Kt5, making difficulties for White.   1 P – K5 allows 2 B – Q3 with a direct menace (P × P ch, R × P; B – B5), causing thus a delay of Black's P – Kt5.

White does not play P × P ch earlier, because the capture frees Black's game, allowing, after R × P, K – K2.

Black cannot close even one of the two open diagonals. The try by 2 . . P – K5 is unsuccessful, for it is not the Bishop but the Knight that takes, and all the threats persist.   If 2 . . Kt – B5, then 3 B × Kt, P × B; 4 Q × P, and the menace of 5 P × P ch, R × P; 6 KR – B1 ch, K – K2; 7 B × P ch forces the win. To escape this line Black has 4 . . Kt – Kt3; but then 5 P × P ch, K – Kt1; 6 Q – Kt3, and wins.

A point which calls for especial attention is that in this variation time is sacrificed for space. White loses time by first B – Q3 and then B × Kt; but this enables him to keep the two diagonals open. By occupying both he forces his opponent to strive after closing one, instead of making an aggressive move. As the closing of the diagonals fails, White's end is attained. The difficulty to be surmounted was great, for it was a matter of pressing an attack with an eye all the while to the defence.

Intermediate Moves

While all moves are intermediate in relation to those which precede and follow them, the name of "intermediate move" (in German, *Zwischenzug*) is given particularly to some presenting special features and falling into a distinct group. We may say that intermediate moves are combinations one or two moves deep; surprise-moves which support the action of the preceding moves to such a degree that they may change the whole course of the game. In every combination there are some moves which seem natural, and required by the position. Suddenly one's opponent breaks the normal run of events with a move so strong—it may be a check— that one can only pursue one's ideas after a defensive stroke; and this "intermediate move" may render one's threats ineffective. It is a combination within a combination.

A few examples will explain what we are trying to say.

In No. 185, after 2 B × B, it would be a blunder on Black's part to reply R × B, for then 3 B × P ch, winning the Rook. It would be the *normal* course of the game. But Black makes an intermediate move, R – Q1, allowing White's QB to go; for after it goes the KB is taken instead, and Black has won a Pawn. If the QB does not retreat it can be captured without risk, Black's Rook at Q4 being defended.

The intermediate move has a still more surprising effect in the course of a combination, which is always a sequence

of dangerous threats. It is the bolt from the blue that
upsets all calculations.

In No. 186 both players make intermediate moves, the
second refuting the first. We see a clash of two combinations, each involving such a move. White begins with a
Knight-sacrifice. Instead of retaking at move 2 he pins,
hoping to regain the piece, whereas 2 P × B would have lost

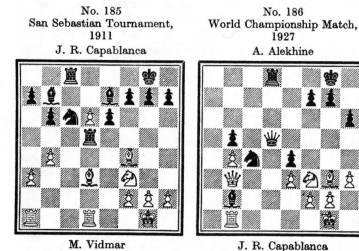

No. 185	No. 186
San Sebastian Tournament, 1911	World Championship Match, 1927
J. R. Capablanca	A. Alekhine

M. Vidmar	J. R. Capablanca
1..B×P; 2 B×B, R−Q1! Drawn game.	1 Kt−Q4, B×Kt; 2 R−Q1, Kt×P. White resigns.

a Pawn at once. Then Black, with a move in hand, sacrifices his Knight in turn, but with such effect that White has
to give up. If 3 P × Kt, B × P ch, and the pinning Rook is
lost. "The trapper trapped!" observed Capablanca once in
similar circumstances.

We could give many simple instances of such departures
from the normal course of the game. We prefer instead to
examine a more complex case.

In No. 187, White having sacrificed a Bishop at KB7,
Black on his 4th move is ready to give it back to save himself—e.g. 5 Q × B ch, Q − K3; 6 R − B1 ch, B − B3; 7 Q − B3,
K − Kt2, etc. But White does not intend matters to go
thus. Instead of 5 Q × B ch he gives an intermediate check,
and now, if 5..B − B3, the win is quick with 6 Q − KR4,

We see the change in the validity of Black's B – B3 through the influence of the intermediate move.

It is not the Bishop on Q5 that White regains, but that on KB6. As a matter of fact, he renounces the regain of a piece, for Black can play 5..K – K3. But then White wins by direct attack: 6 Q – Kt4 ch, K – Q3; 7 Kt – B4 ch. Now the win is secured—the hostile King being in the centre of

No. 187
Dresden Tournament, 1926
M. Blümich

A. Alekhine

1 R × P, R × R; 2 B × R ch, K × B; 3 Q – B4 ch, B – K3; 4 P – Q5, B × QP;
5 R – B1 ch, Kt – B3; 6 Q × B ch, Q – K3; 7 Q – B3, Q – B4; 8 B × Kt,
Black resigns.

the board—but not without some difficulty: *e.g.*, 7..B × Kt; 8 Q × B, P – Kt4; 9 R – Q1 ch, Kt – Q5; 10 Q – K2, Q–B4; 11 Kt – B3, Kt – Kt6; 12 Q – K1, Kt – K5; 13 B – R4, P – Kt4; 14 B – Kt3, etc. (Alekhine's analysis).

This example may serve as a model as regards the order of the moves, for R – B1 ch and Q × B ch might be inverted, but with a very different result.

The False Trail

Combinations are not always free from "duals". There are often several winning lines. The surest, quickest, and most decisive should be chosen. It is even right to give up an involved combination when there is a simpler and more direct variation, though it may be less brilliant.

In No. 188, for instance, White selects the simplest winning line, not the seductive combination with the Rook-sacrifice. That was too complicated to promise certain success in every variation; for instance, in 1 B × Kt, P × B;

No. 188
Moscow Tournament, 1925
F. J. Marshall

J. R. Capablanca

1 KR – Kt1, Q – Kt5; 2 B × Kt, P × B; 3 R × Q, P × R; 4 B × KtP, and wins.

2 Q – Kt4 ch, K – B1; 3 R × P ch, K × R; 4 Q – Kt5, R – KB1; 5 B × RP, B – B3; 6 R – B1 ch, etc. (Capablanca's analysis).

But we must allow æsthetic considerations full play. In No. 187 we should be ungracious if we blamed Alekhine for having chosen the magnificent combination with a Rook-sacrifice in preference to the tame continuation Q – B3, though that would have regained the piece sacrificed.

In the great majority of cases there is only one winning line. We do not take into consideration here the opponent's weak moves or blunders, but merely tempting continuations which seem to win, though they are really unsound. The great difficulty is to make up one's mind, when a choice offers, between the simplest or the most complicated line. We should decide for the precise and strictly accurate variation.

In No. 189 White went astray, probably only contemplating, in answer to his first move, Q × P ch, when he could play 2 K – Kt2. The actual reply 1..P – Kt4! compromised his game. The right line was 1 Q – B7 (with a threat of mate on R5), P – Kt3 (P – Kt4; 2 R × P, etc.); 2 Kt – K6 or P – KKt4. Here was the sure win.

In No. 190 Black had two continuations, that in the text with the Rook-sacrifice, and a sacrifice of the Exchange only,

<table>
<tr><td>No. 189
Moscow Tournament, 1925
E. D. Bogoljuboff</td><td>No. 190
Monte Carlo Tournament, 1903
S. Tarrasch</td></tr>
</table>

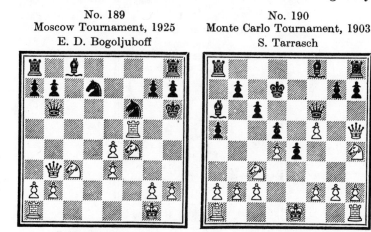

<table>
<tr><td>J. R. Capablanca</td><td>H. N. Pillsbury</td></tr>
</table>

1 P−Kt4?, P−Kt4!; 2 Q × Q, P × Q;
3 R − Q1, and White eventually won.

1 Kt−Kt6, Q × QP; 2 Kt × R, B − B4;
3 Q − R4, R × Kt. Black eventually won.

by 1..P × Kt; 2 Q × R, P × P. The fact that White here has the possibility of castling makes this variation rather doubtful.

On the 2nd move Black has again a choice; the text-move (which finally led to success) and 2..B – Kt5, forcing an immediate draw by perpetual check.

We find this diversity of continuations regularly in combinations. Our next example shows how difficult it sometimes is to choose between lines, all of which apparently lead to a win.

Black makes a lovely Queen-sacrifice in No. 191, with Rook, Bishop, and two Pawns for the Queen. But on the 2nd move, in addition to the continuation chosen, which looked like the most decisive, there was another, in which the menace was not so direct, but of which the latent force might probably have secured the win, *viz.* 2 . . P × P; 3 B – Kt5 (3 B × Kt, P × R(= Q); 4 Q × Q, Kt – B7 ch; 5 K – B2, P × B), P × R(= Q); 4 B × Q, Kt – B7 ch; 5 K – B2, R – Q1; 6 Q – K2, B – B4 ch, followed by Castles, etc.

It is plainly not a question here of the idea, for that is the same in both variations.   Detailed analysis is necessary,

No. 191
Paris Tournament, 1925
A. Alekhine

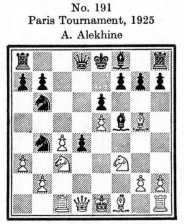

E. Znosko-Borovsky

1 . . P × Kt!; 2 B × Q, R × B?; 3 Q – Kt3, P × P; 4 Q × P, Kt – R5; 5 Q – R1,
Kt – B7 ch; 6 R × Kt, B × R; 7 Kt – Q4, B – Kt3; 8 P – B5, etc.

without neglecting certain general indications of great importance.   As in the preceding example, White must not be allowed to castle.   Black, on the other hand, must castle as soon as possible.   If he could win by direct attack, castling might be omitted; but as there is no such attack the scattered forces must be brought together with all speed to contend successfully against the hostile Queen.   As it was, White took advantage of his opportunity to prevent castling entirely, which secured a draw.

Analysis of a Combination

In order to have a better understanding of the mechanism of a combination, to get the whole idea of what a player must examine and must fathom in the course of his calculations, to put ourselves, in three words, "inside the mind" of the creator of a combination, let us look at a very fine example, which might serve as illustration of a great many of our general considerations.

When he arrived at the position in No. 192, Capablanca says in an illuminative note, it was clear to White that his opponent wished to play Kt – Q2, followed by Kt – K4, or

No. 192
St. Petersburg, 1913
F. Dus-Khotimirsky

J. R. Capablanca

1 P—R3, B×Kt; 2 Q×B, Kt—Q2; 3 KR—B1, Kt—B4; 4 P—QKt4, Kt—R5; 5 R×R, R×R; 6 P—K5!, P—Kt3; 7 P—K6, R—B1; 8 Kt—Kt3, Q—Kt2; 9 Kt—B5, P×P; 10 P×P, Q—B2, continued in No. 193.

by Kt – B4 – R5, forcing the advance of White's QKtP in certain cases, and then by B – B3 and Kt – B6 to restrict White's game so much as to paralyse it entirely. It is against this plan that White must evolve another to counteract it. If it is possible, White may hope to gain the advantage by concentrating, during Black's manœuvres, the forces necessary to attack his QP and QKtP and to win one or the other. The sequel shows the realisation of this scheme.

The ex-champion of the world in his note reveals in luminous fashion not only his own method of play, but also that of all modern masters. No recondite analysis, no pat reply to this or that move, but the elaboration of a complete plan in answer to the opponent's. Against the manœuvre to

create a weakness at his QB3 and to plant a Knight there,
White aims at the weakness of the squares Q4 and QKt5,
to exploit it against the enemy.   But, if that were all that
there were in it, the example would illustrate only positional
play and would not serve us in our study of combinations.
Actually there is a magnificent combination, in a variation
where Black is trying to realise his design in its entirety.   He
could, indeed, have avoided the combination on his 4th move
by Kt × B.   But then his positional inferiority was manifest.
He pursued his plan therefore, and obtained a position
which the masters present when the game was played considered a winning one.   They did not see, remarks Capablanca, that he was about to "turn the position over."

We have here an application of the rule, Do not be content
to discover the position of advantage, but always see at least
a move beyond it.   The move in the present case is superb,
though very simple.   By 6 P – K5 White opens a diagonal
for his Bishop and insinuates an attack on the Black King.
This is a marvellous instance of a move skilfully concealed.
All the action was taking place on the Queen's wing, when,
in a flash, an irresistible attack was launched on the other
side.   Look at the pleasing double threat of Q – B5, attacking the unguarded Rook and the KRP.   The more or less
forced parries have the effect of arresting Black's attack.

Profiting by the fact that after 7 P – K6, P × P is impossible because of 8 Q – Kt4, with another double threat,
against KP and KKtP, White brings up his Knight.   The
sensation comes on the 9th move.   But the Knight cannot
be taken, for then 10 Q × P and mate to follow.   Other
threats are P × P ch, R × P; Kt – R6, winning the Exchange;
and Kt × B ch; Q × Kt; B × QKtP—Black's Queen having
too much to defend, which prevented her on the 8th move
going to B2.   So 9..P × P is forced.   But what a brilliant
reply, 10 P × P!!.   If Q × Q, then 11 Kt × B ch and 12 P × Q,
winning a piece.

It is extremely rare for a player to possess, in such a degree
as we get here exhibited, the two essential qualities of
imagination which gives birth to combinations and that
sane judgement which directs the positional game.

We see the importance of small details in a combination

which is as brilliant as it is daring. The strength of the
Bishop at Q3 is also to be noted. As soon as its longer
diagonal is opened it acts forcefully on two sides, against
the weaknesses at QKt5 and KR7. The Queen aids it
against R7, and takes advantage of the long white diagonal,
which she controls. The intersection-point of the two

No. 193
Same game as No. 192
F. Dus-Khotimirsky

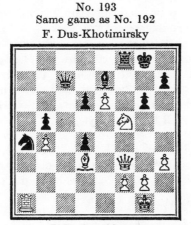

J. R. Capablanca

11 Q – B6!, Q – Q1; 12 Kt × B ch, Q × Kt; 13 B × QKtP, Kt – B6;
14 Q – Q7, Q × Q; 15 B × Q, R – Kt1; 16 P – K7, and wins.

diagonals is K4, showing the importance of the move P – K5.
How many players would have hesitated to sacrifice this
Pawn, being unable to foresee the final outcome of all the
variations! We must admit that there is a difficulty, the
action of the Knight on KB1, which is obliged to make a
quiet move, almost without a threat, to Kt3. But we know
how often such moves are ventured upon in a combination.
We reach in No. 193 the culminating point in Capablanca's
combination, the offer of his Queen. It is a Knight-combination, for if 11 . . Q × Q, 12 Kt × B ch regains the Queen.
(Note that if Black had played 10 . . P – Q4, then 11 Q × P!,
the White Queen and Black King being connected with one
another by a Knight's move.) Black has therefore to lose
another tempo, of which White takes advantage to capture
at last the QKtP, a weak point long aimed at. Now his
KP can no longer be stopped.

This example shows us not only tactical combinations, based on the gain of time, in which appear nearly all the ideas we have been studying, but further, a strategical combination counteracting the opponent's positional scheme. It shows, moreover, the preparation and at the same time the dissimulation of a combination in no way due to chance. If it needs the imagination of genius to conceive it, nevertheless there is to be seen only the logical evolution of the strategical contest between two plans.

One is inclined at times to admit that there is no difference between the positional and combinational games. Genius, indeed, can display itself in both; but in the former the combinations which are not realised remain in the player's mind only, whereas in the latter the combinations are revealed in the full light of day.

[I am tempted to add here an example which shows the difficulty in distinguishing precisely between the positional and combinational games.

No. 194
Hastings Tournament, 1934–5
M. Botvinnik

Sir George Thomas

1 Q–B3, B–K2; 2 Q–Kt3, Q–Kt1;
3 Q–K3, P×P; 4 BP×P, K–K1;
5 Q–Q3, K–B1 (to avoid the ultimate threat of Q×P ch and Kt–B7 ch);
  6 Kt–B3, and wins the QKtP.

In so far as White's immediate object here is to drive Black's Queen and Bishop into less favourable positions than they at present occupy for the defence of his Pawns, the play may be looked upon as purely positional. On the other hand, what White ultimately designs is to win a weak Pawn, of which Black has two (QKtP and KP). White, moreover, on his first and third moves threatens successively Q–B6 and Q–R6 ch—as well as on the latter P×P. Can we not, therefore, speak here of a combination to win a Pawn, though the only strictly combinational phase in it is the sacrificial threat, which is not immediate?—P. W. S.]

CHAPTER III

REFUTING A COMBINATION

The Combination with a Flaw in it

To be strictly accurate, a normal combination can only be refuted when it is incorrect, when it is one of the unsound combinations that have no interest for us. Take those little combinations in two or three moves, where the opponent's immediate answer is unforeseen. In such a case we speak of a flaw in the combination. But when we are considering a long combination, complicated by numerous variations, have we the right to be so exacting if in the end it proves unworkable? In the calm of the positional game is one always sure of success? If stupid fortune will so have it that after a number of moves our opponent surprises us by a continuation which saves the game, can it really be said that our combination is unsound? Must the player, in fact, be blamed for having conceived it and carried it out, when it is admitted that the human brain is incapable of seeing the most remote consequences?

We should praise, rather, the courage of the player who, relying only on his intuition, plunges into a brilliant combination of which the issue does not appear to him too clear. Alekhine's famous combination against Réti, at Baden-Baden in 1925 (our Nos. 95 and 178), takes 20 moves. After various attacks and counter-attacks, Alekhine, faced with a very strong move by Réti, has a difficult problem to solve. His answer is a new combination 10 moves deep. What would have happened if a slight flaw had been present in one of the many schemes? What would be the effect on our verdict as to the magnificence of each of them?

One could name many celebrated combinations in which a defence has been found that casts doubt upon the result, which has not prevented them from still being considered masterpieces. Even "The Immortal Game" may be cited here!

Refutation by Obstinate Defence

In all these cases it may be said that the combination has been refuted. The refutation comes by various ways. Sometimes it is necessity which dictates the choice, often just chance. The method, however, that does honour to the players is a tenacious defence, which at times proves that a combination can be at once sound and unsound.

The difficulty lies precisely in the fact that a combination aims above all at breaking down the opponent's power of resistance. Therefore it seems very bold to cling to the defence against a combination undertaken after mature study. This way of refutation calls for admirable calmness of mind and a self-reliance worthy of all praise.

The following example is all the more characteristic in that the player under attack did not succeed in finding the best continuation, which would have secured him a draw.

The combination here, a masterpiece by the former World Champion, extends to 14 moves, and entails the sacrifice of two Rooks and a Bishop. It ends with a delightful economic mate; but White overlooked the best defence.

No. 195
St. Petersburg Quadrangular Tournament, 1896
Dr. Emanuel Lasker

H. N. Pillsbury

1 P−B5, R×Kt; 2 P×B, R−QR6;
3 P×P ch, R×P; 4 P×R, Q−Kt3 ch;
5 B−Kt5, Q×B ch; 6 K−R1, R−B2;
7 R−Q2, R−B5; 8 KR−Q1, R−B6;
9 Q−B5, Q−B5; 10 K−Kt2, R×P;
11 K×R, Q−B6 ch; 12 K−R4,
P−Kt4 ch; 13 K×P, Q−B5 ch;
14 K−R5, B−Q1 mate.

Instead of 10 K − Kt2 he should have played 10 Q − Kt1, and if R × P; 11 Q − Kt2, R − QB6; 12 K − Kt1, it not being evident that Black retains enough advantage to win. The game might even end abruptly with a perpetual check: 12..P − QKt4; 13 R − QB2, B × P; 14 R × R, B × R; 15 Q − Kt3, Q − K5 ch; 16 Q − B2, Q − Kt 5 ch, etc. An attempt by Black to play for a winning ending here by 15..P − Q5 would have given him no better result; for after

16 Q × Q, P × Q; 17 R – KB1 (threatening R – B5 – B5),
B – R4; 18 R – B1, P – B6; 19 K – B2, Black cannot
win.

So therefore this combination, which is still so much
admired, at one point might only have yielded a draw. We
must not forget, too, the cases where a similar combination
is demolished by the opponent. We have seen an example
in No. 129, where Marshall, sacrificing a piece almost in the
opening, makes a tremendous attack, which his opponent
by obstinate defence succeeds in repelling. Marshall's combination is none the less magnificent, and one sees it sometimes echoed again in master-games.

These last two examples illustrate perfectly the refutation
of a combination by tenacious defence. In No. 129 the
defender succeeds in saving the game, and even wins. In
No. 195 he loses. We may blame the latter for his oversight,
but we must reserve all our admiration for the attacker,
since such combinations almost pass human understanding.
When the defender was unable to keep his mind clear amid
all the complications, how can we reproach the attacker for
not having seen all? Is it reasonable to class so long and
brilliant a combination with unsound combinations of the
ordinary shallow type? We know today that these inspired
manœuvres are incorrect, but to prove it there have been
needed defenders of admirable skill and presence of mind;
for as a rule attacks of this kind are irresistible.

Refutation by Refusal

We may decline a combination like a gambit by not
accepting the sacrifice, or one of the sacrifices, offered. It
is not usually the best refutation, and often the very refusal
leads to loss, because in a combination there is always something inevitable. Moreover, as a capture, of Pawn or piece,
very frequently accompanies the sacrifice, the mere refusal
then leaves a material advantage with the other player.

Nevertheless, in certain cases the combination is not really
sound unless the sacrifice is accepted, and then it is by refusing that the game can be won.

In the position in No. 196 White conceives a combination beginning with a pretty Bishop-sacrifice. If Black accepts it, then 2 Kt × P, followed by P – B4, with a crushing attack. But Black is not obliged to accept the sacrifice, and seizes the attack himself, utilising the time given him by the fact that the Bishop is *en prise*. For White to attempt to save

No. 196
Scheveningen Tournament, 1913
A. Alekhine

A. G. Olland

1 B × BP, B × Kt; 2 Kt × B, R – KKt1; 3 Kt × P, P × Kt; 4 B × B, Q – Kt5; 5 P – Kt3, K × B.

the piece would be fatal, *e.g.* 3 B – K3, R × P ch; 4 K × R, Q – Kt5 ch; 5 K – R2, Q × Kt, and wins.

Here we notice the danger of multiple sacrifices. The attacked player accepts one of them and then defends obstinately, refusing the others, whereas his opponent counted on the acceptance of all and so remains with a material inferiority.

Refutation by Counter-combination

Similia similibus. Counter-attack is often the best defence against an attack, and a counter-combination the best method of meeting a combination. This is true in the first place for psychological reasons, because the player engaged in a combination is an aggressor, who with his heavy blows is sapping his opponent's energy, so as to take advantage of a momentary collapse. In such a state the counter-combination is often unexpected, and no preparation has been made to meet it. On the other hand, the conducing conditions for such a blow rarely present themselves. But when it is really possible it nearly always results in the complete rout of the first aggressor.

The counter-combination is almost always sprung at the

No. 197
Nice Tournament, 1930
E. Znosko-Borovsky

B. Kostich

1 Q—B3, P×P; 2 P×P, P—QKt4; 3 P—K5, P—Kt5; 4 Kt—R4, P×P;
5 P—Q6, Q×P; 6 Q×B, P—K5!; 7 B—K5, Kt×B; 8 P×Kt, Q×P;
9 Kt—B2, R—Q7; 10 Kt—K3, B—Q3; 11 KR—K1. Black mates in 8
moves, beginning with Q×P ch.

end of the combination, in that moment of calm which is so dangerous; for if hopes are then realised and the object attained of an advantage, the future remains dark and enigmatic, and he who sees a little further into it may easily profit by that fact. The golden rule of chess applies again here: Always see a move further than the necessary move.

A counter-combination begun under the storm of the adversary's combination is always very difficult, since it involves the ability to swim against the flood at its full. From the psychological point of view the difficulty is all but insurmountable, so that this counter-combination is exceedingly rare.

No. 197, however, is an example of this type of refutation by counter-combining.

White's comparatively simple combination aims at the win of the Bishop at QKt7. Black prepares a counter-combination with a sacrifice of this piece. After its capture comes an interval of rest. It must not be supposed that White had not analysed the sequel; but he counted on a normal continuation by 6..P × P, which wins a third Pawn for the Bishop—not here a sufficient compensation. Im-

No. 198
World Championship Match, Munich, 1908
Dr. Emanuel Lasker

S. Tarrasch

1..P−B4; 2 Kt−Kt5, P × P; 3 R × P, R × R; 4 P−K5, R × KBP!; 5 P × R, Q−Kt3 ch; 6 K−R1, Q−QKt8 ch; 7 K−Kt2, Q × P ch, and wins.

agining Black to be already half beaten, White had not conceived of the possibility of a counter-combination, which aims at nothing less than the shutting in of the Queen by the central Pawn-advance. It is a position of rare occurrence, where the advantage suddenly passes over to Black, and so decisively that he even has the option of winning the Queen or making a direct attack upon the King.

No. 198 is another example of a counter-combination launched in the middle of a hostile combination. After a bold manœuvre by Black, planting one of his Rooks in enemy territory, White succeeds in imprisoning this Rook, first at his QB4 and then at his QB5, and prepares to capture it. Hence the combination, to which Black replies with a counter-combination. The seemingly lost Rook plays a decisive part, and actually wins the game.

We must never submit to the loss of a piece without trying
to reap some benefit from it.   Lasker even asserts that such
a piece, which he calls a *desperado*, always lends itself to
combinations, and that one must see in it a new combinational idea.   I do not share his opinion.   A lost piece is
generally a piece lost.   We must, however, heed this warn-
ing, that it is quite natural that, when we aim at winning a
piece and accumulate round it a number of our own pieces,
some weaknesses should appear in other parts of the board,
of which our opponent may take advantage.   If the hunted
piece can be set free by sacrifices, it acquires thereby a fresh
access of strength, like every piece once shut in and then
let loose.   Hurling itself against the weakened hostile
position, it may spread ruin there, a *desperado* indeed, inspired with all the courage of despair.

CONCLUSION

WITH our task ended, we must first pay a tribute to the inexhaustible wealth of the game of chess. We have but touched on our subject. How many brilliant combinations have been left unillustrated! There is an untold number still in our stock, to analyse which we should require not one more, but a whole series of volumes.

This humble study only reveals the bare essentials. Destined no doubt to be continued and completed by others, it has none the less, we hope, succeeded in showing that research into the art of combination is both instructive and curious.

We are far from being ambitious to present our work as a learned production. We have, on the contrary, excluded all parade of pedantry, so as to display the art in all its freshness and avoid spoiling its beauties by arid formulas. There was another danger, too, that had to be avoided; the perpetual ecstasy over every sacrifice, contagious in its enthusiasm, but in no way tending to improvement, which affects so many young players, incapable of defining their sentiments when their eyes are confronted with the real work of art. Between these two reefs we have endeavoured to steer a prudent course.

We have not, we believe, in any way depreciated the leading part which imagination plays in combinations. We have rather insisted, often, on the mystery of the creative genius that breathes life into inert matter and gives to our game a touch of the superhuman. After having taken to pieces the mechanism of a brilliant combination, and examining and understanding all its "works", there frequently remains for us something obscure that compels our admiration.

Anatole France observes that imagination sows the seed of all beauty in the world, that through it alone we become great.

Can it reasonably be said that our analysis does injury to one of the finest gifts of the human mind? We know, however, that imagination by itself is not enough for the flowering of genius. There must be labour as well. Often at the chess-board we fail through simple ignorance rather than through the lack of ideas, and on the verge of executing a magnificent combination we sit perplexed, at a loss how to realise it. Inexperience makes the most fertile imagination powerless.

It would be idle, and presumptuous, to wish to imitate the achievements of a Morphy or an Alekhine; but their methods and their manner of expressing themselves are within the reach of all.

May we say, finally, that we have striven to furnish with good tools the excellent workmen that all real chess amateurs should be? It is for them to judge whether we have succeeded. But let them at least admit with us that combination can be learnt, and that to know its general principles is to make easier the upsoaring of creative ideas.

The study of combinations should enrich the analytical spirit of studious amateurs. Thereafter the most gifted among them will be able to catch some sparks of the genius of masters, and in addition some rays of the glory that is the masters'.

POSTSCRIPT

Two Examples from the late Championship Match

N o. 199 presents one of the finest combinations played in the recent World Championship match. The position is after White's 15th move. His King is left in the centre of the board, and naturally becomes the object of attack by all Black's pieces. But he is wonderfully well pro-

No. 199
World Championship Match,
4th Game. October 10, 1935
A. Alekhine

M. Euwe

15..P B4!; 16 B×Kt, Q×B;
17 Kt×P, Q−Kt4; 18 Kt−B4, B−Kt5;
19 P−B3, P−K4!; 20 Kt(B4)−Q3,
P×P; 21 P×B, P×P; 22 B×KP,
Kt×P; 23 B−B4, B−B6 ch; 24 R−Q2,
R×Kt; 25 Kt×R, Q×Kt; 26 B×R,
Q−K2 ch; 27 K−Q1, Kt−K6 ch;
28 K−B1, Kt×Q, and wins.

No. 200
World Championship Match,
30th Game, December 15, 1935
A. Alekhine

M. Euwe

27 Q×P ch, K×Q; ¦28 Kt−B4 ch,
K−B2; 29 Kt×Q, etc.

tected by both pieces and Pawns, and to pierce the defence is far from easy. A series of sacrifices is initiated by Black to crush his opponent's resistance. The first, a Pawn-sacrifice, eliminates a White piece (KB), and puts another (Kt) on the dangerous square QB5, where it is twice attacked, so that the QP cannot move. But the real combination begins

206

with the second Pawn-sacrifice, which is at the same time
a Bishop-sacrifice.   One after another the stones of White's
wall of defence fall, so that after a few moves his King is
without protection!

The whole combination is too complicated to be analysed
here.   But on the 25th move there was another, even more
drastic, solution of the problem for Black, namely
25..R – K ch; 26 Kt – K4 (26 K – Q1, B × R), B × R ch;
27 K × B, Q – Q4 ch, etc.

Black's position in No. 200 (from the game which finally
decided the transference of the World Championship title
to its new holder) is extremely bad.   His Queen had no
escape before his last move, Kt(from Kt3) – R5, which
prevented 27 R – R2 and gave the Queen a flight-square.
But now comes a Knight-combination for White, who
"sacrifices" his Queen and regains his next material move,
putting him another Pawn ahead.   His idea is to bring his
opponent's King to his K3, where he is in relation to his
Queen at KR4 by a Knight's move—White's Knight at B4.
This is an example of the feeling for trigonometry at chess,
such as we should expect to find in a mathematician!

INDEX OF ILLUSTRATIVE EXAMPLES

NO.	PAGE	NO.	PAGE
1 Maróczy—Tartakover .	11	40 Schlechter—Mieses . .	55
2 Cukierman—Znosko-Borovsky	13	41 Bogoljuboff—Mieses .	56
3 Capablanca-Vidmar . .	14	42 Bird—Morphy . . .	56
4 Alekhine—Capablanca .	15	45 Study by Rinck . . .	58
5 Capablanca—Yates . .	18	46 Nenarokoff—Grigorieff .	58
6 Lucena's Mate . . .	19	47 Tarrasch—3 Amateurs .	59
7 X.—Swiderski . . .	21	48 Lövenfisch—Rosenthal .	60
8 Mieses—Taubenhaus .	21	49 Réti—Bogoljuboff . .	60
9 Steinitz—X.	22	50 Chatard—X.	61
10 Rubinstein—Duras . .	24	51 Study by Troitsky . .	61
11 Study by Znosko-Borovsky	25	52 Tylor—Winter . . .	62
		53 Blackburne—Lipschütz	62
12 Mühlock—Kostich . .	25	54 Schulten—Morphy . .	63
13 Tarrasch—Alekhine . .	27	55 Spielmann—Tarrasch .	64
14 Sämisch—Nimzovitch .	27	58 Cukierman—Tartakover	67
15 Alekhine—Bogoljuboff .	28	61 Study by Rinck . . .	71
16 Winter—Sultan Khan .	28	62 Mieses—X.	71
17 Enevoldsen—Thomas .	29	63 Bartolitch—Abkin . .	72
18 Dr. E. Lasker—Loman .	36	64 Study by Stamma . .	73
19 Study by Sehwers . .	36	65 Study by Stamma . .	73
20 Study by Rinck . . .	37	66 Janowski—Marshall .	74
21 X.—Präger . . .	37	67 Paulsen—Morphy . .	74
22 Alekhine—Capablanca .	39	68 Nimzovitch—Tartakover	75
23 Study by Kubbel . .	39	69 Levitzky—Marshall . .	75
24 Znosko-Borovsky—Salwe	40	70 Spielmann—X. . . .	76
25 End of Study by Kubbel	40	71 Schiffers—Tchigorin .	77
26 Study by Kubbel . .	41	72 Study by Anderssen .	77
27 Tarrasch—Walbrodt .	42	73 X.—Znosko-Borovsky .	78
29 Euwe—Davidson . .	45	76 Morphy—Löwenthal .	81
30 Yates—Réti	47	77 Monticelli—Prokes . .	83
31 Atkinson—X. . . .	47	78 Lövenfisch—Freymann .	83
32 Study in the *French Defence*	48	79 Marshall—Kupchik . .	84
		80 Romanovsky — Rabinovitch	84
33 Znosko-Borovsky—Price	48	81 Réti—Alekhine . . .	85
34 Study (original source uncertain)	49	84 Adams—Torre . . .	88
		85 Study by Troitsky . .	88
37 Alekhine—Bogoljuboff .	52	86 Steinitz—Bardeleben .	89
38 Winter—Michell . . .	53	87 Morphy—Worrall . .	90
39 Biscay — Znosko-Borovsky	53	88 Nimzovitch—Marshall .	90
		89 Barnes—Morphy. . .	91

NO.		PAGE
90	Rotlevy—Rubinstein	92
93	Przepiórka—Cohn	95
94	Tchigorin—Gunsberg	95
95	Réti—Alekhine	96
96	Belsitzmann—Rubinstein	97
97	Spielmann—L'Hermet.	97
98	Anderssen—Zukertort	98
99	Piotrowski—Tannenbaum	98
102	Yates—Marin	107
103	Colle—O'Hanlon	108
104	Alekhine—Asgiersson	110
105	Fritz—Mason	111
106	Schlechter—Wolf	112
107	Marshall—Burn	114
108	Capablanca—Becker	115
109	Janowski—Chajes	116
110	Capablanca—Molina	117
113	Dr E. Lasker—Bauer	120
114	Alekhine—Drewitt	122
115	Nimzovitch—Tarrasch	122
118	Yates—Rubinstein	127
119	Brinckmann—Preusse	128
120	Alekhine—Sterk	129
121	Yates—Censer	130
122	Riemann—Pfeifer	132
123	Steinitz—Dr E. Lasker	132
124	Spielmann—Wahle	133
125	Becker—Carls	134
128	Mansfield—Znosko-Borovsky	137
129	Capablanca—Marshall	138
130	Charousek—Engländer	139
131	Burn—Cohn	139
132	Burn—Dr E. Lasker	140
135	Znosko-Borovsky—Noteboom	143
136	Hamlisch—X.	144
137	Holzhausen—Tarrasch	144
138	Alekhine—Feldt	145
139	Bernstein—Stahlberg	146
140	Tylor—Koltanowski	146
141	Hochmair—Heeren	148
142	Leonhardt—X.	148
145	Anderssen—Schallopp	151
146	Spielmann—Flamberg	151
147	Réti—Tartakover	153
148	Nimzovitch—Alapin	153
149	Morphy—Brunswick and Isouard	154
150	Anderssen—Hillel	155
151	Anderssen—Dufresne	156
152	Znosko-Borovsky—X.	157
153	Lilienthal—Capablanca	157
154	Alekhine—Lövenfisch	159
155	Anderssen—Kieseritzky	160
156	Steiner—Szabay	161
157	Steinitz—Winawer	161
160	Znosko-Borovsky—Mattison	164
161	Alekhine—Rubinstein	164
162	Capablanca—Alekhine	165
163	Nimzovitch—Duhm	166
164	Leonhardt—Spielmann	167
165	Albin—Réti	167
166	Vigodchikoff—Alekhine	168
167	Sämisch—Grünfeld	168
168	Viakhireff—Alekhine	169
169	Nimzovitch—Rubinstein	170
170	Blumenfeld—Alekhine	171
171	Vygodchikoff—Alekhine	172
172	Capablanca—Marshall	172
173	Canal—Johner	173
174	Bogoljuboff—Ahues	173
177	Kaufmann—Réti	178
178	Réti—Alekhine	179
179	Alekhine—Prat	181
180	Alekhine—Sterk	182
181	Alekhine—Bogoljuboff	182
182	Dr E. Lasker—Showalter	183
183	Sämisch—Alekhine	185
184	Alekhine—Grünfeld	186
185	Vidmar—Capablanca	188
186	Capablanca—Alekhine	188
187	Alekhine—Blümich	189
188	Capablanca—Marshall	190
189	Capablanca—Bogoljuboff	191
190	Pillsbury—Tarrasch	191
191	Znosko-Borovsky—Alekhine	192
192	Capablanca—Dus-Khotimirsky	193

NO.	PAGE	NO.	PAGE
193 Capablanca—Dus-Khotimirsky	. . 195	197 Kostich — Znosko-Borovsky	 201
194 Thomas—Botvinnik	. 196	198 Tarrasch—Dr E. Lasker	202
195 Pillsbury—Dr E. Lasker	198	199 Euwe—Alekhine	. . 206
196 Olland—Alekhine	. . 200	200 Euwe—Alekhine	. . 206

SOLUTIONS TO EXERCISES

P. 43. No. 28 (Study by Stamma).—1 B – Q4, K × B; 2 P – Kt8(=Q), P – Kt8(=Q); 3 Q – Kt6 ch and 4 Q × Q.

P. 50. No. 35 (Zukertort—Englisch).—1 Q – Kt5, Q × Q; 2 P – B8(=Q) ch, K – B2; 3 Q × Kt ch, K × Q; 4 Kt – B7 ch and 5 Kt × Q.

P. 50. No. 36 (Golombek—Krogius).—1 Kt × BP, Kt – Q6 ch; 2 K – Kt3, Kt × R; 3 Kt × R, P × P; 4 P × P, P – Kt4; 5 B – K4, Resigns.

P. 57. No. 43 (Nimzovitch—Capablanca).—1 . . R – B7; 2 Q – R6, P – K4; 3 B × KP, R(Q1) – Q7; 4 Q – Kt7 (4 R – KB1, Q × KP. Or 4 Q – B1, Q – Q4; 5 B – Q4, Q – KR4; 6 P – KR4, Q – B6), R × P; 5 P – Kt 4, Q – K3; 6 B – Kt3, R × P; 7 Q – B3 (7 B × R, Q × KtP ch; 8 K – R1, Q – R6), R(R7) – Kt7 ch; 8 Q × R, R × Q ch; 9 K × Q, Q × KtP, and wins.

P. 57. No. 44 (Marshall—Stoltz).—1 . . P – K4!; 2 Q × KP (better was 2 Q – Q1), R – B3; 3 P – K4 (if 3 K – R1, then Q – R6; 4 R – KKt1, Q × BP ch; 5 R – Kt2, R – KKt3, and White must give up his Q), P – Q5; 4 R – Q3, Q – R6; 5 R × P, R – Kt3 ch, and wins.

P. 65. No. 56 (Fink—Alekhine).—1 . . B – Kt4, and wins.

P. 65. No. 57 (Znosko-Borovsky—Mattison).—1 . . Kt – R4?; 2 R – R1, Kt – B5 ch; 3 P × Kt, R – KKt1; 4 R – R8, and wins.

P. 68. No. 59 (Johnston—Marshall).—1 Kt – K7 dbl. ch, K – R1; 2 Kt – Kt6 ch, P × Kt; 3 P × Kt dis. ch, and wins.

P. 68. No. 60 (Yonge—Watts).—1 . . B × Kt; 2 P × B, Kt × B; 3 Q × Kt (immediately fatal, but 3 K × Kt also loses quickly), R – K1 ch; 4 Q – K3, Q – R4 ch; 5 P – Kt4, P × P i.p. dbl. ch. mate

P. 79. No. 74 (Botvinnik—Chekover).—1 Kt – Kt5, P × Kt; 2 P × P, Kt(B1) – Q2; 3 Kt × P, K × Kt; 4 P – Kt6 ch,

K – Kt1; 5 Q × P ch, K – R1; 6 Q – R3 ch, K – Kt1;
7 B – B5, Kt – B1; 8 B – K6 ch, Kt × B; 9 Q × Kt ch,
K – R1;   10 Q – R3 ch, K – Kt1;   11 R × Kt, B × R;
12 Q – R7 ch, K – B1; 13 R – K1, B – K4; 14 Q – R8 ch,
K – K2; 15 Q × P ch, K – Q3; 16 Q × B ch, K – Q2;
17 Q – B5 ch, K – B3; 18 P – Q5 ch, K – B4; 19 B – R3 ch,
K × P; 20 Q – K4 ch, K – B6; 21 B – Kt4 ch, K – Kt7;
22 Q – Kt1 mate.

P. 79.   No. 75 (Ed. Lasker—Thomas).—1 Q × P ch, K × Q;
2 Kt × B dbl. ch, K – R3; 3 Kt(K5) – Kt4 ch, K – Kt4;
4 P – R4 ch, K – B5; 5 P – Kt3 ch, K – B6; 6 B – K2 ch.
(This was the move actually played; but 6 K – B1 or
6 Castles K, followed by 7 Kt – R2 mate, would have
shortened the solution by one move), K – Kt2; 7 R – R2
ch, K – Kt8; 8 K – Q2 dis. ch mate.   Or 8 Castles mate.

P. 86.   No. 82 (Bernstein—Znosko-Borovsky).—1 Kt × P,
P × Kt; 2 Q × KP ch, K – R1 (K – Kt2; 3 Q – K7 ch. Or
K – B1; 3 Q – Q6 ch); 3 Q – K7, Q – Kt1; 4 R × P ch,
Q × R; 5 Q × R ch, Kt – B1; 6 Q × Kt ch, Q – Kt1; 7 Q × P
ch, and wins.

P. 86.   No. 83 (Torre—Dr. E. Lasker).—1 B – B6, Q × Q;
2 R × P ch, K – R1; 3 R × P dis. ch, K – Kt1; 4 R – Kt7 ch,
K – R1; 5 R × B dis. ch, K – Kt1; 6 R – Kt7 ch, K – R1;
7 R – Kt5 dis. ch, K – R2; 8 R × Q, K – Kt3; 9 R – R3,
K × B; 10 R × P ch, and wins.

P. 93.   No. 91 (Giertz—Kremser).—1 R – B8 ch, Q × R;
2 Q × P ch, R × Q; 3 R × R mate.

P. 93.   No. 92 (Reggio—Mieses).—1 . . R – Kt6; 2 Q × R, B – R5
and wins the Q; for if 3 Q × B, Q – K6 ch and mate next
move.

P. 99.   No. 100 (Sterk—Marshall).—1 Q × Kt, P × Q; 2 P × P
dbl. ch, K – R2; 3 P – B8(= Kt) ch, K – R1; 4 R – Kt8
mate.

P. 99.   No. 101 (Pollock—Tchigorin).—1 . . B × RP; 2 P × B,
R(K1) × B; 3 P × R, Q × P, and wins.

P. 118.   No. 111 (Schallopp—Gossip).—1 B × P ch, K × B;
2 Kt – Kt5 ch, B × Kt; 3 Q × B ch, B – R3; 4 B × B, P × B;
5 R – B6, and wins.

P. 118.   No. 112 (Richter—Schober).—1 R – R3, P – KKt3;
2 Q × P ch, R – Kt2; 3 Q × Kt, Q × R (Q × Q; 4 Kt – B6 ch,
K – B2; 5 Kt × Q, R – Kt3; 6 R × P ch, K × Kt; 7 R × P,
etc.); 4 B × R, R × Q; 5 Kt – B6 ch, K – B2; 6 P × Q, R – K3;
7 B – R8, P – KR4; 8 P – B3, Resigns.

P. 124.   No. 116 (Sämisch—Janowski).—1 Q – R6, Resigns; for,
if P × Q, then of course 2 R – Kt3 mate.

P. 124.   No. 117 (P. W. Sergeant—Griffith).—1 Kt × RP,
K × Kt; 2 Q – R3 ch, K – Kt1; 3 Kt – B6, P × Kt?; 4 P × P,
Kt – Kt4;   5 Q – R6,   Kt(Q1) – K3;   6 P × B,   P – B3;
7 P × R(= Q) ch, R × Q; 8 B × P, Kt – B6 ch; 9 P × Kt,

K – B2; 10 B – Kt7, Kt × B (R – KKt1; 11 Q – B6 ch,
and Black's R is lost); 11 R – K7 ch, Resigns. This is
not one of those cases where it is advisable to accept all
the sacrifices. 3..B × Kt; 4 P × B, P – Kt3 would have
caused an awkward pause in White's attack.

P. 135. No. 126 (Torre — Verlinsky).—1 B × KtP, B × Q;
2 B – B7 ch, K – R1; 3 B × R, and wins.

P. 135. No. 127 (Charousek—Burn).—1 B × P, P × B;
2 Q – R7 ch, K – B1; 3 Q × P, Q – R8 ch; 4 K – Q2,
Q – R4 ch; 5 P – Kt4 (obtaining a flight-square for his K
without allowing an exchange of Qs), Q × P ch; 6 K – K2,
Q – K2; 7 R – R4, B – K3; 8 Kt – R7 ch, K – Kt1. White
here lost with 9 QR – KR1?; but with 9 Kt – Kt5 he should
have drawn.

P. 141. No. 133 (Nyholm—Post).—1 R × P, P × R; 2 Q – Kt6
ch, K – R1; 3 Q × P ch, K – Kt1; 4 P – Kt6, and wins.

P. 142.   No. 134 (Tartakover—Schlechter).—1 Kt × P, K × Kt;
2 Q – R5 ch, K – Kt1 (K – B1; 3 B × P. Or K – K2;
3 Q – Kt6, R – B1; 4 B × P, P × B; 5 QR – K1 ch); 3 R × Kt,
R – K8 ch; 4 R – B1, R × R ch; 5 B × R, B – B1; 6 B × P,
Q – B3; 7 B – Kt5, Q – B4; 8 Kt – Q6, B × Kt; 9 B – B4 ch,
B – K3; 10 R – KB1, Q × R ch (Q – K4; 11 Q – K8 ch);
11 B × Q, and wins.

P. 149. No. 143 (Colle—Grünfeld).—1 Kt – Kt5, P – Kt3;
2 Kt × BP, K × Kt; 3 Q × P ch, K – Kt2; 4 P – Q5, Kt – B4;
5 Kt – B5 ch, K – B1; 6 Q – K3, P × Kt; 7 Q – R6 ch,
K – B2; 8 B × P, and wins.

P. 149. No. 144 (Gerschenkron—Fischer).—1 Kt × P, K × Kt?
(Q – Kt3 was necessary); 2 Q × P ch, K × Q; 3 Kt – Kt5
mate.

P. 162. No. 158 (Göring—Schallopp).—1..Q × R ch; 2 B × Q,
B – B5 ch; 3 B – Q2, R – K8 mate.

P. 162. No. 159 (Koltanowski—X.).—1 Q – Q8 ch, K × Q;
2 B – R5 dbl. ch and mate next move.

P. 174. No. 175 (Asztalos—Vidmar).—1 R × B, Q × R;
2 P – B7, and wins.

P. 174. No. 176 (Schönmann—Rodatz).—1 R × Kt, P × R;
2 P – B6 ch, K – Kt1; 3 Q – Kt 3, R × Kt; 4 P × R, R – R4;
5 R – B5, K – B1; 6 R × P, R – R1; 7 R – R5, Resigns.

THE END

A CATALOGUE OF SELECTED DOVER BOOKS
IN ALL FIELDS OF INTEREST

A CATALOGUE OF SELECTED DOVER BOOKS
IN ALL FIELDS OF INTEREST

AMERICA'S OLD MASTERS, James T. Flexner. Four men emerged unexpectedly from provincial 18th century America to leadership in European art: Benjamin West, J. S. Copley, C. R. Peale, Gilbert Stuart. Brilliant coverage of lives and contributions. Revised, 1967 edition. 69 plates. 365pp. of text.
21806-6 Paperbound $3.00

FIRST FLOWERS OF OUR WILDERNESS: AMERICAN PAINTING, THE COLONIAL PERIOD, James T. Flexner. Painters, and regional painting traditions from earliest Colonial times up to the emergence of Copley, West and Peale Sr., Foster, Gustavus Hesselius, Feke, John Smibert and many anonymous painters in the primitive manner. Engaging presentation, with 162 illustrations. xxii + 368pp.
22180-6 Paperbound $3.50

THE LIGHT OF DISTANT SKIES: AMERICAN PAINTING, 1760-1835, James T. Flexner. The great generation of early American painters goes to Europe to learn and to teach: West, Copley, Gilbert Stuart and others. Allston, Trumbull, Morse; also contemporary American painters—primitives, derivatives, academics—who remained in America. 102 illustrations. xiii + 306pp.
22179-2 Paperbound $3.50

A HISTORY OF THE RISE AND PROGRESS OF THE ARTS OF DESIGN IN THE UNITED STATES, William Dunlap. Much the richest mine of information on early American painters, sculptors, architects, engravers, miniaturists, etc. The only source of information for scores of artists, the major primary source for many others. Unabridged reprint of rare original 1834 edition, with new introduction by James T. Flexner, and 394 new illustrations. Edited by Rita Weiss. 6⅝ x 9⅝.
21695-0, 21696-9, 21697-7 Three volumes, Paperbound $15.00

EPOCHS OF CHINESE AND JAPANESE ART, Ernest F. Fenollosa. From primitive Chinese art to the 20th century, thorough history, explanation of every important art period and form, including Japanese woodcuts; main stress on China and Japan, but Tibet, Korea also included. Still unexcelled for its detailed, rich coverage of cultural background, aesthetic elements, diffusion studies, particularly of the historical period. 2nd, 1913 edition. 242 illustrations. lii + 439pp. of text.
20364-6, 20365-4 Two volumes, Paperbound $6.00

THE GENTLE ART OF MAKING ENEMIES, James A. M. Whistler. Greatest wit of his day deflates Oscar Wilde, Ruskin, Swinburne; strikes back at inane critics, exhibitions, art journalism; aesthetics of impressionist revolution in most striking form. Highly readable classic by great painter. Reproduction of edition designed by Whistler. Introduction by Alfred Werner. xxxvi + 334pp.
21875-9 Paperbound $3.00

VISUAL ILLUSIONS: THEIR CAUSES, CHARACTERISTICS, AND APPLICATIONS, Matthew Luckiesh. Thorough description and discussion of optical illusion, geometric and perspective, particularly; size and shape distortions, illusions of color, of motion; natural illusions; use of illusion in art and magic, industry, etc. Most useful today with op art, also for classical art. Scores of effects illustrated. Introduction by William H. Ittleson. 100 illustrations. xxi + 252pp.

21530-X Paperbound $2.00

A HANDBOOK OF ANATOMY FOR ART STUDENTS, Arthur Thomson. Thorough, virtually exhaustive coverage of skeletal structure, musculature, etc. Full text, supplemented by anatomical diagrams and drawings and by photographs of undraped figures. Unique in its comparison of male and female forms, pointing out differences of contour, texture, form. 211 figures, 40 drawings, 86 photographs. xx + 459pp. 5⅜ x 8⅜. 21163-0 Paperbound $3.50

150 MASTERPIECES OF DRAWING, Selected by Anthony Toney. Full page reproductions of drawings from the early 16th to the end of the 18th century, all beautifully reproduced: Rembrandt, Michelangelo, Dürer, Fragonard, Urs, Graf, Wouwerman, many others. First-rate browsing book, model book for artists. xviii + 150pp. 8⅜ x 11¼. 21032-4 Paperbound¹ $2.50

THE LATER WORK OF AUBREY BEARDSLEY, Aubrey Beardsley. Exotic, erotic, ironic masterpieces in full maturity: Comedy Ballet, Venus and Tannhauser, Pierrot, Lysistrata, Rape of the Lock, Savoy material, Ali Baba, Volpone, etc. This material revolutionized the art world, and is still powerful, fresh, brilliant. With *The Early Work,* all Beardsley's finest work. 174 plates, 2 in color. xiv + 176pp. 8⅛ x 11. 21817-1 Paperbound $3.75

DRAWINGS OF REMBRANDT, Rembrandt van Rijn. Complete reproduction of fabulously rare edition by Lippmann and Hofstede de Groot, completely reedited, updated, improved by Prof. Seymour Slive, Fogg Museum. Portraits, Biblical sketches, landscapes, Oriental types, nudes, episodes from classical mythology—All Rembrandt's fertile genius. Also selection of drawings by his pupils and followers. "Stunning volumes," *Saturday Review.* 550 illustrations. lxxviii + 552pp. 9⅛ x 12¼. 21485-0, 21486-9 Two volumes, Paperbound $10.00

THE DISASTERS OF WAR, Francisco Goya. One of the masterpieces of Western civilization—83 etchings that record Goya's shattering, bitter reaction to the Napoleonic war that swept through Spain after the insurrection of 1808 and to war in general. Reprint of the first edition, with three additional plates from Boston's Museum of Fine Arts. All plates facsimile size. Introduction by Philip Hofer, Fogg Museum. v + 97pp. 9⅜ x 8¼. 21872-4 Paperbound $2.50

GRAPHIC WORKS OF ODILON REDON. Largest collection of Redon's graphic works ever assembled: 172 lithographs, 28 etchings and engravings, 9 drawings. These include some of his most famous works. All the plates from *Odilon Redon: oeuvre graphique complet,* plus additional plates. New introduction and caption translations by Alfred Werner. 209 illustrations. xxvii + 209pp. 9⅛ x 12¼. 21966-8 Paperbound $4.50

ADVENTURES OF AN AFRICAN SLAVER, Theodore Canot. Edited by Brantz Mayer. A detailed portrayal of slavery and the slave trade, 1820-1840. Canot, an established trader along the African coast, describes the slave economy of the African kingdoms, the treatment of captured negroes, the extensive journeys in the interior to gather slaves, slave revolts and their suppression, harems, bribes, and much more. Full and unabridged republication of 1854 edition. Introduction by Malcom Cowley. 16 illustrations. xvii + 448pp. 22456-2 Paperbound $3.50

MY BONDAGE AND MY FREEDOM, Frederick Douglass. Born and brought up in slavery, Douglass witnessed its horrors and experienced its cruelties, but went on to become one of the most outspoken forces in the American anti-slavery movement. Considered the best of his autobiographies, this book graphically describes the inhuman treatment of slaves, its effects on slave owners and slave families, and how Douglass's determination led him to a new life. Unaltered reprint of 1st (1855) edition. xxxii + 464pp. 22457-0 Paperbound $3.50

THE INDIANS' BOOK, recorded and edited by Natalie Curtis. Lore, music, narratives, dozens of drawings by Indians themselves from an authoritative and important survey of native culture among Plains, Southwestern, Lake and Pueblo Indians. Standard work in popular ethnomusicology. 149 songs in full notation. 23 drawings, 23 photos. xxxi + 584pp. 6⅝ x 9⅜. 21939-9 Paperbound $5.00

DICTIONARY OF AMERICAN PORTRAITS, edited by Hayward and Blanche Cirker. 4024 portraits of 4000 most important Americans, colonial days to 1905 (with a few important categories, like Presidents, to present). Pioneers, explorers, colonial figures, U. S. officials, politicians, writers, military and naval men, scientists, inventors, manufacturers, jurists, actors, historians, educators, notorious figures, Indian chiefs, etc. All authentic contemporary likenesses. The only work of its kind in existence; supplements all biographical sources for libraries. Indispensable to anyone working with American history. 8,000-item classified index, finding lists, other aids. xiv + 756pp. 9¼ x 12¾. 21823-6 Clothbound $30.00

TRITTON'S GUIDE TO BETTER WINE AND BEER MAKING FOR BEGINNERS, S. M. Tritton. All you need to know to make family-sized quantities of over 100 types of grape, fruit, herb and vegetable wines; as well as beers, mead, cider, etc. Complete recipes, advice as to equipment, procedures such as fermenting, bottling, and storing wines. Recipes given in British, U. S., and metric measures. Accompanying booklet lists sources in U. S. A. where ingredients may be bought, and additional information. 11 illustrations. 157pp. 5⅝ x 8⅛. 22090-7 **Paperbound $2.00**

GARDENING WITH HERBS FOR FLAVOR AND FRAGRANCE, Helen M. Fox. How to grow herbs in your own garden, how to use them in your cooking (over 55 recipes included), legends and myths associated with each species, uses in medicine, perfumes, etc.—these are elements of one of the few books written especially for American herb fanciers. Guides you step-by-step from soil preparation to harvesting and storage for each type of herb. 12 drawings by Louise Mansfield. xiv + 334pp. 22540-2 Paperbound $2.50

JOHANN SEBASTIAN BACH, Philipp Spitta. One of the great classics of musicology, this definitive analysis of Bach's music (and life) has never been surpassed. Lucid, nontechnical analyses of hundreds of pieces (30 pages devoted to St. Matthew Passion, 26 to B Minor Mass). Also includes major analysis of 18th-century music. 450 musical examples. 40-page musical supplement. Total of xx + 1799pp.
(EUK) 22278-0, 22279-9 Two volumes, Clothbound $25.00

MOZART AND HIS PIANO CONCERTOS, Cuthbert Girdlestone. The only full-length study of an important area of Mozart's creativity. Provides detailed analyses of all 23 concertos, traces inspirational sources. 417 musical examples. Second edition. 509pp.
21271-8 Paperbound $4.50

THE PERFECT WAGNERITE: A COMMENTARY ON THE NIBLUNG'S RING, George Bernard Shaw. Brilliant and still relevant criticism in remarkable essays on Wagner's Ring cycle, Shaw's ideas on political and social ideology behind the plots, role of Leitmotifs, vocal requisites, etc. Prefaces. xxi + 136pp.
(USO) 21707-8 Paperbound $1.75

DON GIOVANNI, W. A. Mozart. Complete libretto, modern English translation; biographies of composer and librettist; accounts of early performances and critical reaction. Lavishly illustrated. All the material you need to understand and appreciate this great work. Dover Opera Guide and Libretto Series; translated and introduced by Ellen Bleiler. 92 illustrations. 209pp.
21134-7 Paperbound $2.00

BASIC ELECTRICITY, U. S. Bureau of Naval Personel. Originally a training course, best non-technical coverage of basic theory of electricity and its applications. Fundamental concepts, batteries, circuits, conductors and wiring techniques, AC and DC, inductance and capacitance, generators, motors, transformers, magnetic amplifiers, synchros, servomechanisms, etc. Also covers blue-prints, electrical diagrams, etc. Many questions, with answers. 349 illustrations. x + 448pp. 6½ x 9¼.
20973-3 Paperbound $3.50

REPRODUCTION OF SOUND, Edgar Villchur. Thorough coverage for laymen of high fidelity systems, reproducing systems in general, needles, amplifiers, preamps, loudspeakers, feedback, explaining physical background. "A rare talent for making technicalities vividly comprehensible," R. Darrell, *High Fidelity*. 69 figures
iv + 92pp.
21515-6 Paperbound $1.35

HEAR ME TALKIN' TO YA: THE STORY OF JAZZ AS TOLD BY THE MEN WHO MADE IT, Nat Shapiro and Nat Hentoff. Louis Armstrong, Fats Waller, Jo Jones, Clarence Williams, Billy Holiday, Duke Ellington, Jelly Roll Morton and dozens of other jazz greats tell how it was in Chicago's South Side, New Orleans, depression Harlem and the modern West Coast as jazz was born and grew. xvi + 429pp.
21726-4 Paperbound $3.95

FABLES OF AESOP, translated by Sir Roger L'Estrange. A reproduction of the very rare 1931 Paris edition; a selection of the most interesting fables, together with 50 imaginative drawings by Alexander Calder. v + 128pp. 6½x9¼.
21780-9 Paperbound $1.50

"ESSENTIAL GRAMMAR" SERIES

All you really need to know about modern, colloquial grammar. Many educational shortcuts help you learn faster, understand better. Detailed cognate lists teach you to recognize similarities between English and foreign words and roots—make learning vocabulary easy and interesting. Excellent for independent study or as a supplement to record courses.

ESSENTIAL FRENCH GRAMMAR, Seymour Resnick. 2500-item cognate list. 159pp.
(EBE) 20419-7 Paperbound $1.50

ESSENTIAL GERMAN GRAMMAR, Guy Stern and Everett F. Bleiler. Unusual shortcuts on noun declension, word order, compound verbs. 124pp.
(EBE) 20422-7 Paperbound $1.25

ESSENTIAL ITALIAN GRAMMAR, Olga Ragusa. 111pp.
(EBE) 20779-X Paperbound $1.25

ESSENTIAL JAPANESE GRAMMAR, Everett F. Bleiler. In Romaji transcription; no characters needed. Japanese grammar is regular and simple. 156pp.
21027-8 Paperbound $1.50

ESSENTIAL PORTUGUESE GRAMMAR, Alexander da R. Prista. vi + 114pp.
21650-0 Paperbound $1.35

ESSENTIAL SPANISH GRAMMAR, Seymour Resnick. 2500 word cognate list. 115pp.
(EBE) 20780-3 Paperbound $1.25

ESSENTIAL ENGLISH GRAMMAR, Philip Gucker. Combines best features of modern, functional and traditional approaches. For refresher, class use, home study. x + 177pp.
21649-7 Paperbound $1.75

A PHRASE AND SENTENCE DICTIONARY OF SPOKEN SPANISH. Prepared for U. S. War Department by U. S. linguists. As above, unit is idiom, phrase or sentence rather than word. English-Spanish and Spanish-English sections contain modern equivalents of over 18,000 sentences. Introduction and appendix as above. iv + 513pp.
20495-2 Paperbound $3.50

A PHRASE AND SENTENCE DICTIONARY OF SPOKEN RUSSIAN. Dictionary prepared for U. S. War Department by U. S. linguists. Basic unit is not the word, but the idiom, phrase or sentence. English-Russian and Russian-English sections contain modern equivalents for over 30,000 phrases. Grammatical introduction covers phonetics, writing, syntax. Appendix of word lists for food, numbers, geographical names, etc. vi + 573 pp. 6⅛ x 9¼.
20496-0 Paperbound $5.50

CONVERSATIONAL CHINESE FOR BEGINNERS, Morris Swadesh. Phonetic system, beginner's course in Pai Hua Mandarin Chinese covering most important, most useful speech patterns. Emphasis on modern colloquial usage. Formerly *Chinese in Your Pocket*. xvi + 158pp.
21123-1 Paperbound $1.75

ОшибокЭ

TWO LITTLE SAVAGES; BEING THE ADVENTURES OF TWO BOYS WHO LIVED AS INDIANS AND WHAT THEY LEARNED, Ernest Thompson Seton. Great classic of nature and boyhood provides a vast range of woodlore in most palatable form, a genuinely entertaining story. Two farm boys build a teepee in woods and live in it for a month, working out Indian solutions to living problems, star lore, birds and animals, plants, etc. 293 illustrations. vii + 286pp.

20985-7 Paperbound $2.50

PETER PIPER'S PRACTICAL PRINCIPLES OF PLAIN & PERFECT PRONUNCIATION. Alliterative jingles and tongue-twisters of surprising charm, that made their first appearance in America about 1830. Republished in full with the spirited woodcut illustrations from this earliest American edition. 32pp. 4½ x 6⅜.

22560-7 Paperbound $1.00

SCIENCE EXPERIMENTS AND AMUSEMENTS FOR CHILDREN, Charles Vivian. 73 easy experiments, requiring only materials found at home or easily available, such as candles, coins, steel wool, etc.; illustrate basic phenomena like vacuum, simple chemical reaction, etc. All safe. Modern, well-planned. Formerly *Science Games for Children*. 102 photos, numerous drawings. 96pp. 6⅛ x 9¼.

21856-2 Paperbound $1.25

AN INTRODUCTION TO CHESS MOVES AND TACTICS SIMPLY EXPLAINED, Leonard Barden. Informal intermediate introduction, quite strong in explaining reasons for moves. Covers basic material, tactics, important openings, traps, positional play in middle game, end game. Attempts to isolate patterns and recurrent configurations. Formerly *Chess*. 58 figures. 102pp. (USO) 21210-6 Paperbound $1.25

LASKER'S MANUAL OF CHESS, Dr. Emanuel Lasker. Lasker was not only one of the five great World Champions, he was also one of the ablest expositors, theorists, and analysts. In many ways, his Manual, permeated with his philosophy of battle, filled with keen insights, is one of the greatest works ever written on chess. Filled with analyzed games by the great players. A single-volume library that will profit almost any chess player, beginner or master. 308 diagrams. xli x 349pp.

20640-8 Paperbound $2.75

THE MASTER BOOK OF MATHEMATICAL RECREATIONS, Fred Schuh. In opinion of many the finest work ever prepared on mathematical puzzles, stunts, recreations; exhaustively thorough explanations of mathematics involved, analysis of effects, citation of puzzles and games. Mathematics involved is elementary. Translated by F. Göbel. 194 figures. xxiv + 430pp. 22134-2 Paperbound $4.00

MATHEMATICS, MAGIC AND MYSTERY, Martin Gardner. Puzzle editor for Scientific American explains mathematics behind various mystifying tricks: card tricks, stage "mind reading," coin and match tricks, counting out games, geometric dissections, etc. Probability sets, theory of numbers clearly explained. Also provides more than 400 tricks, guaranteed to work, that you can do. 135 illustrations. xii + 176pp.

20335-2 Paperbound $2.00

THE ARCHITECTURE OF COUNTRY HOUSES, Andrew J. Downing. Together with Vaux's *Villas and Cottages* this is the basic book for Hudson River Gothic architecture of the middle Victorian period. Full, sound discussions of general aspects of housing, architecture, style, decoration, furnishing, together with scores of detailed house plans, illustrations of specific buildings, accompanied by full text. Perhaps the most influential single American architectural book. 1850 edition. Introduction by J. Stewart Johnson. 321 figures, 34 architectural designs. xvi + 560pp.
22003-6 Paperbound $5.00

LOST EXAMPLES OF COLONIAL ARCHITECTURE, John Mead Howells. Full-page photographs of buildings that have disappeared or been so altered as to be denatured, including many designed by major early American architects. 245 plates. xvii + 248pp. 7⅞ x 10¾.
21143-6 Paperbound $3.50

DOMESTIC ARCHITECTURE OF THE AMERICAN COLONIES AND OF THE EARLY REPUBLIC, Fiske Kimball. Foremost architect and restorer of Williamsburg and Monticello covers nearly 200 homes between 1620-1825. Architectural details, construction, style features, special fixtures, floor plans, etc. Generally considered finest work in its area. 219 illustrations of houses, doorways, windows, capital mantels. xx + 314pp. 7⅞ x 10¾.
21743-4 Paperbound $4.00

EARLY AMERICAN ROOMS: 1650-1858, edited by Russell Hawes Kettell. Tour of 12 rooms, each representative of a different era in American history and each furnished, decorated, designed and occupied in the style of the era. 72 plans and elevations, 8-page color section, etc., show fabrics, wall papers, arrangements, etc. Full descriptive text. xvii + 200pp. of text. 8⅜ x 11¼.
21633-0 Paperbound $5.00

THE FITZWILLIAM VIRGINAL BOOK, edited by J. Fuller Maitland and W. B. Squire. Full modern printing of famous early 17th-century ms. volume of 300 works by Morley, Byrd, Bull, Gibbons, etc. For piano or other modern keyboard instrument; easy to read format. xxxvi + 938pp. 8⅜ x 11.
21068-5, 21069-3 Two volumes, Paperbound $12.00

KEYBOARD MUSIC, Johann Sebastian Bach. Bach Gesellschaft edition. A rich selection of Bach's masterpieces for the harpsichord: the six English Suites, six French Suites, the six Partitas (Clavierübung part I), the Goldberg Variations (Clavierübung part IV), the fifteen Two-Part Inventions and the fifteen Three-Part Sinfonias. Clearly reproduced on large sheets with ample margins; eminently playable. vi + 312pp. 8⅛ x 11.
22360-4 Paperbound $5.00

THE MUSIC OF BACH: AN INTRODUCTION, Charles Sanford Terry. A fine, nontechnical introduction to Bach's music, both instrumental and vocal. Covers organ music, chamber music, passion music, other types. Analyzes themes, developments, innovations. x + 114pp.
21075-8 Paperbound $1.95

BEETHOVEN AND HIS NINE SYMPHONIES, Sir George Grove. Noted British musicologist provides best history, analysis, commentary on symphonies. Very thorough, rigorously accurate; necessary to both advanced student and amateur music lover. 436 musical passages. vii + 407 pp.
20334-4 Paperbound $4.00

PLANETS, STARS AND GALAXIES: DESCRIPTIVE ASTRONOMY FOR BEGINNERS, A. E. Fanning. Comprehensive introductory survey of astronomy: the sun, solar system, stars, galaxies, universe, cosmology; up-to-date, including quasars, radio stars, etc. Preface by Prof. Donald Menzel. 24pp. of photographs. 189pp. 5¼ x 8¼.
21680-2 Paperbound $2.50

TEACH YOURSELF CALCULUS, P. Abbott. With a good background in algebra and trig, you can teach yourself calculus with this book. Simple, straightforward introduction to functions of all kinds, integration, differentiation, series, etc. "Students who are beginning to study calculus method will derive great help from this book." Faraday House Journal. 308pp. 20683-1 Clothbound $2.50

TEACH YOURSELF TRIGONOMETRY, P. Abbott. Geometrical foundations, indices and logarithms, ratios, angles, circular measure, etc. are presented in this sound, easy-to-use text. Excellent for the beginner or as a brush up, this text carries the student through the solution of triangles. 204pp. 20682-3 Clothbound $2.00

BASIC MACHINES AND HOW THEY WORK, U. S. Bureau of Naval Personnel. Originally used in U.S. Naval training schools, this book clearly explains the operation of a progression of machines, from the simplest—lever, wheel and axle, inclined plane, wedge, screw—to the most complex—typewriter, internal combustion engine, computer mechanism. Utilizing an approach that requires only an elementary understanding of mathematics, these explanations build logically upon each other and are assisted by over 200 drawings and diagrams. Perfect as a technical school manual or as a self-teaching aid to the layman. 204 figures. Preface. Index. vii + 161pp. 6½ x 9¼. 21709-4 Paperbound $2.50

THE FRIENDLY STARS, Martha Evans Martin. Classic has taught naked-eye observation of stars, planets to hundreds of thousands, still not surpassed for charm, lucidity, adequacy. Completely updated by Professor Donald H. Menzel, Harvard Observatory. 25 illustrations. 16 x 30 chart. x + 147pp. 21099-5 Paperbound $2.00

MUSIC OF THE SPHERES: THE MATERIAL UNIVERSE FROM ATOM TO QUASAR, SIMPLY EXPLAINED, Guy Murchie. Extremely broad, brilliantly written popular account begins with the solar system and reaches to dividing line between matter and nonmatter; latest understandings presented with exceptional clarity. Volume One: Planets, stars, galaxies, cosmology, geology, celestial mechanics, latest astronomical discoveries; Volume Two: Matter, atoms, waves, radiation, relativity, chemical action, heat, nuclear energy, quantum theory, music, light, color, probability, antimatter, antigravity, and similar topics. 319 figures. 1967 (second) edition. Total of xx + 644pp. 21809-0, 21810-4 Two volumes, Paperbound $5.75

OLD-TIME SCHOOLS AND SCHOOL BOOKS, Clifton Johnson. Illustrations and rhymes from early primers, abundant quotations from early textbooks, many anecdotes of school life enliven this study of elementary schools from Puritans to middle 19th century. Introduction by Carl Withers. 234 illustrations. xxxiii + 381pp.
21031-6 Paperbound $4.00

A HISTORY OF COSTUME, Carl Köhler. Definitive history, based on surviving pieces of clothing primarily, and paintings, statues, etc. secondarily. Highly readable text, supplemented by 594 illustrations of costumes of the ancient Mediterranean peoples, Greece and Rome, the Teutonic prehistoric period; costumes of the Middle Ages, Renaissance, Baroque, 18th and 19th centuries. Clear, measured patterns are provided for many clothing articles. Approach is practical throughout. Enlarged by Emma von Sichart. 464pp. 21030-8 Paperbound $3.50

ORIENTAL RUGS, ANTIQUE AND MODERN, Walter A. Hawley. A complete and authoritative treatise on the Oriental rug—where they are made, by whom and how, designs and symbols, characteristics in detail of the six major groups, how to distinguish them and how to buy them. Detailed technical data is provided on periods, weaves, warps, wefts, textures, sides, ends and knots, although no technical background is required for an understanding. 11 color plates, 80 halftones, 4 maps. vi + 320pp. 6⅛ x 9⅛. 22366-3 Paperbound $5.00

TEN BOOKS ON ARCHITECTURE, Vitruvius. By any standards the most important book on architecture ever written. Early Roman discussion of aesthetics of building, construction methods, orders, sites, and every other aspect of architecture has inspired, instructed architecture for about 2,000 years. Stands behind Palladio, Michelangelo, Bramante, Wren, countless others. Definitive Morris H. Morgan translation. 68 illustrations. xii + 331pp. 20645-9 Paperbound . $3.00

THE FOUR BOOKS OF ARCHITECTURE, Andrea Palladio. Translated into every major Western European language in the two centuries following its publication in 1570, this has been one of the most influential books in the history of architecture. Complete reprint of the 1738 Isaac Ware edition. New introduction by Adolf Placzek, Columbia Univ. 216 plates. xxii + 110pp. of text. 9½ x 12¾. 21308-0 Clothbound $12.50

STICKS AND STONES: A STUDY OF AMERICAN ARCHITECTURE AND CIVILIZATION, Lewis Mumford.One of the great classics of American cultural history. American architecture from the medieval-inspired earliest forms to the early 20th century; evolution of structure and style, and reciprocal influences on environment. 21 photographic illustrations. 238pp. 20202-X Paperbound $2.00

THE AMERICAN BUILDER'S COMPANION, Asher Benjamin. The most widely used early 19th century architectural style and source book, for colonial up into Greek Revival periods. Extensive development of geometry of carpentering, construction of sashes, frames, doors, stairs; plans and elevations of domestic and other buildings. Hundreds of thousands of houses were built according to this book, now invaluable to historians, architects, restorers, etc. 1827 edition. 59 plates. 114pp. 7⅞ x 10¾. 22236-5 Paperbound $4.00

DUTCH HOUSES IN THE HUDSON VALLEY BEFORE 1776, Helen Wilkinson Reynolds. The standard survey of the Dutch colonial house and outbuildings, with constructional features, decoration, and local history associated with individual homesteads. Introduction by Franklin D. Roosevelt. Map. 150 illustrations. 469pp. 6⅝ x 9¼. 21469-9 Paperbound $5.00

DESIGN BY ACCIDENT; A BOOK OF "ACCIDENTAL EFFECTS" FOR ARTISTS AND DESIGNERS, James F. O'Brien. Create your own unique, striking, imaginative effects by "controlled accident" interaction of materials: paints and lacquers, oil and water based paints, splatter, crackling materials, shatter, similar items. Everything you do will be different; first book on this limitless art, so useful to both fine artist and commercial artist. Full instructions. 192 plates showing "accidents," 8 in color. viii + 215pp. 8⅜ x 11¼.   21942-9 Paperbound $3.75

THE BOOK OF SIGNS, Rudolf Koch. Famed German type designer draws 493 beautiful symbols: religious, mystical, alchemical, imperial, property marks, runes, etc. Remarkable fusion of traditional and modern. Good for suggestions of timelessness, smartness, modernity. Text. vi + 104pp. 6⅛ x 9¼.
                    20162-7 Paperbound $1.50

HISTORY OF INDIAN AND INDONESIAN ART, Ananda K. Coomaraswamy. An unabridged republication of one of the finest books by a great scholar in Eastern art. Rich in descriptive material, history, social backgrounds; Sunga reliefs, Rajput paintings, Gupta temples, Burmese frescoes, textiles, jewelry, sculpture, etc. 400 photos. viii + 423pp. 6⅜ x 9¾.   21436-2 Paperbound $5.00

PRIMITIVE ART, Franz Boas. America's foremost anthropologist surveys textiles, ceramics, woodcarving, basketry, metalwork, etc.; patterns, technology, creation of symbols, style origins. All areas of world, but very full on Northwest Coast Indians. More than 350 illustrations of baskets, boxes, totem poles, weapons, etc. 378 pp.
                    20025-6 Paperbound $3.00

THE GENTLEMAN AND CABINET MAKER'S DIRECTOR, Thomas Chippendale. Full reprint (third edition, 1762) of most influential furniture book of all time, by master cabinetmaker. 200 plates, illustrating chairs, sofas, mirrors, tables, cabinets, plus 24 photographs of surviving pieces. Biographical introduction by N. Bienenstock. vi + 249pp. 9⅞ x 12¾.   21601-2 Paperbound $5.00

AMERICAN ANTIQUE FURNITURE, Edgar G. Miller, Jr. The basic coverage of all American furniture before 1840. Individual chapters cover type of furniture—clocks, tables, sideboards, etc.—chronologically, with inexhaustible wealth of data. More than 2100 photographs, all identified, commented on. Essential to all early American collectors. Introduction by H. E. Keyes. vi + 1106pp. 7⅞ x 10¾.
                    21599-7, 21600-4 Two volumes, Paperbound $11.00

PENNSYLVANIA DUTCH AMERICAN FOLK ART, Henry J. Kauffman. 279 photos, 28 drawings of tulipware, Fraktur script, painted tinware, toys, flowered furniture, quilts, samplers, hex signs, house interiors, etc. Full descriptive text. Excellent for tourist, rewarding for designer, collector. Map. 146pp. 7⅞ x 10¾.
                    21205-X Paperbound $3.00

EARLY NEW ENGLAND GRAVESTONE RUBBINGS, Edmund V. Gillon, Jr. 43 photographs, 226 carefully reproduced rubbings show heavily symbolic, sometimes macabre early gravestones, up to early 19th century. Remarkable early American primitive art, occasionally strikingly beautiful; always powerful. Text. xxvi + 207pp. 8⅜ x 11¼.   21380-3 Paperbound $4.00

THE PHILOSOPHY OF THE UPANISHADS, Paul Deussen. Clear, detailed statement of upanishadic system of thought, generally considered among best available. History of these works, full exposition of system emergent from them, parallel concepts in the West. Translated by A. S. Geden. xiv + 429pp.

21616-0 Paperbound $3.50

LANGUAGE, TRUTH AND LOGIC, Alfred J. Ayer. Famous, remarkably clear introduction to the Vienna and Cambridge schools of Logical Positivism; function of philosophy, elimination of metaphysical thought, nature of analysis, similar topics. "Wish I had written it myself," Bertrand Russell. 2nd, 1946 edition. 160pp.

20010-8 Paperbound $1.50

THE GUIDE FOR THE PERPLEXED, Moses Maimonides. Great classic of medieval Judaism, major attempt to reconcile revealed religion (Pentateuch, commentaries) and Aristotelian philosophy. Enormously important in all Western thought. Unabridged Friedländer translation. 50-page introduction. lix + 414pp.

(USO) 20351-4 Paperbound $4.50

OCCULT AND SUPERNATURAL PHENOMENA, D. H. Rawcliffe. Full, serious study of the most persistent delusions of mankind: crystal gazing, mediumistic trance, stigmata, lycanthropy, fire walking, dowsing, telepathy, ghosts, ESP, etc., and their relation to common forms of abnormal psychology. Formerly *Illusions and Delusions of the Supernatural and the Occult.* iii + 551pp. 20503-7 Paperbound $4.00

THE EGYPTIAN BOOK OF THE DEAD: THE PAPYRUS OF ANI, E. A. Wallis Budge. Full hieroglyphic text, interlinear transliteration of sounds, word for word translation, then smooth, connected translation; Theban recension. Basic work in Ancient Egyptian civilization; now even more significant than ever for historical importance, dilation of consciousness, etc. clvi + 377pp. 6½ x 9¼.

21866-X Paperbound $4.95

PSYCHOLOGY OF MUSIC, Carl E. Seashore. Basic, thorough survey of everything known about psychology of music up to 1940's; essential reading for psychologists, musicologists. Physical acoustics; auditory apparatus; relationship of physical sound to perceived sound; role of the mind in sorting, altering, suppressing, creating sound sensations; musical learning, testing for ability, absolute pitch, other topics. Records of Caruso, Menuhin analyzed. 88 figures. xix + 408pp.

21851-1 Paperbound $3.50

THE I CHING (THE BOOK OF CHANGES), translated by James Legge. Complete translated text plus appendices by Confucius, of perhaps the most penetrating divination book ever compiled. Indispensable to all study of early Oriental civilizations. 3 plates. xxiii + 448pp. 21062-6 Paperbound $3.50

THE UPANISHADS, translated by Max Müller. Twelve classical upanishads: Chandogya, Kena, Aitareya, Kaushitaki, Isa, Katha, Mundaka, Taittiriyaka, Brhadaranyaka, Svetasvatara, Prasna, Maitriyana. 160-page introduction, analysis by Prof. Müller. Total of 670pp. 20992-X, 20993-8 Two volumes, Paperbound $7.50

ALPHABETS AND ORNAMENTS, Ernst Lehner. Well-known pictorial source for decorative alphabets, script examples, cartouches, frames, decorative title pages, calligraphic initials, borders, similar material. 14th to 19th century, mostly European. Useful in almost any graphic arts designing, varied styles. 750 illustrations. 256pp. 7 x 10.
21905-4 Paperbound $4.00

PAINTING: A CREATIVE APPROACH, Norman Colquhoun. For the beginner simple guide provides an instructive approach to painting: major stumbling blocks for beginner; overcoming them, technical points; paints and pigments; oil painting; watercolor and other media and color. New section on "plastic" paints. Glossary. Formerly *Paint Your Own Pictures.* 221pp.
22000-1 Paperbound $1.75

THE ENJOYMENT AND USE OF COLOR, Walter Sargent. Explanation of the relations between colors themselves and between colors in nature and art, including hundreds of little-known facts about color values, intensities, effects of high and low illumination, complementary colors. Many practical hints for painters, references to great masters. 7 color plates, 29 illustrations. x + 274pp.
20944-X Paperbound $3.00

THE NOTEBOOKS OF LEONARDO DA VINCI, compiled and edited by Jean Paul Richter. 1566 extracts from original manuscripts reveal the full range of Leonardo's versatile genius: all his writings on painting, sculpture, architecture, anatomy, astronomy, geography, topography, physiology, mining, music, etc., in both Italian and English, with 186 plates of manuscript pages and more than 500 additional drawings. Includes studies for the Last Supper, the lost Sforza monument, and other works. Total of xlvii + 866pp. $7\frac{7}{8}$ x $10\frac{3}{4}$.
22572-0, 22573-9 Two volumes, Paperbound $12.00

MONTGOMERY WARD CATALOGUE OF 1895. Tea gowns, yards of flannel and pillow-case lace, stereoscopes, books of gospel hymns, the New Improved Singer Sewing Machine, side saddles, milk skimmers, straight-edged razors, high-button shoes, spittoons, and on and on . . . listing some 25,000 items, practically all illustrated. Essential to the shoppers of the 1890's, it is our truest record of the spirit of the period. Unaltered reprint of Issue No. 57, Spring and Summer 1895. Introduction by Boris Emmet. Innumerable illustrations. xiii + 624pp. $8\frac{1}{2}$ x $11\frac{5}{8}$.
22377-9 Paperbound $8.50

THE CRYSTAL PALACE EXHIBITION ILLUSTRATED CATALOGUE (LONDON, 1851). One of the wonders of the modern world—the Crystal Palace Exhibition in which all the nations of the civilized world exhibited their achievements in the arts and sciences—presented in an equally important illustrated catalogue. More than 1700 items pictured with accompanying text—ceramics, textiles, cast-iron work, carpets, pianos, sleds, razors, wall-papers, billiard tables, beehives, silverware and hundreds of other artifacts—represent the focal point of Victorian culture in the Western World. Probably the largest collection of Victorian decorative art ever assembled— indispensable for antiquarians and designers. Unabridged republication of the Art-Journal Catalogue of the Great Exhibition of 1851, with all terminal essays. New introduction by John Gloag, F.S.A. xxxiv + 426pp. 9 x 12.
22503-8 Paperbound $5.00

THE PRINCIPLES OF PSYCHOLOGY, William James. The famous long course, complete and unabridged. Stream of thought, time perception, memory, experimental methods—these are only some of the concerns of a work that was years ahead of its time and still valid, interesting, useful. 94 figures. Total of xviii + 1391pp.
20381-6, 20382-4 Two volumes, Paperbound $9.00

THE STRANGE STORY OF THE QUANTUM, Banesh Hoffmann. Non-mathematical but thorough explanation of work of Planck, Einstein, Bohr, Pauli, de Broglie, Schrödinger, Heisenberg, Dirac, Feynman, etc. No technical background needed. "Of books attempting such an account, this is the best," Henry Margenau, Yale. 40-page "Postscript 1959." xii + 285pp.
20518-5 Paperbound $3.00

THE RISE OF THE NEW PHYSICS, A. d'Abro. Most thorough explanation in print of central core of mathematical physics, both classical and modern; from Newton to Dirac and Heisenberg. Both history and exposition; philosophy of science, causality, explanations of higher mathematics, analytical mechanics, electromagnetism, thermodynamics, phase rule, special and general relativity, matrices. No higher mathematics needed to follow exposition, though treatment is elementary to intermediate in level. Recommended to serious student who wishes verbal understanding. 97 illustrations. xvii + 982pp.
20003-5, 20004-3 Two volumes, Paperbound$10.00

GREAT IDEAS OF OPERATIONS RESEARCH, Jagjit Singh. Easily followed non-technical explanation of mathematical tools, aims, results: statistics, linear programming, game theory, queueing theory, Monte Carlo simulation, etc. Uses only elementary mathematics. Many case studies, several analyzed in detail. Clarity, breadth make this excellent for specialist in another field who wishes background. 41 figures. x + 228pp.
21886-4 Paperbound $2.50

GREAT IDEAS OF MODERN MATHEMATICS: THEIR NATURE AND USE, Jagjit Singh. Internationally famous expositor, winner of Unesco's Kalinga Award for science popularization explains verbally such topics as differential equations, matrices, groups, sets, transformations, mathematical logic and other important modern mathematics, as well as use in physics, astrophysics, and similar fields. Superb exposition for layman, scientist in other areas. viii + 312pp.
20587-8 Paperbound $2.75

GREAT IDEAS IN INFORMATION THEORY, LANGUAGE AND CYBERNETICS, Jagjit Singh. The analog and digital computers, how they work, how they are like and unlike the human brain, the men who developed them, their future applications, computer terminology. An essential book for today, even for readers with little math. Some mathematical demonstrations included for more advanced readers. 118 figures. Tables. ix + 338pp.
21694-2 Paperbound $2.50

CHANCE, LUCK AND STATISTICS, Horace C. Levinson. Non-mathematical presentation of fundamentals of probability theory and science of statistics and their applications. Games of chance, betting odds, misuse of statistics, normal and skew distributions, birth rates, stock speculation, insurance. Enlarged edition. Formerly "The Science of Chance." xiii + 357pp.
21007-3 Paperbound $2.50

AMERICAN FOOD AND GAME FISHES, David S. Jordan and Barton W. Evermann. Definitive source of information, detailed and accurate enough to enable the sportsman and nature lover to identify conclusively some 1,000 species and sub-species of North American fish, sought for food or sport. Coverage of range, physiology, habits, life history, food value. Best methods of capture, interest to the angler, advice on bait, fly-fishing, etc. 338 drawings and photographs. 1 + 574pp. 6⅝ x 9⅜.
22196-2 Paperbound $5.00

THE FROG BOOK, Mary C. Dickerson. Complete with extensive finding keys, over 300 photographs, and an introduction to the general biology of frogs and toads, this is the classic non-technical study of Northeastern and Central species. 58 species; 290 photographs and 16 color plates. xvii + 253pp.
21973-9 Paperbound $4.00

THE MOTH BOOK: A GUIDE TO THE MOTHS OF NORTH AMERICA, William J. Holland. Classical study, eagerly sought after and used for the past 60 years. Clear identification manual to more than 2,000 different moths, largest manual in existence. General information about moths, capturing, mounting, classifying, etc., followed by species by species descriptions. 263 illustrations plus 48 color plates show almost every species, full size. 1968 edition, preface, nomenclature changes by A. E. Brower. xxiv + 479pp. of text. 6½ x 9¼.
21948-8 Paperbound $6.00

THE SEA-BEACH AT EBB-TIDE, Augusta Foote Arnold. Interested amateur can identify hundreds of marine plants and animals on coasts of North America; marine algae; seaweeds; squids; hermit crabs; horse shoe crabs; shrimps; corals; sea anemones; etc. Species descriptions cover: structure; food; reproductive cycle; size; shape; color; habitat; etc. Over 600 drawings. 85 plates. xii + 490pp.
21949-6 Paperbound $4.00

COMMON BIRD SONGS, Donald J. Borror. 33⅓ 12-inch record presents songs of 60 important birds of the eastern United States. A thorough, serious record which provides several examples for each bird, showing different types of song, individual variations, etc. Inestimable identification aid for birdwatcher. 32-page booklet gives text about birds and songs, with illustration for each bird.
21829-5 Record, book, album. Monaural. $3.50

FADS AND FALLACIES IN THE NAME OF SCIENCE, Martin Gardner. Fair, witty appraisal of cranks and quacks of science: Atlantis, Lemuria, hollow earth, flat earth, Velikovsky, orgone energy, Dianetics, flying saucers, Bridey Murphy, food fads, medical fads, perpetual motion, etc. Formerly "In the Name of Science." x + 363pp.
20394-8 Paperbound $3.00

HOAXES, Curtis D. MacDougall. Exhaustive, unbelievably rich account of great hoaxes: Locke's moon hoax, Shakespearean forgeries, sea serpents, Loch Ness monster, Cardiff giant, John Wilkes Booth's mummy, Disumbrationist school of art, dozens more; also journalism, psychology of hoaxing. 54 illustrations. xi + 338pp.
20465-0 Paperbound $3.50

AGAINST THE GRAIN (A REBOURS), Joris K. Huysmans. Filled with weird images, evidences of a bizarre imagination, exotic experiments with hallucinatory drugs, rich tastes and smells and the diversions of its sybarite hero Duc Jean des Esseintes, this classic novel pushed 19th-century literary decadence to its limits. Full unabridged edition. Do not confuse this with abridged editions generally sold. Introduction by Havelock Ellis. xlix + 206pp.   22190-3 Paperbound $2.50

VARIORUM SHAKESPEARE: HAMLET. Edited by Horace H. Furness; a landmark of American scholarship. Exhaustive footnotes and appendices treat all doubtful words and phrases, as well as suggested critical emendations throughout the play's history. First volume contains editor's own text, collated with all Quartos and Folios. Second volume contains full first Quarto, translations of Shakespeare's sources (Belleforest, and Saxo Grammaticus), Der Bestrafte Brudermord, and many essays on critical and historical points of interest by major authorities of past and present. Includes details of staging and costuming over the years. By far the best edition available for serious students of Shakespeare. Total of xx + 905pp.
21004-9, 21005-7, 2 volumes, Paperbound $7.00

A LIFE OF WILLIAM SHAKESPEARE, Sir Sidney Lee. This is the standard life of Shakespeare, summarizing everything known about Shakespeare and his plays. Incredibly rich in material, broad in coverage, clear and judicious, it has served thousands as the best introduction to Shakespeare. 1931 edition. 9 plates. xxix + 792pp.   21967-4 Paperbound $4.50

MASTERS OF THE DRAMA, John Gassner. Most comprehensive history of the drama in print, covering every tradition from Greeks to modern Europe and America, including India, Far East, etc. Covers more than 800 dramatists, 2000 plays, with biographical material, plot summaries, theatre history, criticism, etc. "Best of its kind in English," *New Republic*. 77 illustrations. xxii + 890pp.
20100-7 Clothbound $10.00

THE EVOLUTION OF THE ENGLISH LANGUAGE, George McKnight. The growth of English, from the 14th century to the present. Unusual, non-technical account presents basic information in very interesting form: sound shifts, change in grammar and syntax, vocabulary growth, similar topics. Abundantly illustrated with quotations. Formerly *Modern English in the Making*. xii + 590pp.
21932-1 Paperbound $3.50

AN ETYMOLOGICAL DICTIONARY OF MODERN ENGLISH, Ernest Weekley. Fullest, richest work of its sort, by foremost British lexicographer. Detailed word histories, including many colloquial and archaic words; extensive quotations. Do not confuse this with the Concise Etymological Dictionary, which is much abridged. Total of xxvii + 830pp. 6½ x 9¼.
21873-2, 21874-0 Two volumes, Paperbound $7.90

FLATLAND: A ROMANCE OF MANY DIMENSIONS, E. A. Abbott. Classic of science-fiction explores ramifications of life in a two-dimensional world, and what happens when a three-dimensional being intrudes. Amusing reading, but also useful as introduction to thought about hyperspace. Introduction by Banesh Hoffmann. 16 illustrations. xx + 103pp.   20001-9 Paperbound $1.00

JIM WHITEWOLF: THE LIFE OF A KIOWA APACHE INDIAN, Charles S. Brant, editor. Spans transition between native life and acculturation period, 1880 on. Kiowa culture, personal life pattern, religion and the supernatural, the Ghost Dance, breakdown in the White Man's world, similar material. 1 map. xii + 144pp.
22015-X Paperbound $1.75

THE NATIVE TRIBES OF CENTRAL AUSTRALIA, Baldwin Spencer and F. J. Gillen. Basic book in anthropology, devoted to full coverage of the Arunta and Warramunga tribes; the source for knowledge about kinship systems, material and social culture, religion, etc. Still unsurpassed. 121 photographs, 89 drawings. xviii + 669pp.
21775-2 Paperbound $5.00

MALAY MAGIC, Walter W. Skeat. Classic (1900); still the definitive work on the folklore and popular religion of the Malay peninsula. Describes marriage rites, birth spirits and ceremonies, medicine, dances, games, war and weapons, etc. Extensive quotes from original sources, many magic charms translated into English. 35 illustrations. Preface by Charles Otto Blagden. xxiv + 685pp.
21760-4 Paperbound $4.00

HEAVENS ON EARTH: UTOPIAN COMMUNITIES IN AMERICA, 1680-1880, Mark Holloway. The finest nontechnical account of American utopias, from the early Woman in the Wilderness, Ephrata, Rappites to the enormous mid 19th-century efflorescence; Shakers, New Harmony, Equity Stores, Fourier's Phalanxes, Oneida, Amana, Fruitlands, etc. "Entertaining and very instructive." *Times Literary Supplement.* 15 illustrations. 246pp.
21593-8 Paperbound $2.00

LONDON LABOUR AND THE LONDON POOR, Henry Mayhew. Earliest (c. 1850) sociological study in English, describing myriad subcultures of London poor. Particularly remarkable for the thousands of pages of direct testimony taken from the lips of London prostitutes, thieves, beggars, street sellers, chimney-sweepers, street-musicians, "mudlarks," "pure-finders," rag-gatherers, "running-patterers," dock laborers, cab-men, and hundreds of others, quoted directly in this massive work. An extraordinarily vital picture of London emerges. 110 illustrations. Total of lxxvi + 1951pp. 6⅝ x 10.
21934-8, 21935-6, 21936-4, 21937-2 Four volumes, Paperbound $16.00

HISTORY OF THE LATER ROMAN EMPIRE, J. B. Bury. Eloquent, detailed reconstruction of Western and Byzantine Roman Empire by a major historian, from the death of Theodosius I (395 A.D.) to the death of Justinian (565). Extensive quotations from contemporary sources; full coverage of important Roman and foreign figures of the time. xxxiv + 965pp. 20398-0, 20399-9 Two volumes, Paperbound $7.00

AN INTELLECTUAL AND CULTURAL HISTORY OF THE WESTERN WORLD, Harry Elmer Barnes. Monumental study, tracing the development of the accomplishments that make up human culture. Every aspect of man's achievement surveyed from its origins in the Paleolithic to the present day (1964); social structures, ideas, economic systems, art, literature, technology, mathematics, the sciences, medicine, religion, jurisprudence, etc. Evaluations of the contributions of scores of great men. 1964 edition, revised and edited by scholars in the many fields represented. Total of xxix + 1381pp. 21275-0, 21276-9, 21277-7 Three volumes, Paperbound $10.50

THE RED FAIRY BOOK, Andrew Lang. Lang's color fairy books have long been children's favorites. This volume includes Rapunzel, Jack and the Bean-stalk and 35 other stories, familiar and unfamiliar. 4 plates, 93 illustrations x + 367pp.
21673-X Paperbound $2.50

THE BLUE FAIRY BOOK, Andrew Lang. Lang's tales come from all countries and all times. Here are 37 tales from Grimm, the Arabian Nights, Greek Mythology, and other fascinating sources. 8 plates, 130 illustrations. xi + 390pp.
21437-0 Paperbound $2.75

HOUSEHOLD STORIES BY THE BROTHERS GRIMM. Classic English-language edition of the well-known tales — Rumpelstiltskin, Snow White, Hansel and Gretel, The Twelve Brothers, Faithful John, Rapunzel, Tom Thumb (52 stories in all). Translated into simple, straightforward English by Lucy Crane. Ornamented with headpieces, vignettes, elaborate decorative initials and a dozen full-page illustrations by Walter Crane. x + 269pp.
21080-4 Paperbound **$2.00**

THE MERRY ADVENTURES OF ROBIN HOOD, Howard Pyle. The finest modern versions of the traditional ballads and tales about the great English outlaw. Howard Pyle's complete prose version, with every word, every illustration of the first edition. Do not confuse this facsimile of the original (1883) with modern editions that change text or illustrations. 23 plates plus many page decorations. xxii + 296pp.
22043-5 Paperbound $2.75

THE STORY OF KING ARTHUR AND HIS KNIGHTS, Howard Pyle. The finest children's version of the life of King Arthur; brilliantly retold by Pyle, with 48 of his most imaginative illustrations. xviii + 313pp. 6⅛ x 9¼.
21445-1 Paperbound $2.50

THE WONDERFUL WIZARD OF OZ, L. Frank Baum. America's finest children's book in facsimile of first edition with all Denslow illustrations in full color. The edition a child should have. Introduction by Martin Gardner. 23 color plates, scores of drawings. iv + 267pp.
20691-2 Paperbound $3.50

THE MARVELOUS LAND OF OZ, L. Frank Baum. The second Oz book, every bit as imaginative as the Wizard. The hero is a boy named Tip, but the Scarecrow and the Tin Woodman are back, as is the Oz magic. 16 color plates, 120 drawings by John R. Neill. 287pp.
20692-0 Paperbound $2.50

THE MAGICAL MONARCH OF MO, L. Frank Baum. Remarkable adventures in a land even stranger than Oz. The best of Baum's books not in the Oz series. 15 color plates and dozens of drawings by Frank Verbeck. xviii + 237pp.
21892-9 Paperbound $2.25

THE BAD CHILD'S BOOK OF BEASTS, MORE BEASTS FOR WORSE CHILDREN, A MORAL ALPHABET, Hilaire Belloc. Three complete humor classics in one volume. Be kind to the frog, and do not call him names . . . and 28 other whimsical animals. Familiar favorites and some not so well known. Illustrated by Basil Blackwell. 156pp.
(USO) 20749-8 Paperbound $1.50

LAST AND FIRST MEN AND STAR MAKER, TWO SCIENCE FICTION NOVELS, Olaf Stapledon. Greatest future histories in science fiction. In the first, human intelligence is the "hero," through strange paths of evolution, interplanetary invasions, incredible technologies, near extinctions and reemergences. Star Maker describes the quest of a band of star rovers for intelligence itself, through time and space: weird inhuman civilizations, crustacean minds, symbiotic worlds, etc. Complete, unabridged. v + 438pp. (USO) 21962-3 Paperbound $3.00

THREE PROPHETIC NOVELS, H. G. WELLS. Stages of a consistently planned future for mankind. *When the Sleeper Wakes*, and *A Story of the Days to Come*, anticipate *Brave New World* and *1984*, in the 21st Century; *The Time Machine*, only complete version in print, shows farther future and the end of mankind. All show Wells's greatest gifts as storyteller and novelist. Edited by E. F. Bleiler. x + 335pp. (USO) 20605-X Paperbound $3.00

THE DEVIL'S DICTIONARY, Ambrose Bierce. America's own Oscar Wilde— Ambrose Bierce—offers his barbed iconoclastic wisdom in over 1,000 definitions hailed by H. L. Mencken as "some of the most gorgeous witticisms in the English language." 145pp. 20487-1 Paperbound $1.50

MAX AND MORITZ, Wilhelm Busch. Great children's classic, father of comic strip, of two bad boys, Max and Moritz. Also Ker and Plunk (Plisch und Plumm), Cat and Mouse, Deceitful Henry, Ice-Peter, The Boy and the Pipe, and five other pieces. Original German, with English translation. Edited by H. Arthur Klein; translations by various hands and H. Arthur Klein. vi + 216pp. 20181-3 Paperbound $2.00

PIGS IS PIGS AND OTHER FAVORITES, Ellis Parker Butler. The title story is one of the best humor short stories, as Mike Flannery obfuscates biology and English. Also included, That Pup of Murchison's, The Great American Pie Company, and Perkins of Portland. 14 illustrations. v + 109pp. 21532-6 Paperbound $1.50

THE PETERKIN PAPERS, Lucretia P. Hale. It takes genius to be as stupidly mad as the Peterkins, as they decide to become wise, celebrate the "Fourth," keep a cow, and otherwise strain the resources of the Lady from Philadelphia. Basic book of American humor. 153 illustrations. 219pp. 20794-3 Paperbound $2.00

PERRAULT'S FAIRY TALES, translated by A. E. Johnson and S. R. Littlewood, with 34 full-page illustrations by Gustave Doré. All the original Perrault stories— Cinderella, Sleeping Beauty, Bluebeard, Little Red Riding Hood, Puss in Boots, Tom Thumb, etc.—with their witty verse morals and the magnificent illustrations of Doré. One of the five or six great books of European fairy tales. viii + 117pp. 8⅛ x 11. 22311-6 Paperbound $2.00

OLD HUNGARIAN FAIRY TALES, Baroness Orczy. Favorites translated and adapted by author of the *Scarlet Pimpernel*. Eight fairy tales include "The Suitors of Princess Fire-Fly," "The Twin Hunchbacks," "Mr. Cuttlefish's Love Story," and "The Enchanted Cat." This little volume of magic and adventure will captivate children as it has for generations. 90 drawings by Montagu Barstow. 96pp. (USO) 22293-4 Paperbound $1.95

INCIDENTS OF TRAVEL IN YUCATAN, John L. Stephens. Classic (1843) exploration of jungles of Yucatan, looking for evidences of Maya civilization. Stephens found many ruins; comments on travel adventures, Mexican and Indian culture. 127 striking illustrations by F. Catherwood. Total of 669 pp.

20926-1, 20927-X Two volumes, Paperbound $5.50

INCIDENTS OF TRAVEL IN CENTRAL AMERICA, CHIAPAS, AND YUCATAN, John L. Stephens. An exciting travel journal and an important classic of archeology. Narrative relates his almost single-handed discovery of the Mayan culture, and exploration of the ruined cities of Copan, Palenque, Utatlan and others; the monuments they dug from the earth, the temples buried in the jungle, the customs of poverty-stricken Indians living a stone's throw from the ruined palaces. 115 drawings by F. Catherwood. Portrait of Stephens. xii + 812pp.

22404-X, 22405-8 Two volumes, Paperbound $6.00

A NEW VOYAGE ROUND THE WORLD, William Dampier. Late 17-century naturalist joined the pirates of the Spanish Main to gather information; remarkably vivid account of buccaneers, pirates; detailed, accurate account of botany, zoology, ethnography of lands visited. Probably the most important early English voyage, enormous implications for British exploration, trade, colonial policy. Also most interesting reading. Argonaut edition, introduction by Sir Albert Gray. New introduction by Percy Adams. 6 plates, 7 illustrations. xlvii + 376pp. 6½ x 9¼.

21900-3 Paperbound $3.00

INTERNATIONAL AIRLINE PHRASE BOOK IN SIX LANGUAGES, Joseph W. Bátor. Important phrases and sentences in English paralleled with French, German, Portuguese, Italian, Spanish equivalents, covering all possible airport-travel situations; created for airline personnel as well as tourist by Language Chief, Pan American Airlines. xiv + 204pp.

22017-6 Paperbound $2.25

STAGE COACH AND TAVERN DAYS, Alice Morse Earle. Detailed, lively account of the early days of taverns; their uses and importance in the social, political and military life; furnishings and decorations; locations; food and drink; tavern signs, etc. Second half covers every aspect of early travel; the roads, coaches, drivers, etc. Nostalgic, charming, packed with fascinating material. 157 illustrations, mostly photographs. xiv + 449pp.

22518-6 Paperbound $4.00

NORSE DISCOVERIES AND EXPLORATIONS IN NORTH AMERICA, Hjalmar R. Holand. The perplexing Kensington Stone, found in Minnesota at the end of the 19th century. Is it a record of a Scandinavian expedition to North America in the 14th century? Or is it one of the most successful hoaxes in history. A scientific detective investigation. Formerly *Westward from Vinland*. 31 photographs, 17 figures. x + 354pp.

22014-1 Paperbound $2.75

A BOOK OF OLD MAPS, compiled and edited by Emerson D. Fite and Archibald Freeman. 74 old maps offer an unusual survey of the discovery, settlement and growth of America down to the close of the Revolutionary war: maps showing Norse settlements in Greenland, the explorations of Columbus, Verrazano, Cabot, Champlain, Joliet, Drake, Hudson, etc., campaigns of Revolutionary war battles, and much more. Each map is accompanied by a brief historical essay. xvi + 299pp. 11 x 13¾.

22084-2 Paperbound $7.00

POEMS OF ANNE BRADSTREET, edited with an introduction by Robert Hutchinson. A new selection of poems by America's first poet and perhaps the first significant woman poet in the English language. 48 poems display her development in works of considerable variety—love poems, domestic poems, religious meditations, formal elegies, "quaternions," etc. Notes, bibliography. viii + 222pp.

22160-1 Paperbound $2.50

THREE GOTHIC NOVELS: THE CASTLE OF OTRANTO BY HORACE WALPOLE; VATHEK BY WILLIAM BECKFORD; THE VAMPYRE BY JOHN POLIDORI, WITH FRAGMENT OF A NOVEL BY LORD BYRON, edited by E. F. Bleiler. The first Gothic novel, by Walpole; the finest Oriental tale in English, by Beckford; powerful Romantic supernatural story in versions by Polidori and Byron. All extremely important in history of literature; all still exciting, packed with supernatural thrills, ghosts, haunted castles, magic, etc. xl + 291pp.

21232-7 Paperbound $3.00

THE BEST TALES OF HOFFMANN, E. T. A. Hoffmann. 10 of Hoffmann's most important stories, in modern re-editings of standard translations: Nutcracker and the King of Mice, Signor Formica, Automata, The Sandman, Rath Krespel, The Golden Flowerpot, Master Martin the Cooper, The Mines of Falun, The King's Betrothed, A New Year's Eve Adventure. 7 illustrations by Hoffmann. Edited by E. F. Bleiler. xxxix + 419pp. 21793-0 Paperbound $3.00

GHOST AND HORROR STORIES OF AMBROSE BIERCE, Ambrose Bierce. 23 strikingly modern stories of the horrors latent in the human mind: The Eyes of the Panther, The Damned Thing, An Occurrence at Owl Creek Bridge, An Inhabitant of Carcosa, etc., plus the dream-essay, Visions of the Night. Edited by E. F. Bleiler. xxii + 199pp. 20767-6 Paperbound $2.00

BEST GHOST STORIES OF J. S. LeFANU, J. Sheridan LeFanu. Finest stories by Victorian master often considered greatest supernatural writer of all. Carmilla, Green Tea, The Haunted Baronet, The Familiar, and 12 others. Most never before available in the U. S. A. Edited by E. F. Bleiler. 8 illustrations from Victorian publications. xvii + 467pp. 20415-4 Paperbound $3.00

MATHEMATICAL FOUNDATIONS OF INFORMATION THEORY, A. I. Khinchin. Comprehensive introduction to work of Shannon, McMillan, Feinstein and Khinchin, placing these investigations on a rigorous mathematical basis. Covers entropy concept in probability theory, uniqueness theorem, Shannon's inequality, ergodic sources, the E property, martingale concept, noise, Feinstein's fundamental lemma, Shanon's first and second theorems. Translated by R. A. Silverman and M. D. Friedman. iii + 120pp. 60434-9 Paperbound $2.00

SEVEN SCIENCE FICTION NOVELS, H. G. Wells. The standard collection of the great novels. Complete, unabridged. *First Men in the Moon, Island of Dr. Moreau, War of the Worlds, Food of the Gods, Invisible Man, Time Machine, In the Days of the Comet.* Not only science fiction fans, but every educated person owes it to himself to read these novels. 1015pp. **(USO)** 20264-X Clothbound $6.00

How to Know the Wild Flowers, Mrs. William Starr Dana. This is the classical book of American wildflowers (of the Eastern and Central United States), used by hundreds of thousands. Covers over 500 species, arranged in extremely easy to use color and season groups. Full descriptions, much plant lore. This Dover edition is the fullest ever compiled, with tables of nomenclature changes. 174 full-page plates by M. Satterlee. xii + 418pp. 20332-8 Paperbound $3.00

Our Plant Friends and Foes, William Atherton DuPuy. History, economic importance, essential botanical information and peculiarities of 25 common forms of plant life are provided in this book in an entertaining and charming style. Covers food plants (potatoes, apples, beans, wheat, almonds, bananas, etc.), flowers (lily, tulip, etc.), trees (pine, oak, elm, etc.), weeds, poisonous mushrooms and vines, gourds, citrus fruits, cotton, the cactus family, and much more. 108 illustrations. xiv + 290pp. 22272-1 Paperbound $2.50

How to Know the Ferns, Frances T. Parsons. Classic survey of Eastern and Central ferns, arranged according to clear, simple identification key. Excellent introduction to greatly neglected nature area. 57 illustrations and 42 plates. xvi + 215pp. 20740-4 Paperbound $2.00

Manual of the Trees of North America, Charles S. Sargent. America's foremost dendrologist provides the definitive coverage of North American trees and tree-like shrubs. 717 species fully described and illustrated: exact distribution, down to township; full botanical description; economic importance; description of subspecies and races; habitat, growth data; similar material. Necessary to every serious student of tree-life. Nomenclature revised to present. Over 100 locating keys. 783 illustrations. lii + 934pp. 20277-1, 20278-X Two volumes, Paperbound $7.00

Our Northern Shrubs, Harriet L. Keeler. Fine non-technical reference work identifying more than 225 important shrubs of Eastern and Central United States and Canada. Full text covering botanical description, habitat, plant lore, is paralleled with 205 full-page photographs of flowering or fruiting plants. Nomenclature revised by Edward G. Voss. One of few works concerned with shrubs. 205 plates, 35 drawings. xxviii + 521pp. 21989-5 Paperbound $3.75

The Mushroom Handbook, Louis C. C. Krieger. Still the best popular handbook: full descriptions of 259 species, cross references to another 200. Extremely thorough text enables you to identify, know all about any mushroom you are likely to meet in eastern and central U. S. A.: habitat, luminescence, poisonous qualities, use, folklore, etc. 32 color plates show over 50 mushrooms, also 126 other illustrations. Finding keys. vii + 560pp. 21861-9 Paperbound $4.50

Handbook of Birds of Eastern North America, Frank M. Chapman. Still much the best single-volume guide to the birds of Eastern and Central United States. Very full coverage of 675 species, with descriptions, life habits, distribution, similar data. All descriptions keyed to two-page color chart. With this single volume the average birdwatcher needs no other books. 1931 revised edition. 195 illustrations. xxxvi + 581pp. 21489-3 Paperbound $5.00

EAST O' THE SUN AND WEST O' THE MOON, George W. Dasent. Considered the best of all translations of these Norwegian folk tales, this collection has been enjoyed by generations of children (and folklorists too). Includes True and Untrue, Why the Sea is Salt, East O' the Sun and West O' the Moon, Why the Bear is Stumpy-Tailed, Boots and the Troll, The Cock and the Hen, Rich Peter the Pedlar, and 52 more. The only edition with all 59 tales. 77 illustrations by Erik Werenskiold and Theodor Kittelsen. xv + 418pp.   22521-6 Paperbound $3.50

GOOPS AND HOW TO BE THEM, Gelett Burgess. Classic of tongue-in-cheek humor, masquerading as etiquette book. 87 verses, twice as many cartoons, show mischievous Goops as they demonstrate to children virtues of table manners, neatness, courtesy, etc. Favorite for generations. viii + 88pp. $6\frac{1}{2}$ x $9\frac{1}{4}$.
                                                        22233-0 Paperbound $1.50

ALICE'S ADVENTURES UNDER GROUND, Lewis Carroll. The first version, quite different from the final Alice in Wonderland, printed out by Carroll himself with his own illustrations. Complete facsimile of the "million dollar" manuscript Carroll gave to Alice Liddell in 1864. Introduction by Martin Gardner. viii + 96pp. Title and dedication pages in color.   21482-6 Paperbound $1.25

THE BROWNIES, THEIR BOOK, Palmer Cox. Small as mice, cunning as foxes, exuberant and full of mischief, the Brownies go to the zoo, toy shop, seashore, circus, etc., in 24 verse adventures and 266 illustrations. Long a favorite, since their first appearance in St. Nicholas Magazine. xi + 144pp. $6\frac{5}{8}$ x $9\frac{1}{4}$.
                                                        21265-3 Paperbound $1.75

SONGS OF CHILDHOOD, Walter De La Mare. Published (under the pseudonym Walter Ramal) when De La Mare was only 29, this charming collection has long been a favorite children's book. A facsimile of the first edition in paper, the 47 poems capture the simplicity of the nursery rhyme and the ballad, including such lyrics as I Met Eve, Tartary, The Silver Penny. vii + 106pp. (USO) 21972-0 Paperbound
                                                                         $1.25

THE COMPLETE NONSENSE OF EDWARD LEAR, Edward Lear. The finest 19th-century humorist-cartoonist in full: all nonsense limericks, zany alphabets, Owl and Pussycat, songs, nonsense botany, and more than 500 illustrations by Lear himself. Edited by Holbrook Jackson. xxix + 287pp.   (USO) 20167-8 Paperbound $2.00

BILLY WHISKERS: THE AUTOBIOGRAPHY OF A GOAT, Frances Trego Montgomery. A favorite of children since the early 20th century, here are the escapades of that rambunctious, irresistible and mischievous goat—Billy Whiskers. Much in the spirit of Peck's Bad Boy, this is a book that children never tire of reading or hearing. All the original familiar illustrations by W. H. Fry are included: 6 color plates, 18 black and white drawings. 159pp.   22345-0 Paperbound $2.00

MOTHER GOOSE MELODIES. Faithful republication of the fabulously rare Munroe and Francis "copyright 1833" Boston edition—the most important Mother Goose collection, usually referred to as the "original." Familiar rhymes plus many rare ones, with wonderful old woodcut illustrations. Edited by E. F. Bleiler. 128pp. $4\frac{1}{2}$ x $6\frac{3}{8}$.   22577-1 Paperbound $1.00

MATHEMATICAL PUZZLES FOR BEGINNERS AND ENTHUSIASTS, Geoffrey Mott-Smith. 189 puzzles from easy to difficult—involving arithmetic, logic, algebra, properties of digits, probability, etc.—for enjoyment and mental stimulus. Explanation of mathematical principles behind the puzzles. 135 illustrations. viii + 248pp.
20198-8 Paperbound $2.00

PAPER FOLDING FOR BEGINNERS, William D. Murray and Francis J. Rigney. Easiest book on the market, clearest instructions on making interesting, beautiful origami. Sail boats, cups, roosters, frogs that move legs, bonbon boxes, standing birds, etc. 40 projects; more than 275 diagrams and photographs. 94pp.
20713-7 Paperbound $1.00

TRICKS AND GAMES ON THE POOL TABLE, Fred Herrmann. 79 tricks and games— some solitaires, some for two or more players, some competitive games—to entertain you between formal games. Mystifying shots and throws, unusual caroms, tricks involving such props as cork, coins, a hat, etc. Formerly *Fun on the Pool Table.* 77 figures. 95pp.
21814-7 Paperbound $1.25

HAND SHADOWS TO BE THROWN UPON THE WALL: A SERIES OF NOVEL AND AMUSING FIGURES FORMED BY THE HAND, Henry Bursill. Delightful picturebook from great-grandfather's day shows how to make 18 different hand shadows: a bird that flies, duck that quacks, dog that wags his tail, camel, goose, deer, boy, turtle, etc. Only book of its sort. vi + 33pp. 6½ x 9¼. 21779-5 Paperbound $1.00

WHITTLING AND WOODCARVING, E. J. Tangerman. 18th printing of best book on market. "If you can cut a potato you can carve" toys and puzzles, chains, chessmen, caricatures, masks, frames, woodcut blocks, surface patterns, much more. Information on tools, woods, techniques. Also goes into serious wood sculpture from Middle Ages to present, East and West. 464 photos, figures. x + 293pp.
20965-2 Paperbound $2.50

HISTORY OF PHILOSOPHY, Julián Marías. Possibly the clearest, most easily followed, best planned, most useful one-volume history of philosophy on the market; neither skimpy nor overfull. Full details on system of every major philosopher and dozens of less important thinkers from pre-Socratics up to Existentialism and later. Strong on many European figures usually omitted. Has gone through dozens of editions in Europe. 1966 edition, translated by Stanley Appelbaum and Clarence Strowbridge. xviii + 505pp. 21739-6 Paperbound $3.50

YOGA: A SCIENTIFIC EVALUATION, Kovoor T. Behanan. Scientific but non-technical study of physiological results of yoga exercises; done under auspices of Yale U. Relations to Indian thought, to psychoanalysis, etc. 16 photos. xxiii + 270pp.
20505-3 Paperbound $2.50

Prices subject to change without notice.
Available at your book dealer or write for free catalogue to Dept. GI, Dover Publications, Inc., 180 Varick St., N. Y., N. Y. 10014. Dover publishes more than 150 books each year on science, elementary and advanced mathematics, biology, music, art, literary history, social sciences and other areas.